BETWEEN HEAVEN AND EARTH

BETWEEN HEAVEN AND EARTH

THE RELIGIOUS WORLDS
PEOPLE MAKE AND THE SCHOLARS
WHO STUDY THEM

Robert A. Orsi

PRINCETON UNIVERSITY PRESS

PRINCETON AND OXFORD

COPYRIGHT © 2005 BY PRINCETON UNIVERSITY PRESS

PUBLISHED BY PRINCETON UNIVERSITY PRESS, 41 WILLIAM STREET,

PRINCETON, NEW JERSEY 08540

IN THE UNITED KINGDOM: PRINCETON UNIVERSITY PRESS,

3 MARKET PLACE, WOODSTOCK, OXFORDSHIRE OX20 1SY

ALL RIGHTS RESERVED

SECOND PRINTING, AND FIRST PAPERBACK PRINTING, 2007

PAPERBACK ISBN-13: 978-0-691-12776-7

PAPERBACK ISBN-10: 0-691-12776-X

THE LIBRARY OF CONGRESS HAS CATALOGED THE CLOTH EDITION

OF THIS BOOK AS FOLLOWS

ORSI, ROBERT A.

BETWEEN HEAVEN AND EARTH : THE RELIGIOUS WORLDS PEOPLE MAKE

AND THE SCHOLARS WHO STUDY THEM / ROBERT A. ORSI.

P.   CM.

INCLUDES BIBLIOGRAPHICAL REFERENCES AND INDEX.

ISBN 0-691-04903-3 (ALK. PAPER)

1. CATHOLIC CHURCH—UNITED STATES—CUSTOMS AND PRACTICES—

CASE STUDIES. 2. CATHOLICS—RELIGIOUS LIFE—UNITED STATES—CASE STUDIES.

3. CHRISTIAN SAINTS—CULT—UNITED STATES—CASE STUDIES. 4. RELIGION—

METHODOLOGY. I. TITLE.

BX1406.3.O77 2004

235′.2′071—dc22   2004043414

BRITISH LIBRARY CATALOGING-IN-PUBLICATION DATA IS AVAILABLE

THIS BOOK HAS BEEN COMPOSED IN SABON TYPEFACE

PRINTED ON ACID-FREE PAPER. ∞

PUP.PRINCETON.EDU

PRINTED IN THE UNITED STATES OF AMERICA

3   5   7   9   10   8   6   4   2

For My Friend, Jeff Keller

CONTENTS

ACKNOWLEDGMENTS

ONE OF THE ARGUMENTS of this book is that the world is made and sustained within networks of relationships, and so are books. Many of the chapters were first written in response to invitations from other writers and scholars, and I am grateful to them for these opportunities: Thomas J. Ferraro (I initially wrote "Mildred, Is It Fun to Be a Cripple?" for his collection *Catholic Lives, Contemporary America*, and I am especially grateful for Tom's support of the chapter's experiment in religious studies poetics); Melissa Katz (who asked me to contribute an essay to her catalogue for the exhibition at Wellesley College called "Divine Mirrors," and which appears here in revised form as chapter 2); James Hudnut-Beumler (who supervised the Lilly project on material religion that was the occasion for chapter 3); Rudolph Bell (who invited me to contribute to his and Cristina Mazzoni's volume on Gemma Galgani, although I finally decided to keep the essay out until I could rewrite it to my own satisfaction—I appreciate Rudy's generous understanding of this choice); Russell Richey and R. Bruce Mullin (who invited me to participate in their conference on denominationalism that led me to write the first draft of chapter 5); and Richard Wightman Fox and Robert B. Westbrook (I wrote a version of chapter 6 for their conference on moral reasoning across the disciplines and I owe a special thanks to Richard Fox for his careful critique of an early draft of it).

All these essays have been rewritten for this volume, except for "Mildred," which appears as it was first published. I wish to thank Duke University Press for permission to reproduce "Mildred," which originally appeared in its publication of Thomas J. Ferraro's aforementioned *Catholic Lives, Contemporary America* (1994). Thank you as well to Oxford University Press for permission to publish a new version of "The Many Names of the Mother of God," which first appeared in *Divine Mirrors: The Virgin Mary in the Visual Arts*, ed. Melissa Katz (2001).

I was generously funded at various stages of this work by the Lilly Endowment, the Guggenheim Foundation, Indiana University, and, most recently, Harvard University. I owe particular thanks to Craig Dykstra at Lilly, who has supported and encouraged my ongoing research on American Catholic memory and on American Catholic childhoods. J. Bryan Hehir, then Acting Dean of Harvard Divinity School, gave me the time I needed for the final preparation of this volume.

Whoever the patron saint of graduate assistants might be, I owe him or her an enormous gift. This project has been absolutely blessed by simply the most talented and committed assistants any scholar can hope for: at Indiana University, Kristy Nabhan-Warren, and at Harvard Divinity School, Stephanie Stillman and Amy Sitar. With grace, humor, and enormous professional skill, Amy assumed the considerable tasks of readying the manuscript for submission.

The book enjoyed the encouragement of a number of colleagues and the benefit of their critical acumen. I first began thinking about modern Catholic memory when I was preparing to give the Albert Cardinal Meyer Lecture Series, Mundelein University, Chicago, which are generously funded by Andrew Greeley, who has been a constant source of support and encouragement. Colleen McDannell, Leigh Schmidt and Marie Griffith read an early version of the chapter on children, filling the margins of the text with helpful notes and suggestions. Michael Satlow and Constance Furey gave me invaluable assistance in rethinking the chapter on my grandmother and Saint Gemma. Fred Appel at Princeton University Press supported the project when I had almost given up on it. For almost twenty years I had breakfast every Friday with political theorist Jeff Isaac, whose moral and intellectual passion have been an inspiration to me and whose friendship has sustained me. John Efron joined us when he came to Indiana University, and from him I learned not only what real *matzobrei* is but a clearer understanding of the work of history too. I love these two men dearly. The Department of Religious Studies at Indiana University in the 1990s was an extraordinary place of warm collegiality and intense conversation about religion. I thank my colleagues there for all those years of good food and good talk—Jan Nattier, John McRae, David Haberman and his wife Sandy Ducey, Connie Furey (who came later) and her husband Jason Fickel (for the songs too), Rebecca Manring, Steve Weitzman, the late Sam Preus, Patrick Olivelle, Greg Schopen, and Steve Stein. A special thanks to Meagan Haberman-Ducey for the laughter. Harvard Divinity School welcomed me graciously and warmly into its conversations and for this I thank Stephanie Paulsell, Kevin Madigan, Anne Monius, Ron Thiemann, Claudia Highbaugh, Belva Brown Jordan, and Ann Braude. Catherine Sasanov, a poet who has a strikingly intimate and deep knowledge of Saint Gemma Galgani, read through chapter 4 and corrected its errors of fact concerning Gemma's life. (Catherine's poem "Reassembling the Bodily Relics of St. Gemma Galgani (Italy 1878–1903)" is a stunning meditation on the dangers and beauty of sanctity.) David Hall and his wife Hannah Jones opened their home to me, for which I will be forever grateful. For reasons too numerous to list I also thank Bill Reese, Amy Koehlinger, Julie Berger, Rich Remsberg (who among other things tracked down many of the illustrations for this volume) and

Lisa Nilsson, Valerie Keller, Betty De Berg, Martha Cooley, Michael Jackson, Sarah Pike, Kathy King, Joanne Gumo, and Jason Bivins. As always my deepest gratitude goes to my daughter, Claire Harlan-Orsi. The book is dedicated to Jeff Keller, whose enduring friendship has been the ground beneath my feet for more than three decades.

BETWEEN HEAVEN AND EARTH

Introduction

JESUS HELD HIM SO CLOSE IN HIS LOVE FOR HIM THAT HE LEFT THE MARKS OF HIS PASSION ON HIS BODY

> They say someone has invented you
> but to me this does not sound convincing
> for humans invented themselves as well.
> *Czeslaw Milosz, "On Angels"*

MY MOTHER became gravely ill in the months when I was finishing this book, and I found myself with my father and brother spending long and frightening days in the hospital walking up and down confusing corridors and waiting for word from the doctors. On the morning of the procedure that determined her cancer was inoperable my mother lay in her hospital bed holding a tiny blue statue of Our Lady of Fatima tightly in one hand, and from the fingers of her other hand she trailed the beads of her favorite rosary. After the operation my mother kept mistaking Fatima for the pain button. A nurse's aide tapping on the back of my mother's hand in search of a vein told us when she heard my father speaking Italian how much she loved the recently canonized Padre Pio—who makes a brief appearance in this book in chapter 3—and prayed to him every day, which gave my father the opportunity to tell us all again his story about the time he was in the army in Italy and went to confession to Padre Pio in San Giovanni Rotundo and the old friar miraculously discerned my father's troubles and anxieties without him having to say a word. The aide was unable to find a vein in my mother's thin hands, so she called in a surgical nurse who was immediately successful. "Oh, I always say a prayer to Saint Jude," she told us when we congratulated her, "before I start looking, and he never fails me." I noticed as my mother was being wheeled to surgery that someone had tucked a holy card of Our Lady of Lourdes into a corner of the bulletin board on which was also posted the pain chart to assist patients in identifying the level of their distress. So in the hour and a half before a surgical procedure four holy figures crowded in with the humans around my mother's bed—Our Lady of Fatima, Padre Pio, Saint Jude, and Our Lady of Lourdes—and this was not a Catholic hospital. The saints came in rounds of stories and their presence on this day became another story in those rounds.

The first four chapters of this book explore the relationships that form between humans and holy figures and the consequences of these bonds for the everyday lives of men, women, and children. Religion is commonly thought of among modern people and by many scholars in the West (although this has been challenged recently, as I will discuss in chapter 4) as a medium for explaining, understanding, and modeling reality, but this book offers religion as a network of relationships between heaven and earth involving humans of all ages and many different sacred figures together. These relationships have all the complexities—all the hopes, evasions, love, fear, denial, projections, misunderstandings, and so on—of relationships between humans. My examples are drawn from American Catholic history in the twentieth century, but I believe what I have to say about religion as relationships between heaven and earth is relevant for other cultures as well. I can think of no religious world—not even Buddhism!—that does not offer practitioners opportunities to form deep ties with saints, ancestors, demons, gods, ghosts, and other special beings, in whose company humans work on the world and on themselves. For better or worse: what humans do with the saints is not always, or even often, good for themselves, does not make their lives easier or even more comprehensible, does not smooth out their relationships with the significant persons in their lives, with their parents and children, spouses or friends, does not make driving safer, raising sons and daughters less challenging, work easier, or love simpler. This is a theme that recurs again and again in the pages of this book. Thinking of religion as relationships between heaven and earth with the specific shapes that relationships take in particular times and places—the history of love in a certain part of the world at a certain time, or the nature of parenting, for example—frees us from any notion of religious practices as *either* good *or* bad. Religions are as ambiguous and ambivalent as the bonds that constitute them, and their effects cannot be generally anticipated but known in practice and experience. One challenge of writing about religion is to figure out how to include figures of special power as agents in history and actors of consequence in historical persons' lives and experiences.

Fundamental to the approach to religion and to research in religion taken in this volume is the notion that all cultural idioms are intersubjective, including and especially religious ones. Men, women, and children *together* make religious worlds in relationship with special beings and with each other. Intersubjectivity is not only a local or intimate matter: such relational ties structure religious practice and experience in a global context too. Immigrants and migrants establish connections between heaven and earth that stretch as well between one environment and another and among families, friends, teachers, and others around the world, in their new homes and in the ones they left. Networks of connections between heaven and earth map the globe.

The chapters in this book are concerned with intersubjectivity in two ways or on two levels. First, there is the intersubjective nature of particular social, cultural, and religious identities and indeed of reality itself—hence the importance of understanding the bonds of love and hate within which religious actors, including those drawn to violence, make their lives. Second, there is the intersubjective nature of research on religion, which is the focus of chapters 5 and 6. Our lives and our stories are not simply implicated in our work; they are among the media through which we scholars of religion encounter and engage the religious worlds of others. "Research is a relationship," I quote Jean-Paul Sartre in chapter 5. This is no less so for historians than for ethnographers. As Richard Fox says in his book on a late-nineteenth-century religious and sexual scandal in the United States, "we historians have not done enough to let our subjects speak in their own voices," in response to which he proposes a historiography of "attentive listening" in the archive "to hear what the tellers are saying about their selves, their relationships, their culture." This is why this book so often takes the form of stories told and attended to and retold.[1]

Chapters 5 and 6 explore in this context a paradox of understanding in the study of religion: others (in the past or in different cultures) become at once both closer and more distinct in their separateness and difference. The challenge is to balance carefully and self-reflectively on the border between familiarity and difference, strangeness and recognizability, whether in relation to people in the past or in another cultural world. This is the tension with which the book closes.

The first chapter of this book tells the story of my uncle Sal, who had cerebral palsy and lived into his eighties, confounding all expectations for men of his generation so afflicted. I wrote the first incarnation of this chapter when my uncle was still alive. He read the article and liked it, which I knew among other ways because he kept a stack of offprints in his room to distribute to visitors. Sal died in October 1997. He was admitted to the hospital with dangerously low blood pressure as a result of the obscure intestinal illness I refer to in the first chapter.

My emphasis on religion as relationship does not preclude attention to the realities of power, the complexities of society, or the impress of history (nor is it meant to mask the intricacies of the relationships between a researcher in religion and the people he or she studies). "Relationship" is a friendly word, but this is not how I use it throughout this book, nor am I focused on relationships as intimate realities apart from the arrangements of the social world in which they exist. Children, women, and "cripples" (as Catholics called persons with physical disabilities in the middle years of the last century), who are the subjects of the first four chapters of this book, were vulnerable and exposed to the fantasies of adults, of male church officials, and of persons without physical handicaps, and they were invited into relationships with holy figures—with the Virgin Mother of God, the angels and the saints—that endorsed and deepened these discrepancies of agency and power. The saints could be dangerous enforcers of cultural structures, norms, and expectations, as we will see in the first four chapters, wielded by the culture against women, children, and handicapped persons. At the same time, however, youngsters, women, and persons with disabilities themselves called on the saints to assist them to live against what others would make of them in this religious world, meaning that the very same figures who were called into play against them could become their allies in resistance and subversion. But this is to draw things in too starkly oppositional terms: rarely is it a simple matter of either resistance or submission, but rather of negotiating compromises that are often tragic in their inevitability. Culture is a hard taskmaster, and the saints and humans must find their way as best they can. The saints are never innocent, nor are the effects of their presence singular. It is impossible to say that the saints and the Mother of God are either on the side of those with power in any social world or those without it. Instead, another theme of the first four chapters is that these holy figures get caught up and implicated in struggles on earth. They bear the marks of history. How they are positioned, what they do for whom or to whom requires close local analysis, historical and social psychological study to figure out, because it varies from situation to situation. This is all the subject of the first four chapters of the book.

On Halloween night five years or so ago I set out from my parents' home in New York, where I had stopped by to visit on my way to meeting Karen McCarthy Brown, a leading scholar of Haitian religions (whose work is discussed briefly in chapter 6), in lower Manhattan to go with her to a vodou celebration in honor of Papa Gede in Brooklyn. My parents were terrified for my spiritual and physical welfare. What was going to happen to me? My mother paced nervously around the apartment as the hour for my departure drew near, threading her rosary loudly through her fingers. Finally she couldn't stand it any more. She sat down, reached into her handbag and pulled out a fat bundle of two- by three-inch cards wrapped with thick colored rubber bands. These were the memorial images of Jesuits she had known in her many years working at Fordham University printed by the order at their death and distributed at their wakes. She snapped off the rubber bands. Each card was bordered in black and showed a close-up of a priest's face in black and white. "They worship the dead," she said darkly of the people I was going to visit in Brooklyn as she laid out the cards in rows in front of her, as if she were playing a kind of celestial solitaire. The cards of the priests who had died many years ago were worn and frayed from being handled by my mother at prayer; some had been raggedly taped back together. Soon the table was covered with the faces of dead Jesuits, "my friends in heaven" as my mother called them. Now she was ready to do battle for me. She addressed her anxieties to her friends. "They've never let me down," she told me once about her dead Jesuits. In some cases she roughly correlated her prayers with what a particular Jesuit did in life: a priest who worked in Fordham's student counseling office gets called on in situations of psychological distress, for instance, but she was not systematic about this.

Later that night as the ceremony was winding down in the early hours of the morning in Brooklyn, Papa Gede asked to speak to me. Earlier in the evening, just after he had made his appearance, Papa Gede had said something extremely rude and sexual to me involving my mouth and mustache that was translated with great delicacy and dignity by a Haitian doctor standing next to me who still could not resist joining in the general laughter at my expense when he was done (nor could I really). This was how Papa Gede was generally treating folks that night, even those who came to bring serious dilemmas to his attention, because one of his messages to those who serve him is about the redemptive and healing powers of a strong and fearless sense of humor. So when Karen McCarthy Brown came out of the room where Papa Gede was holding court to tell me that he wanted to talk with me, I expected the worst. Gede was sitting on a low stool in the hot and crowded room. He motioned me close. Karen McCarthy Brown leaned in to translate from the Creole. Speaking in a low voice, Papa Gede, who was also Mama Lola, who had already during an earlier visit the year before heard from me stories about dilemmas in my life, addressed me with the most tender and solicitous concern and offered me encouragement and support. I was deeply moved. Do I believe in Papa Gede, students have asked me about this story, do I think he was really in the room?

Once religion is understood as a web not of meanings but of relationships between heaven and earth, then scholars of religion take their places as participants in these networks too, together with the saints and in the company of practitioners. We get caught up in these bonds, whether we want to or not. This is the issue for chapters 5 and 6. Scholars of religion become preoccupied with themselves as interpreters of meanings, and so they forget that we do our work of interpretation within the network of relationships between heaven and earth, in the company of those among whom we have gone to study, in the field or in the archives. Again this is not innocent and I accord no special heuristic power to the notion of research as "relationship." To be in relationship with someone, as we all know, is not necessarily to understand him or her; but the relationship, which arises always on a particular social field and is invariably inflected by needs, desires, and feelings, conscious and not, that draw on both parties' histories and experiences, becomes the context for understanding. Scholars get implicated in the socially structured struggles among people on earth into which the saints are drawn too; we are asked to take sides at the intersection of heaven and earth and within sight of the saints. Chapter 5 looks at some of the dilemmas facing a scholar who works in his or her own religious culture—although what "one's own religious culture" means is part of the problem to be examined there—and chapter 6 considers some of the dangers that may attend relationships that form between practitioners and scholars of religion.

Chapter 6 asks another question too: how is it that religious studies as an area of scholarly inquiry is possible given all that we have come to know about the limits of knowing another person's inner world, about the politics of knowledge, about the distinct interests (and prejudices) that researchers bring to their subjects, about the implication of Western reason in strategies of domination, and so on? This is a huge question and I offer one take on it that begins by paying attention to the specific history of the construction of religion as an object of inquiry in the American university within the circumstances of United States society in the late nineteenth and twentieth centuries. The study of religion is an international enterprise, but it is also the case that its local practice is inflected by immediate histories. The distinctive shape of French sociology of religion, Danièle Hervieu-Léger has argued for instance, is the product of French engagement with the developing international discipline and "the historical and political circumstances peculiar to France," in particular the long effort by the Catholic Church to impose its authority on the educational system. Whether contemporary Americans working to understand particular religious phenomena know it or not, they bring to their inquiries local histories of talk about religion in the United States over time both within and outside the academy. Built into the very tools of analysis are hidden normativities, implicit distinctions between "good" and "bad" religions, and these need to be unpacked.[2]

Attending to such normativities is especially urgent now in American history. After the horror of September 11, 2001, scholars of religion in the United States found themselves called on to help delineate the threat facing the nation from religious others. There was tremendous pressure to define a normative "Islam" in contradistinction from whatever it was that motivated the men who flew their planes into the World Trade Center, who we were told (by the president of the United States among others) did not represent "real" Islam. This insistence was motivated by the most admirable and necessary concern not to vilify an entire religious world and to protect Muslim fellow citizens. But this was also an act of extraordinary political and religious hubris, to claim to define what "real" or "true" Islam may or may not be! In talk of "real Islam" I heard the voice of the 1893 Parliament of Religions (which will be discussed in chapter 6) resonating within contemporary American global power assuring us that real Islam conformed to the dictates of Western modernity. There was a good Islam that we recognized as like ourselves (just as nineteenth- and early-twentieth-century scholarship on Buddhism, Hinduism, and other religious cultures recreated normative versions of these worlds in conformity with Western expectations, values, and desires) and a bad distorted something else that existed in Middle Eastern lands but had nothing to do with Islam and was our enemy, and once it was so designated, we lost any interest in this other thing other than to bring it within the range of our weapons. The purpose of the study of religions is not to contribute to projects of surveillance or to reassure our fellow citizens; it certainly is to contribute to the work of educating the public about religion, but our engagements with the media and with government agencies are much more complicated than this benign and admirable description suggests, and I think we need to be more cautious of them than we sometimes are, especially in times of political panic. One of the moral and intellectual imperatives of this volume is to underscore the importance of studying and thinking about despised religious idioms, practices that make us uncomfortable, unhappy, frightened—and not just to study them but to bring ourselves into close proximity to them, and not to resolve the discomfort they occasion by imposing a normative grid. This is the challenge of chapter 6.

The way of approaching religion proposed in chapters 5 and 6 is meant to eliminate the comfort of academic distance and to undermine the confidence and authority of the claims, "We are not them" and "They are not us." We may not condone or celebrate the religious practices of others—and let me emphasize this here because it is always misunderstood: to work toward some understanding(s) of troubling religious phenomena is not to endorse or sanction them (an issue that became of great personal significance, as I explain in chapter 5)—but we cannot dismiss them as inhuman, so alien to us that they cannot be understood or approached, only contained or obliterated (which is what the language of good/bad religion accomplishes, the obliteration of the other by desire, need, or fear). The point is rather to bring the other into fuller focus within the circumstances of his or her history, relationships, and experiences. It is chastening and liberating to stand in an attitude of disciplined openness and attentiveness before a religious practice or idea of another era or culture on which we do not impose our wishes, dreams, or anxieties.

A woman whose elderly father lived in the Catholic residence that was Sal's home too and whose husband had just died wrote my mother after Sal's death: "I am so sorry for the loss of your beloved brother, Sal. I'll miss seeing him in the lobby, waiting for his mail, in the cafeteria, waiting for his lunch, when he was going out, telling him to be careful going down the ramp. I think I'll miss him most on Sundays, that special smile on his face . . . God and His Blessed Mother are going to have a special place for him in heaven because that is what he deserves."

The Catholic practices and imaginings I discuss in this volume for the most part occurred in the middle years of the twentieth century, a time of extraordinary transformations in American Catholic life. Twice Catholics made the passage from one way of life to another. First, the old inner-city immigrant communities born of the industrial era began to disappear as second, third, and fourth generations, born or raised in the United States, moved to other areas of cities and to the new rings of suburbs. Second, liturgical reforms initiated by the Second Vatican Council—the replacement of the Latin Mass by vernacular celebrations, the end of certain customs publicly characteristic of Catholic life (the prohibition on Friday meat-eating, for example, or the hugely popular Tuesday night novena ceremonies), the waning of the cult of saints (and the attendant removal of the tools of the cult of saints—statues, medals, blessed liquids, car and bicycle medallions, kitchen shrines, and on and on and on—from the Catholic landscape)—introduced new ways of relating to and thinking about the sacred among Catholics worldwide and in the United States.

But the language of passages *from . . . to* here masks a more staggered and intricate historical, social, psychological, and religious reality. American Catholicism did not simply become an assimilated community in the late twentieth century, for example, among other reasons because this was also the time when large numbers of migrants from Central and South America and the Caribbean made their way into the American church and newcomers from Mexico joined their longer-established kin and friends. The old neighborhoods did not simply disappear. Individual families and family members made painful and difficult choices to stay or leave that had profound personal, political, religious, and psychological consequences. It was in part out of this ambivalence that the powerfully mixed mood of the ethnic revival of the 1970s emerged with its incendiary combination of aggressive assertiveness, bitter nostalgia, loss, and defensiveness. Children were especially vulnerable in such fraught times of change because adults sought to enlist them in the effort to secure an otherwise elusive stability and order, as we will see in chapter 3.

It is better, then, to think of the historical period at issue in this volume as a braided one: many Catholics moved to the suburbs, many others moved into city neighborhoods or held fast there, some members of a family entered the white-collar workforce while others continued in industry and manual labor, the old European languages disappeared from the churches and schools just as priests and nuns found themselves challenged to learn Spanish. Braiding means that the linear narratives so beloved of modernity—from immigration to assimilation, from premodern to modern, from a simple faith to a more sophisticated faith and so on— are not simply wrong but that they mask the sources of history's dynamics, culture's pain, and the possibilities of innovation and change. Braiding alerts us to look for improbable intersections, incommensurable ways of living, discrepant imaginings, unexpected movements of influence, and inspiration existing side by side—within families and neighborhoods, as well as psychological, spiritual, and intellectual knots within the same minds and hearts. The religious idioms discussed in the chapters of this book were engagements with the complexities and ambiguities of the times, not adaptations to a normative trajectory toward the modern.[3]

This is especially true of the history of the sacred in late-twentieth-century American Catholicism. Here the lure of the modernist paradigm has been most powerful: from this perspective, Catholics "mature" in the 1960s from an infantile faith focused on bodies and things to a rational faith concerned above all else with justice, from superstition to morality, from the polytheism of the cult of saints to the monotheism of a Christ-centered faith. This dream of upward religious movement is not unique to Catholics: it is as old as the Enlightenment in the West and as current as the developmental models of faith stages popular among religious educators and psychologists today. The modernist story only barely masks its prescriptive edge: modernity is the norm, religions must conform, and it is true that Catholics around the world in the twentieth century began to look more and more like well-behaved moderns. But the history of the sacred is braided too. Catholics labored in memory and practice to uproot the saints, a topic of chapters 2 and 5, but the power of presence in things and places, and in memory, turned out to be stronger than they had anticipated. New devotions arose to take the place of the old. Just when it seemed that the Blessed Mother had been successfully subordinated to her son, the Virgin began appearing *everywhere* in the United States; newly arrived Catholics from Mexico brought a compelling devotion to Our Lady of Guadalupe that was then adopted by others; the children and grandchildren of the modernizing generation rediscovered old devotional practices. Removed from the normative modernist from-to paradigm, this all looks like the enduring engagement of a distinctly Catholic imagination that spans and transcends the categories of modern and premodern and renders them otiose with the changing circumstances of life in contemporary America. The saints were there in my mother's hospital room among Catholics of different ages, ethnic backgrounds, and professions. Most powerfully, as I will argue in chapter 5, sacral presence—the literal presence of the holy in things and places—migrates into Catholic memory. As historian Leigh Eric Schmidt writes of the modern ambivalence toward sacred presences, "those who denied the presence of voices and the mystery of sounds often continued to pursue them in spite of their incredulity."[4]

"Now," my father said, looking down at Sally in his coffin, "he's not a cripple anymore."

The men and women who crowded together onto hillsides and into grottoes in Europe over the last two centuries to watch children interact with a sacred being only the youngsters could see, or the people lining the interstate in Clearwater, Florida, not too long ago to view the Virgin Mary reflecting back from the windows of an office building, understood these to be sites of the literal presence of the Mother of God on earth. So too the children who left cookies beside the tabernacle in church for Jesus or who made room for their guardian angels on their desk seats at school. Relics, holy cards, medals, oils, and statues brought holy figures into the places of everyday life. My uncle Sal did not think that the little statue of Blessed Margaret of Castello he kept on his bureau *was* the saint, but then again the statue did make Margaret really present to him and could be addressed as such. This is another theme of the book, the realness of sacred presence in the imaginations and experiences of religious practitioners and its fate in the modern world. Again I focus on Catholics, but some version of the problem of the presence of the sacred—of holy figures present to the senses and to relationship—is there among all religions in modernity.

No one any longer holds the secularization thesis to be universally true: there has been too much evidence to the contrary for the idea to stand that over the last two centuries religious belief and commitment have been slowly but inexorably disappearing from the modern world, religion's authority contracting and its explanatory reach diminishing in proportion to the spread of science and critical scholarship. This was surely not how modernity played out in the United States or in the cultures of Asia and Africa, and even in Europe the history of religion varies by region and

Figure 1. Apparition of the Virgin Mary on the side of an office building in Clearwater, Florida, mid-1990s. (Photo courtesy of Guss Wilder III.)

according to different national historical circumstances. Abandoning the outlines of a single story, scholars now talk of alternative modernities and of varying patterns of negotiation across the globe in the encounter of inherited religions with the social, political, and economic circumstances of modernity. Scholars no longer have to present the powerful religious idioms of the modern world as atavistic holdovers of a vanishing time or as distorted reactions against modernity, which makes a richer religious history of modernity possible.

But this revision should not obscure the deep antipathy between modern cultures all over the world and the practice and experience of sacred presence. Of all aspects of religion, the one that has been clearly most out of place in the modernizing world—the one that has proven least tolerable to modern societies—has been the radical presence of the gods to practitioners. The modern world has assiduously and systematically disciplined the senses not to experience sacred presence; the imaginations of moderns are trained toward sacred absence. So while it is true that religious faith has not gone away, sacred presences have acquired an unsavory and disreputable aura, and this clings to practices and practitioners of presence alike. Catholics came late to this repositioning of presence. For most of the twentieth century, Catholic education in the United States consisted of a sustained disciplining of children toward presence, as chapter 3 describes, and among the venues of sacred presence in the culture were children's bodies. The tense dynamics of this encounter of modern life with inherited religious idioms of presence is one of the major topics of the book. I am also concerned throughout with developing social psychological and social historical frames for examining presence: how can historians and scholars of culture talk about the *realness* of presence within particular social worlds at particular times but always within the limits of our modern disciplines? And how does serious engagement with the cultural realities of presence allow us to push against the limits of modern scholarship in religion? My hope is that by asking critical, analytical questions about presence (which, I have to admit, religious practitioners usually do not like to hear) I can contribute to grinding a sharper critical lens on the constraints and disavowals of modern scholarly methods in the study of religion (which, I have to recognize, modern scholars may not like).

My uncle was tiny in his coffin like one of Saint Francis's little dark birds or like the body of Blessed Margaret exposed each year on her feast day, her brown leathery skin tight over her small bones. On the way to the funeral we drove past two apartment buildings where Sally had lived with his family many years ago before moving out on his own, first to the House of the Holy Comforter and then to the Catholic residence at the

Figure 2. The body of Blessed Margaret of Castello, believed to be incorrupt by her devout, under the main altar in the church of San Domenico, Città di Castello, Italy

end of his life. The priest saying the mass clearly had loved my uncle. God knew before all time, he began his eulogy, that God was giving Sally an especially "steep hill" to climb when God put him on earth. All men and women must work out their salvations, he said, but Sal's road was going to be hard. Sal had made the best of what he was given. Sal had made, in the priest's phrase, "a tolerable life for himself."

I tell many family stories in the pages ahead, as I already have in this introduction. This makes the book an ambiguous entity, because it is not really an autobiography—even in the most autobiographical chapters, 1, 4, and 5, I refer to other sources and literatures—but then again readers will become familiar with my grandmothers and uncles and aunts together with Saint Gemma Galgani, Blessed Margaret of Castello, the Sacred Heart of Jesus, the souls in purgatory, and the guardian angels. I decided to work like this, first, because presence in Catholic cultures is enacted among other ways within families; family dynamics are one spring of sacred presences—the saints and the Mother of God draw on the intimate histories of relationships within family worlds (always as these are shaped and inflected by culture and society). The saints borrow dimensions of their identities from family members who in turn become associated with particular saints. The communion of saints, in other words, is a matter of bonds within families and between heaven and earth, and my use of family stories makes this point. Because I wanted to trace the implications of these bonds at the most intimate levels of experience, moreover, in the psychological and social histories of particular families, I turned to my own, which I know (at least in some ways) especially well and because I have experienced some of these implications myself. Where it was possible or seemed necessary, I secured permission to tell these stories, but they were always my stories to tell too.

I also did this in order to uncover the grounds of my own interest in religions. A deep reticence about revealing anything of our own religious stories is very much a part of the discipline and ethos of religious studies. I have spent years playing with students' inevitable questions—"What is your religious faith?" "How did you come to study religion?" "What do you believe?"—turning them around to explore the nature of religious scholarship, insisting that knowledge of my religious past is irrelevant for my work. I have often heard colleagues in the discipline say (and I have agreed with them) that it is a matter of pride when their students at the end of a semester still do not know what religious worlds their professor comes from. But I've also long thought that the time has come in the history of the discipline for a season of public autobiographical self-reflection when we explore the social, psychological, and cultural grounds of our work, just as anthropologists no longer occlude themselves in the field. Such critical self-examination I now see as part of the necessary ongoing precritical work of the discipline, the intimate analogue of the deepening historical self-consciousness of religious studies today, its intensifying awareness of the ambiguities of its own history that I will discuss in chapter 6. Certainly our religious pasts haunt the discipline: the hallways of religious studies departments are thick with ghosts—the minister father, the tongue-speaking mother, the nuns and priests who taught us, the born-again brother—who are our invisible conversation partners, as real as the saints and spirits and ancestors of the religious worlds we study. We'd probably better acknowledge them. If sexual relations in the field is the great taboo subject of anthropology, our own religious histories is the great taboo of religious studies, and so with the family stories in this book, which are always also stories about the saints and about the realness of the presence of the sacred in the circumstances of everyday life, I take a step in the direction of this critical self-reflection.[5]

"Now God has gathered Sally up to God's self," Father continued. " 'When I rise,' Jesus had said to his disciples, 'I will gather you all up to me,' " said Father, "and when God gathers us up, God presses into us the marks of his pain and suffering. He embraces us and holds us close, but this embrace marks us, we are lifted up but pressed deep with pain. This was especially true of Uncle Sally," Father went on. "Jesus held him so close in his love for him that he left the marks of his passion on his body. This was Sal's life. But Sal never complained about the life God had given him, and sometimes he even joked about it." At the end of his sermon, Father looked over at the shrouded coffin holding my uncle and said, "Sal, enjoy the eternal rest you have now in Paradise."

Finally, I want to say something about chapter 3, the chapter on the place of Catholic children in the webs of relationships between heaven and earth. I drafted successive versions of this chapter as the dreadful crisis of the abuse of children by priests and its cover-up by bishops and cardinals was unfolding in the American Catholic Church. Whatever else this moment was about in the history of Catholicism, it has fundamentally been about *children*, about children's vulnerability to adult power and adult fantasy in religious contexts and about the absence of real children in these settings—real children as opposed to "children" as the projection of adult needs and desires or "children" as extensions of adult religious interiority. The necessary response to the crisis must be about children too, and I believe that the study of the history of children's lives in the church makes a fundamental contribution both to understanding what cultural sources converged on the making of this shameful scandal and to constructing the measures necessary to prevent it from happening again.

History and *culture* have not been the operative or salient terms in efforts to understand the abuse of children by priests and the hierarchy's response to it, however. The *Charter for the Protection of Children and Young People* drafted by the U.S. Conference of Catholic Bishops at its meeting in Dallas in the early summer 2002 is unconcerned with the distinctive history of children in the church. The overriding tendency has been to sexualize the problem, to see it as the consequence of the celibate body or of sexual perversion. Defining the crisis as one of biological urges works to take it out of history and culture. One exception to this has been the suggestion in Rome and by some conservative American Catholic thinkers that the American crisis—and there seems to be little doubt in Rome that this is a distinctly *American* Catholic crisis—reflects the American culture of rights and specifically the liberation movements of the 1960s. In this view, the crisis of child abuse is the result of the historically disordered bodies and body of the modern liberal state as represented by proponents of rights, especially rights for homosexuals. Thus the abused bodies of children are being appropriated and mobilized to substantiate a critique of liberal Catholicism and of homosexuality in the United States, and many Catholics fearfully anticipate a crackdown on gay priests. This is the second abuse of children by the church. It poses a question for historical and cultural analysis: how is it that children, and specifically perhaps children in pain and distress, are so effective to think with in this culture and to think with in this way?

Any number of issues come into play in the crisis of the clerical abuse of children: the nature of authority in the church, the history and practice of the episcopacy, relations between clergy and laity, the unfinished business of the Second Vatican Council, and—although this is hardly a complete list—the history of anti-Catholicism in the United States, Catholic sensitivity to and acute awareness of how other Americans are looking at them, and the resulting postures of extreme self-protection that have often enough led to complicity and avoidance as responses to incidents of child abuse in particular communities. Adults and children both could be persuaded to keep silent about abusive priests by the argument that disclosure would satisfy and authorize the enemies of the church. So the crisis raises a range of questions for historical and cultural analysis.

But again this is a story about children's lives in the church, about the stories told about children in Christian history over time, about their "innocence" or "depravity," and the serious consequences of these stories for real-life children in particular times and places, about the kinds of relationships that formed between children and adults in the spaces of the sacred, about children's lives in Catholic settings, their vulnerability and exposure, their bodies, their experiences of themselves as persons (including religious persons and moral subjects), and the boundaries they were and were not able to maintain around themselves in the culture as it was made for and with them. "Boundaries" here refers to the necessary but socially and historically variable ways that relations among people are structured in a culture, the possibilities and limits of what people can do, feel, say, or imagine in relation to others, and the ways that separateness and connectedness are imagined and enacted. Children have been largely missing from commentary on the crisis. The victims are all adults now and what has seemed most urgent or legally relevant and appropriate has been their postchildhood trauma and difficulties (or else children have been present only long enough to be appropriated for others' agendas). So the very least that scholars of U.S. Catholic history and culture can do is to put children back into this story.

But to say "children" is not enough here: we need to put back into the story children in their ongoing relationships with adults, because children do not live and grow as persons alone or only in relation to their peers. Relationships among adults and children—especially adult religious and children—were at the heart of American Catholicism in the twentieth century, for reasons I will discuss in chapter 3. The distinctive quality of American Catholic life and identity over the past century was fundamentally shaped by and in relationships between adults and children. I have come to think of American Catholic culture as a kind of three-dimensional dynamic structure comprised of interconnected, mutually implicated relational triangles (with all the tension implied by the term). The relational configurations included priest/nun/child; parent/child/adult religious; child/adult religious/saint; child/parent/saint; family member/child/adult religious; and so on. The figures in these bonds—"Father," "Sister," "Grandmother"—were always both real and imaginary, experienced and desired or feared at the same time. This is all more schematic than I want it to be, but I am trying to develop an image of the rich and dynamic psychological and religious structure of American Catholicism in the mid–twentieth century. These were real bonds, intense psychological and religious connections on earth and between heaven and earth, within the changing circumstances and places of American Catholic life over time. Chapter 3 charts some of the parameters of these relationships. Catholics need to think about the kinds of relationships into which they have invited children in religious settings in the past and continue to invite them and what becomes of children in adult religious fantasies of them.

Chapter 3 pays attention to the boundaries between children and adults in Catholic contexts, the limits of the permissible and especially to the ways that issues of religious exigency rendered these boundaries porous. Again my focus is on Catholic culture, but its implications and intentions are wider. Parents and religious figures very often feel themselves possessed of a special authority and permission to breach children's boundaries for reasons of religious urgency. The matter of deciding which children had vocations to the religious life, as I describe in chapter 3, makes this clear. The Catholic Church in particular, but other religious communities as well, is challenged by the contemporary crisis to reflect theologically, historically, and practically on the appropriate balance between autonomy and authority in children's experiences and about the necessary boundaries that must be maintained around children's bodies and minds. The very notion of children's rights in religious contexts almost always strikes religiously committed people as an inappropriate curtailment of legitimate, indeed socially and spiritually necessary, parental and religious authority and control. But children clearly must be seen as entities separate from adults in religious environments. Any religious community's effort to identify and authorize such boundaries must recognize that this work of taking care of children occurs in the context of well-established histories of intimacy between adults and children within these various communities that have an enduring impact on contemporary experience. To this work of uncovering the past for the benefit of the present chapter 3 is a contribution.

In the hospital on the night he died Sal heard an announcement over the loudspeaker. "Is Doctor Blank on the floor?" the amplified voice asked. Sally, who was so weak he couldn't speak above the barest whisper, beckoned my father over to the bed and spoke into his ear. "Tell them if he's on the floor, they should pick him up." Later, after drowsing a bit, he told my father to make sure that the people running a special dinner for the handicapped at Saint Patrick's Cathedral the following week got his order right—he wanted the linguine with clam sauce, he insisted. Then he slipped into sleep again which became a coma and then death.

I have not changed the tense in which I initially wrote the first chapter, however. Sal still lives in its present, because I wanted readers to encounter him as he went about his days in the company of his friends and of the saints.

Do I believe in Papa Gede? Do I believe in Gemma Galgani, the guardian angels, the souls in purgatory, or any of the other special figures that appear in this book in relationships with people and between heaven and earth? A note of incredulity sounds in the questions—surely you don't believe . . . This suggests that what I am being asked is if I believe in the real *presence* of these beings. Do I think they are really there? Are they real? This is what would be so incomprehensible and so scandalous. The word *belief* bears heavy weight in public talk about religion in contemporary America: to "believe in" a religion means that one has deliberated over and then assented to its propositional truths, has chosen this religion over other available options, a personal choice unfettered by authority, tradition, or society. What matters about religion from this perspective are its ideas and not its things, practices, or presences. This is not necessarily how Americans actually are religious, of course, but this account of religion carries real normative force.

The people who appear in these pages clearly think about their religion; to emphasize practice is not to deny reflection. They also make choices, although they do so in the more modest sense of choosing on the field of what is already given to them. (That I even have to write these things indicates how strong the normative public discourse of religion is in this culture.) But belief has always struck me as the wrong question, especially when it is offered as a diagnostic for determining the realness of the gods. The saints, gods, demons, ancestors, and so on are real in experience and practice, in relationships between heaven and earth, in the circumstances of people's lives and histories, and in the stories people tell about them. Realness imagined this way may seem too little for some and too much for others. But it has always seemed real enough to me.

Chapter One

"MILDRED, IS IT FUN TO BE A CRIPPLE?"
THE CULTURE OF SUFFERING IN
MID-TWENTIETH CENTURY AMERICAN
CATHOLICISM

> A shut-in should let people know he is the same as other
> people and not from another planet.
> *Sal Cavallaro, "A Shut-in's Day"*

> To be a handicap does not mean that you are sick or
> mentally retarded. A handicap can have a full, healthy,
> happy life, just like their fellow human beings. There is no
> need for them to be put or live in the back room.
> *Sal Cavallaro, "Who Is Handicapped[?]"*

O N THE FIRST SATURDAY of every month in the 1960s my uncle
Sally, who has cerebral palsy, used to go to a different parish in
New York City or its suburbs for Mass and devotions in honor
of Our Lady of Fatima and then afterwards to a Communion breakfast
sponsored by that month's host church. These special outings for "shut-
ins" and "cripples"[1] were organized by the Blue Army of Mary, an association of men and women dedicated to spreading the messages of apoca-
lyptic anti-Communism and personal repentance delivered by Mary at
Fatima in 1917.[2] My uncle would be waiting for my father and me in the
hallway of his mother's apartment, dressed in a jacket and tie and smoking cigarettes in a long, imitation tortoiseshell holder that my grandmother fitted between the knotted fingers of his left hand. He smoked by
holding his forearm stiff on the green leatherette armrest of his wheelchair,
then bending his torso forward and bringing his legs up until his lips
reached the burning cigarette. He was always afraid that my father
wouldn't show up, and as his anxiety mounted, my uncle clenched again
and again over his cigarettes so that by the time we got there—always
early—the foyer was dense with smoke.

We laid Sally down on his back on the front seat of the car. My grandmother, in an uncharacteristic moment of hope and trust, had taken my

uncle as a boy to a mysterious doctor on the Lower East Side who said he could make him walk. Instead, he had locked Sally's legs at the knees, sticking straight out in front of him, fusing him into a ninety-degree angle, and then had vanished. Sally reached back, hooked his right wrist into the steering wheel, and pulled himself in while we pushed. When he was in the car up to his legs, my father leaned in over him and drew him up. He angled my uncle's stiff limbs under the dashboard and wedged them in.

My father went around the car and dropped in the other side. He looked over at his brother-in-law, the two of them sweating and panting. "Okay?" he asked. My uncle nodded back.

We drove to a designated meeting place, usually another church's parking lot, where members of the Blue Army, wearing sky-blue armbands printed with an image of the Virgin of Fatima and the legend "Legion of Mary," helped us pull my uncle out of the car. Other cripples were arriving. The members of the Blue Army knew who wanted to sit next to each other, and they wheeled my uncle's friends over to him, locking them in place beside him. He greeted them solemnly, not saying very much. From here a big yellow school bus would take the cripples out to the church; we'd follow in the car. My uncle was anxious to get going.

The wheelers teased him in loud voices whenever they brought a woman over. "Here's your girlfriend!" they shouted. "I saw her talking to So-and-So yesterday! Aren't you jealous?! You're gonna lose this beautiful girl! Come on, Sal, wake up." They pounded my uncle on the back. "Don't you know a good thing when you got it?" Their voices and gestures were exaggerated, as if they were speaking to someone who couldn't understand their language.

The women rolled their heads back and laughed with bright, moaning sounds, while their mothers fussed at their open mouths with little embroidered handkerchiefs, dabbing at saliva. "Calm down, calm down," they admonished their daughters, "don't get so excited."

My uncle laughed too, but he always looked over at me and shook his head.

There was a statue of San Rocco on a side altar of the Franciscan church of my childhood. The saint's body was covered with open, purple sores; tending to the bodies of plague victims, he had been infected himself. A small dog licked the open sores on his hands. The Franciscans told us that Saint Francis kissed a leper's sores. Once he drank the water he had just used to bathe a leper.

One woman, a regular of the First Saturday outings, came on a stretcher covered with clean sheets in pale, pastel colors; her body was immobile. She twisted her eyes up and looked out at us through a mirror fixed to the side of the stretcher, while her mother tugged at her dress to make sure it stayed down around her thin ankles.

These were special people, God's children, chosen by him for a special destiny. Innocent victims, cheerful sufferers, God's most beloved—this was the litany of the handicapped on these First Saturdays. Finding themselves in front of an unusual congregation, priests were moved to say from the pulpit at mass that the prayers of cripples were more powerful than anyone else's because God listened most attentively to these, his special children. Nuns circulated among the cripples, touching their limbs kindly and reverently, telling them how blessed they were, and how wonderful. To be standing these mornings in a parking lot or church basement was to be on ground made holy by the presence of beds and wheelchairs and twisted bodies.

At breakfast, the mothers of the cripples hovered over them. They held plastic straws, bent in the middle like my uncle, while their children drank coffee or juice; they cut Danishes into bite-sized pieces; they cleaned up spills. Volunteers from the parish and members of the Blue Army brought out plates of eggs and sausage.

"You have such a big appetite this morning!"

"Can you eat all that? God bless you!"

"If I ate like you I'd be even fatter than I am!"

But why had God done this to his most beloved children? What kind of love was this? What kind of God?

When he was done with his coffee, my uncle cupped himself around his cigarette.

Physical distress of all sorts, from conditions like cerebral palsy to the unexpected agonies of accidents and illness, was understood by American Catholics in the middle years of the last century as an individual's main opportunity for spiritual growth.[3] Pain purged and disciplined the ego, stripping it of pride and self-love; it disclosed the emptiness of the world. Without it, human beings remained pagans; in physical distress, they might find their way back to the Church, and to sanctity. "Suffering makes saints," one hospital chaplain told his congregation of sick people, "of many who in health were indifferent to the practices of their holy religion."[4] Pain was a ladder to heaven. The saints were unhappy unless they were in physical distress of some sort. Catholic nurses were encouraged to watch for opportunities on their rounds to help lapsed Catholics renew their faith and even to convert non-Catholics in the promising circumstances of physical distress.[5]

Pain was always the thoughtful prescription of the Divine Physician. The cancer afflicting Thomas Dooley, the handsome young doctor and

On suffering

missionary to Southeast Asia in the 1950s who completely captured American Catholic hearts, was celebrated in Catholic popular culture as a grace, a mark of divine favor. Dooley himself wrote, "God has been good to me. He has given me the most hideous, painful cancer at an extremely young age."[6] So central was pain to the American Catholic ethos that devotional writers sometimes went as far as to equate it with life itself—"The good days are a respite," declared a laywoman writing in a devotional magazine in 1950, "granted to us so that we can endure the bad days."[7]

Catholics thrilled to describe the body in pain. Devotional prose was generally overwrought, but on this subject it exceeded itself. There was an excess of a certain kind of sensuous detail in Catholic accounts of pain and suffering, a delicious lingering over and savoring of other people's pain. A dying man is presented in a story in a 1937 issue of the devotional magazine *Ave Maria* as having "lain [for twenty-one years] on the broad of his back, suffering from arthritis . . . his hands and fingers so distorted that he could not raise them more than an inch . . . his teeth set . . . so physically handicapped that in summer he could not brush away a fly or mosquito from his face because of his condition." It was never enough in this aesthetic to say simply "cancer," stark as that word is. Instead, it had to be the "cancer that is all pain."[8] Wounds always "throbbed," suffering was always "untold," pain invariably took its victims to the very limits of endurance.

The body-in-pain was thrilling. Flushed, feverish, and beautiful—"The sick room is rather a unique beauty shop," one priest mused, where "pain has worked more wonders than cosmetics"[9]—it awaited its lover. A woman visiting a Catholic hospital in 1929 came upon a little Protestant girl who was dying and reported:

> He has set His mark upon her. Somehow you guess; those frail little shoulders are shaped for a cross, those eyes are amber chalices deep enough for pain, that grave little courteous heart is big enough to hold Him! He will yet be her tremendous lover, drawing her gently into His white embrace, bestowing on her the sparkling, priceless pledge of His love—suffering.[10]

Pain had the character of a sacrament, offering the sufferer a uniquely immediate and intimate experience of Jesus' presence.[11] Walking amid the "couches of pain" laid out for the sunset service at Lourdes, an American visitor suddenly sensed that "he is here now. . . . Almost I can hear him speak,—almost I can reach out and touch his garment." Another writer reported that she knew "a very holy nun who is herself one of God's chosen ones" (meaning that she is afflicted with the most severe pain), "and one day she said something to me that I have never forgotten. She said, 'Sometimes God's hand seems to rest so heavily upon our shoulder, and we try to squirm away, and we cry, Oh, let me be! And then we begin to realize how tender as well as how heavy is His hand, and we want it there.' "[12]

This was a darkly erotic aesthetic of pain, one expression of the wider romanticism of American Catholicism in this period.[13] But for all this culture's fascination with physical distress, the sensual pleasure it took in feverish descriptions of suffering, it was also deeply resentful and suspicious of sick persons. A nasty edge of retribution and revenge is evident in these accounts. In one priest's typical cautionary tale of pain, "a young woman of Dallas, Texas, a scandal to her friends for having given up her faith because it interfered with her sinful life, was severely burned in an explosion. Before her death, through the grace of God, she returned to the Church."[14] According to a nursing sister, writing in the leading American Catholic journal for hospital professionals, *Hospital Progress*, in 1952: "Physical disability wears off the veneer of sophistication and forces the acceptance of reality. It is difficult for a patient imprisoned for weeks in a traction apparatus to live in a state of illusion."[15] Pain gives people their comeuppance. It serves as chastisement and judgment.

The Catholic tradition was ambivalent about the moral status of the sick. Despite constant injunctions to the contrary, a persistent identification was made between sickness and sin—not only sin in general or Original Sin, but the specific sinfulness of the person in pain—and the suspicion of all physical suffering as merited was never completely absent from devotional culture.[16] "You may complain and moan about a single toothache," Father Boniface Buckley chided the readers of *Sign* in 1945, but be "woefully forgetful of the fact that this particular pain may be due in justice for some sin of that very day."[17] God always has a reason for sending pain. Theology's restraint is evident here in Father Buckley's use of the conditional. More commonly, devotional writers threw such cautions to the winds in order to score some moral points with pain. Learn to take your pain the way a man takes his hangover, another priest scolded, and admit that "you asked for it."[18]

The association between physical sickness and moral corruption was reinforced throughout American Catholic popular literature by the persistent use of metaphors of illness to describe threats to the social fabric and sources of political and moral decay. As the editor of *Ave Maria* put it, aphoristically, in 1932, "Error is due to thought germs," against which only mental and moral hygiene is an effective prophylactic.[19] Another writer even suggested that to visit the sick was to "stand by the bedside of our soul-sick world."[20] The persistent metaphorical use of leprosy to excoriate various moral dangers was so egregious in the Catholic press that missionaries among sufferers of Hansen's disease regularly complained of the effect this usage was having on the people in their care.[21]

This was not an unusual rhetorical device, of course, but it achieved its own peculiar, disorienting resonance in Catholic devotionalism, where images of the body-in-pain were used to suggest both the depths of corruption and the highest reaches of spiritual glory. In the case of the leper, the two discrepant usages converged: the leper was at once physically—and morally—scrofulous and (potentially) sacred.[22]

As American Catholics interpreted an ancient tradition in their contemporary circumstances, the idea that sickness was punishment for something the sufferer had done took deeper hold. The more sentimental view of sickness as the training ground for saintliness was commonly reserved for people with genetic or birth trauma conditions, such as Sal and his friends. Their suffering, at least, could not be attributed to any moral failure since they were born this way. The innocence of people born with disabilities made them central to the elaboration of the gothic romance of suffering; because they were "innocent," unalloyed spiritual pleasure could be taken in the brokenness of their bodies. There was a cult of the "shut-in" among American Catholics in the middle years of the twentieth century, a fascination with "cripples" and a desire to be in some relation to them, which was thought to carry spiritual advantages. In the summer of 1939, *Catholic Women's World*, one of the most modern and upbeat of the Catholic magazines, set up a pen-pal system so that readers going away on vacation could write to shut-ins about their trips. The project was so popular that "many readers have written to us requesting that we put them in touch not only with one, but as many as three or four shut-ins."[23] There were a number of organizations dedicated to harnessing the spiritual power of shut-ins and putting it to work for the rest of the church, such as the Catholic Union of the Sick in America (CUSA), which formed small cells of isolated handicapped persons who communicated through a round-robin letter and whose assignment was to direct their petitions, more powerful by virtue of their pain, toward some specific social good.[24] The spiritual pleasure taken by the volunteers on the First Saturdays in their proximity to the handicapped was a reflection of this cult as well.

But the mistrust of the sick, the suspicion that their physical distress was the manifestation of a moral failing, lurked just below the surface of even the fantasy of the holy cripple. The eleventh-century "cripple" Hermann, who composed the Marian hymn "Salve Regina," is described in one article as having been "pleasant, friendly, always laughing, never criticizing, so that everybody *loved* him." Concluding, "What a record for a cripple!" the author implies that just the opposite could have been expected from a man like this.[25] The subtext here is that if Hermann had not been so delightful, he would not have deserved love—there was nothing unconditional about this culture's affection for cripples.

Apart from these "fortunate unfortunates," a favorite Catholic term for people with disabilities, however ambivalently construed, sick people were guilty people, and, not surprisingly, they behaved as such. Sick people were generally depicted as malingering, whining, selfish, overly preoccupied with their own problems, indolent, maladjusted, and self-destructive. They exaggerated the extent of their distress. They were quick to yield to despair and loneliness. Wake up to the fact that life is a vale of tears, one priest scolded the ill, and get rid of your "Pollyanna attitude," by which he meant stop hoping for relief. Above all, the sick could not be trusted. Without the astringent of religion, for example, lepers—even beloved lepers—would be "spiteful, cynical, and debauched," according to one visitor to Molokai, and this was maintained as generally true of all sick people.[26] As late as 1965, a Dominican priest writing in *Ave Maria* derided a sick person as a "spoiled child" and warned against "the tendency to remain in our suffering, to exaggerate the injustice, to pout."[27]

But what exactly constituted complaint? Were devotional teachers warning in these passages against the sometimes dark and self-defeating human impulse to protest the will of God or to rebel against the facts of life?

One Saturday the bus didn't come. Something had happened somewhere along its route. The hot summer's morning dragged on; the sidewalk around Sal's chair was littered with cigarette butts; and the garbled messages—there'd been a crash, no, it was just a flat tire, he'll be here any minute, he's upstate—from the people in charge of the outing, meant to be reassuring, just made the confusion and anxiety worse.

A man I didn't recognize, not one of the Blue Army regulars, strolled over to the back of Sal's chair and gripped its rubber handles as if he were going to push my uncle off someplace. He winked at me and my father. Maybe Sal knew him from someplace. "So, Sal," he boomed at the back of my uncle's head, sounding pleased with his own cheerfulness, "looks like you're gonna have to spend the night in this parking lot, hunh?"

My uncle gave an angry wave of dismissal, but the man behind him, comfortably resting his weight on his chair, went on. "Hey, Sal, you hear what I said? You're gonna have to spend the night out here in the parking lot! I hope you got your blankets! Maybe we can get the girls over there to sing you a lullaby."

My uncle rocked himself from side to side in his seat, as if he wanted to dislodge the man's grip on his chair and move him out from behind his back. Bored with the game, the man let go. "Jesus, I hope we get the hell out of here soon," he said to my father, and walked away.

Sal smacked the brakes off his chair with his hard, calloused hands and began to spin himself around in circles. My father tried to calm him down.

"Sally," he said, "the bus'll be here any minute, I know it. It's probably just a flat tire. Come on, don't get like this, you're gonna make yourself sick." But my uncle went on spinning. "Ahhhhhh," he roared, "ahhhhhh."

Everyone teased the cripples, joked with them, and needled them almost all the time. This may have been what the man behind Sally's chair was doing, but I don't think so. He was sweaty and angry. Maybe he was only there that morning because of his wife's devotion to Our Lady of Fatima; maybe he hated cripples and the stories they told about the human body, of all that could and did go wrong with it. He had bent forward, over the back of Sally's head and stared down at his bald crown and coarse gray hair. Maybe he hated the way the cripples drooled when they sucked up their coffee and juice on these Saturday mornings or the mess they made of Communion breakfast.

My uncle began to push himself along the parking lot's chain-link fence, hitting the wheels of his chair with hard shoves. When he got to the end of the fence, where it connected with the church, he spun himself around and began pounding his way back.

Maybe the man found it hard to sustain the idea that Sal and his friends were holier than he was, closer to heaven, when they sprayed him with saliva and bits of egg.

My uncle wheeled around again and started back along the fence.

"This is the only guy I know," my father said to me, "who can pace in a wheelchair."

Someone came over and demanded that Sal stop. "Control yourself! These things happen, Sal," she yelled at him, bending to lock his chair in place, but my uncle pushed her hand away and kept moving.

The morning wore on, and the fortunate unfortunates, disappointed and upset, got on everybody's nerves.

"Complaint" meant any sound that the sick might make, any use of their voices, whether it was to ask for a glass of water in the middle of the night, to question a doctor's decisions, to express a spiritual doubt, or to request that their bodies be shifted in bed. Hospitalized sick people who complained of physical discomfort were referred to in the *Voice of Saint Jude*, a periodical published at the Chicago shrine of the patron saint of hopeless causes, as "c.t.m.p.'s" ("cantankerous, tempestuous, maladjusted patients").[28] There was only one officially sanctioned way to suffer even the most excruciating distress: with bright, upbeat, uncomplaining, submissive endurance.[29] A woman dying horribly of an unspecified cancer was commended by *Ave Maria* for having written "cheerful, newsy notes" home from the hospital, with "only casual references to her illness."[30] In the spirit of a fashion editor, one devotional writer counseled the chronically ill to "learn to wear [your] sickness becomingly. It can be done. It has been done. Put a blue ribbon bow on your bedjacket and smile."[31] Visitors were instructed to urge their sick friends and kin to make the best use of their time; the sick should be happily busy and productive even in the most extreme pain.[32] "Only two percent of the various types of pain are permanent and continual," wrote Mary O'Connor in an *Ave Maria* article for the sick in 1951. She was onto their games. She knew they were likely to "wallow in the muck of self-pity or sympathy": "If the sieges of pain let up a little now and then, take up an interesting hobby and throw yourself into it with all you've got. You'll be delighted to find that your pain is lessening as a result." Her own experience was exemplary in this regard: since the onset of her pain a decade earlier, she had written over two thousand poems, articles, and stories.[33]

If such pitiless badgering failed to arouse the sick, against their sinful inclinations, to saintliness, there was always the scourge of the suffering of Jesus and Mary: no matter how severe your suffering, the sick were told, Jesus' and Mary's were worse, and *they* never complained. What is a migraine compared to the crown of thorns?[34] Who could ever suffer a loss like Mary's? Jesus' suffering served the same purpose as Mary's virtue in devotional culture: to diminish the integrity and meaning of ordinary persons' difficulties and experiences. Indeed, there was a hierarchy of scorn for sick people: just as Jesus' suffering outweighed all human pain, so truly awful pain was used to diminish anything less, and all physical distress was greater than any psychological trouble, in a pyramid of suffering with Jesus, all bloody, and Mary, modestly sorrowing, at its top. Leprosy, in particular, functioned in this ethos as a means of denying other forms of physical distress, which partially accounts for its ubiquity. The message to sick people was: someone else is always suffering more than you are—look at the lepers!—and besides, Jesus suffered most of all, so be quiet!

In this way, the priests, nuns, and laypeople writing for the many devotional magazines and diocesan newspapers that made up the popular literary culture of American Catholicism waged a campaign against men and women in physical or emotional distress. The saint offered as patron to the sick in this century was Gemma Galgani, who used violence against herself when she was ill, adding self-inflicted pain to the distress of disease so that she might "subdue even the faintest suggestion of rebellion on the part of the flesh against the spirit";[35] and if sick people would not subdue their own flesh as Saint Gemma had done hers, if they could not bedeck their own pain in ribbons, it would be done for them. (I will return to Saint Gemma Galgani in chapter 4.) The language used against people in pain was harsh and cruel, devoid of compassion or understanding, and dismissive of their experience. As one priest demanded, if a child spends "seven or nine years" in an iron lung, "what of it?"[36] There was only scorn, never sympathy, for the sick who failed to become saintly through pain.[37] Bending the idioms and images of popular religion against them so that even the suffering of Christ emerged as a reproach, devotional writers crafted a rhetoric of mortification and denial for the sick. This was particularly cruel since they were doing so in the language and venues of popular devotionalism, to which sick people customarily turned for spiritual and emotional comfort.

The consequence of this rhetoric was that pain itself—the awful, frightening reality of something going wrong in the body—disappeared. It was hidden behind the insistence that the sick be cheerful, productive, orderly; it was masked by the condescending assurances offered to the shut-in handicapped, offered by those who were not, that it was better to be a cripple; it was occluded by the shimmering, overheated prose, the excited fascination with physical torment, and the scorn and contempt for the sick.[38] There is not nearly as much suffering in the world as people complain of, chided a writer in the pages of *Ave Maria*—two years after the end of the First World War.[39] "I enjoyed my week with the lepers of Molokai," a traveler exclaimed as if he had not been sojourning among people he had just described as looking "more like corpses than human beings."[40] Chronic illness brought families together in special joy and intimacy, according to these writers.[41] Even Jesus' pain could be denied: lest they find in his Passion an expression of the reality of their own experience, the sick were occasionally reminded that, since he had been conceived without Original Sin, Jesus himself was never sick—the risk of Docetism apparently less troubling than that of compassion.[42] It was in this spirit that William P. McCahill, executive secretary of the President's Committee on National Employ the Physically Handicapped Week, could report with approval a child's question to a handicapped person, "Mildred, is it fun to be a cripple?" Yes, it is! McCahill assured his readers.[43]

Physical distress that had been thus purged of its everyday messiness, of the limits it imposed on the body, and of the dreariness of its persistence could be transmuted into its opposite. "Pain" became a "harvest" ripe for the gathering, a spiritual "powerhouse" that could light the church, a vein of gold to be mined, minted, and spent. "It isn't suffering that's the tragedy," one of CUSA's mottoes proclaims, "only wasted suffering."[44] In a 1953 meditation that mixed several of these transformative metaphors, Florence Waters urged the readers of *Ave Maria* to "travel the length and breadth of the country and add them up—the cardiacs, and arthritics, the cerebral palsied, the paraplegics, the amputees, the blind, the congenitally malformed, and the victims of countless other ills that tie human bodies to beds, wheelchairs, crutches, to one room or one house." What does all this add up to?—"A vast storehouse of spiritual power." In "stark, unadorned pain, mental and physical," Waters concluded, there is "a subtle but true coin that may be exchanged for spiritual goods for ourselves."[45]

So pain was alienable: coined from the bodies of the (untrustworthy) sick, it could be taken away and applied to the welfare of the healthy in a redistributive economy of distress.[46] God apparently sent pain to some people so that others might be edified, making the bodies of the sick conduits of communications and benefits from heaven to earth. But, again, actual sick people, the real persons suffering from specific illnesses in precise ways, got lost in this process.

Since all pain was God-sent and good, and since it was never in any case as bitter as weak, whining sick people made it out to be, there was no need to account for its place in the universe, to respond to the spiritual and intellectual distress it might have occasioned. Protestants required this, perhaps, but not Catholics, who knew that God sent pain always for a purpose;[47] and priests, who might have been expected to sympathize most compassionately with the spiritual and physical dilemmas of the sick, were said to be always cheerful in the presence of suffering because, unlike their counterparts in other faiths, they knew that the problem of pain had been "solved."[48] In any case, as American devotional writers reminded the sick, comprehensible suffering was not real suffering. Catholics were said to prefer to suffer humbly and submissively, in recognition of their own guilt, rather than attempting to lessen the sting of it through understanding. Only spoiled children required such reassurance.[49]

The crew of Italian, Irish, Puerto Rican, and West Indian janitors, kitchen workers, handymen, and gardeners who hid out from their supervisors in the boiler room of the House of the Holy Comforter (a residence on the Grand Concourse in the Bronx to which my uncle moved in the mid-1960s) had a lot to say about the sexuality of the cripples in the rooms above them. A soft-voiced Italian American man named Aldo usually started these conversations. "Hey, I was up there the other night, they had them in the showers—Jesus Christ, have you ever seen Jimmy's dick? It's like this . . ." He opened his hands about a foot wide. "They all got big dicks," someone else affirmed knowledgeably, and then the men would speculate about whether or not having such huge organs was another consequence of their being cripples, as if nature compensated there for the ravages elsewhere. Aldo was always kind and extremely attentive to the men with cerebral palsy who lived at the "home," stopping on his rounds through the floors to talk with them, bringing them things to eat from the kitchen between meals, but in the boiler room he returned again and again to the subject of cripples and sex. I was shocked, when I went to work at the House of the Holy Comforter in the summer after my first year of college, to encounter this other Aldo, so different from the one I knew upstairs, and he didn't spare me his fantasies of my uncle's sex life.

Often Aldo, less frequently one of the other men, sat next to Sally on the long back porch of the home and commented on the women walking past them along the garden walkways below. Leaning into Sally, he'd murmur, "Look at that one, Sal. What would you like to do with her?" He made a cupping motion with his hands. "Just one night, hah, Sally, what we couldn't do. Jesus, Mary, and Saint Anthony." My uncle seemed comfortable and happy during these conversations, apparently delighted with Aldo's company and enjoying their salacious bond, although I'm not sure of this.

The men in the boiler room claimed that in the early hours of the morning, the cripples crawled out of bed and wheeled themselves into the shadows for blow jobs from the few women with cerebral palsy living at the home. This was absolutely impossible, of course, if only for practical reasons: none of the residents could get out of their criblike beds by themselves, and there were no deep shadows in the well-lit building and no times when there were not nurses and orderlies everywhere. But none of the men in the boiler room, who were cynical and skeptical about everything else, ever questioned Aldo's tales of the cripples' nocturnal sexual carnival.

Devotional writers did not shrink from the hard God implied by their celebrations of pain; indeed, they delighted in him. In the winter of 1949, Jerry Filan, a man with cerebral palsy who was slightly younger than Sally, was badly burned in a fire at his home in Brooklyn. Filan had made two arduous trips to Lourdes in the hope of a miracle sometime before this, capturing the imaginations of devotional writers so that, by the time of the fire, Jerry Filan was a well-known "shut-in," admired and loved in the culture (in the way that shut-ins were admired and loved). The young man died after two months of excruciating pain. In their stories of his last days, Jerry Filan's admirers calmly affirmed, with the pride that American Catholics took in making such hard statements, that the fire was God's will. God's burning to death a young man in a wheelchair never seems to have occasioned any doubt or grief.[50]

This God reflected all the anger, resentment, scorn, and denial of the Catholic ethos of suffering and pain. A paralyzed woman, bedridden since she was seventeen, admonished herself to remember that "it is God who sends such things as cold toast."[51] Writing about a nun dying slowly of cancer, a priest concluded that God "had planned to fill her last days on earth with pain so that she might have greater glory in heaven."[52] The family of a little girl stricken with polio was told to marvel that God loved them (not necessarily her) so much as to send them this gift.[53] If anyone dared to register dismay at the handiwork of a deity who was mean-spirited and petty enough to chill a sick woman's toast, he or she would have met with derision from devotional writers, and with even harsher injunctions to silence. American Catholic religious teachers practiced an especially rough theodicy in which a cheerful, compliant silence was deemed the only appropriate response to human sorrow.

But what was it like to believe that this mean God wanted you to suffer like this? Or to hear from the mouths of the ambulatory and the healthy calm affirmations of your distress, to receive from them the word that you were better off bedridden, poor, and alone?

"They hid us away," my uncle shouted at me one afternoon on the back porch of the home, long after my days there as a summertime janitor. He lifted himself off his chair by his elbows and rasped at me, "You don't know what it was like!"

We were in the middle of a conversation—an "interview," I was calling it—about Sal's favorite saints for a new project of mine when he began telling me how the families of his friends, ashamed of them, hid them away in the back rooms so that their neighbors wouldn't see them. "We talk to each other about these things," Sal said over and over to me. "You don't know what I know."

My grandmother never hid Sal away. Before the operation on his knees, he used to crawl out of the apartment and slide down the building's steps on his rear end, then sit on the stoop watching over First Avenue. Later on, his brothers carried him downstairs or he would lean sideways out his bedroom window on a pillow. But not all the neighbors were comfortable with the sight of him. One crazy woman taunted my grandmother constantly about Sal. She called him "a diseased piece of meat." "May the doors of Calvary"—a cemetery in Queens, New York—"close behind you," she screamed at my grandmother on the street, announcing to the stoops and sidewalks that Sally was a judgment on his family.

"They left them alone all day in dark rooms. I know these things—they told me about them—you don't know."

Sal has always had many friends, male and female, all over the city, and he's had a number of extended, monogamous, romantic engagements over time, as have most of his acquaintances. Sal's closest friends belong to the United Cerebral Palsy Federation, which has a large, modern building on Twenty-third Street between Lexington and Park Avenues where Sal and the others go for classes and social events. This is where Sal said he'd heard stories of people being abandoned in back rooms, left all day without even water to drink.

The UCP has been Sal's special domain for many years, his place away, like his younger brothers' offices and social haunts. A couple of times a week he dresses up in his good clothes and wheels himself out to the curb to wait for the van that takes him to his downtown world. Whenever I visited him at the House of the Holy Comforter, I heard stories about the UCP, about the pretty girls volunteering there, whose pictures Sal sometimes put up on his dresser, about a discussion of abortion he had with his friends in psychology class or some hilarious tale of woe involving one or the other of his more maladroit or flamboyant friends.

"You know Irving, right?" Sally'd start, wheezing with laughter, his eyes tearing. "The other night, down at the UCP . . ."

He's asked me to come and visit him there, but I've never gone; for some reason, I feel uncomfortable about dropping in on him at that place. Recently, I passed by there on a wet summer night, very late in the evening. A solitary figure was sitting under the blue fluorescent lights of the building's entryway, waiting to go home. I thought I recognized the silhouette, and I stopped, standing just off to the side. The man didn't move; he stared ahead, gently nodding his head in response to some inner thought. His face was smooth, his forehead uncreased. He seemed to be supremely at peace.

I did know him, actually, or I think I did—he looked like Jimmy, from the old House of the Holy Comforter. When the home closed some years ago, the men and women with cerebral palsy had moved to other residences across the city. My uncle still saw them all at the UCP, but I didn't anymore. Jimmy was a man of astounding self-confidence. For all of the many years that I knew him, he was working on an autobiography, a book that combined—he told me once—his understanding of things, his life's philosophy, with stories about what it was like growing up with cerebral palsy. Whenever he was not at the UCP or visiting in the garden of the home with his girlfriend, whose parents brought her every week from another residence across the city, Jimmy was in his room, working on his autobiography.

A West Indian orderly would come in after breakfast and fix a tight elastic band around Jimmy's head; his forehead was permanently grooved at this spot, like a trumpeter's lips. Affixed to this band so that it stuck out from the middle of Jimmy's forehead was a long, thin rod with a round, cushioned button at the tip. Jimmy was now ready to work. Bending forward again and again over his electric typewriter, he touched the tip of the rod to the keys. The last time I checked with Jimmy, his manuscript was more than eight hundred pages long.

At a time when several American industries were dedicated to the desperate work of helping people avoid or deny pain, which was increasingly understood as an obstacle to performance, achievement, and consumption in a culture that has treated physical distress as a source of embarrassment and shame as well as a sign of personal failure, the Catholic ethos posed (as Catholics themselves recognized) a powerful alternative. Catholics offered a storehouse for what everyone else was disposing of: the notion of sickness as a source of spiritual energy for the whole church recast the uselessness and isolation of sickness into participation and belonging. Organizations like the Catholic Union of the Sick in America assigned the physically distressed a privileged place in the spiritual economy and offered them a way to reconnect themselves to the world around them literally *through*, not despite, their illnesses.[54]

American Catholics in these years were enraptured and enthralled by physical distress. They presented themselves to the rest of the nation as a people experienced in pain. This was what set Catholics apart and above others: in such an elitism of pain, rebelling against illness, whining, and complaining were seen as characteristically Protestant responses, while Catholics were stronger, better able to endure, better prepared to suffer. "It's how I react to cancer" that is important, Dooley wrote, not the suffering itself, because "people will see how I react" and draw spiritual lessons from it.[55] This was one of the things that Catholics could teach American Protestants and, beyond them, the world.[56] There was a specular quality about the way in which Catholics understood their suffering. The devotional press severely and coldly admonished Catholics to suffer well in the sight of others, particularly Protestants, as if everyone were taking note of how they handled their distress. Pain served in this way as both a test of Catholic presence in the United States and a guarantee of it.

But there is an irony here: these romantic evocations of pain without analgesia and of the spiritual glories of leprosy were appearing just when the children and grandchildren of Catholic immigrants were beginning to leave the old ethnic neighborhoods of the Northeast and Midwest for the middle-class suburbs and American way of life beyond, just when the fantasy that scientific medicine could cure almost anything was becoming pervasive and Catholics themselves were developing a sophisticated network of up-to-date hospitals. The ethos of pain was being elaborated in Catholic magazines alongside tips for arranging new furniture, recipes, beauty hints, and ways to throw successful birthday parties for children, all written in the upbeat prose of women's magazines.

Elaborated in a particular way, physical distress was regularly counterposed in devotional culture to middle-class achievement. What good is success, money, power, or fame in this vale of tears? Catholic writers asked, over and over again—in the same periodicals that regularly celebrated the success, money, power, and fame of Catholic film stars, business tycoons, and athletes. One historian has suggested that the pervasive preoccupation with pain in American Catholic culture of this time was a way for the children of immigrants to articulate and respond to their uneasiness with their success in the United States.[57] Young American Catholics with southern European or eastern European or Irish parents and grandparents were caught in a terrible double bind after the First World War. American culture, as they encountered it in advertising, films, school, and the workplace, proclaimed that ambition was good, that material achievement and consumption were worthy goals. But this generation had grown up in cultures, religious and ethnic, that advocated self-control and self-denial, sacrifice and delayed gratification. These were the values of the Catholic family economy taught by parish priests and nuns, expressed in the stories of the saints and the old countries told to children, and evident in the iconography surrounding them in church. They may have begun to "disdain" the culture of the enclaves, as James T. Fisher writes, but the immigrants' children could not free themselves of it. This clash of moral sensibilities was exacerbated, furthermore, by the fact that the immigrants' children were trying to make it—and were by then succeeding—in a society that had not welcomed their parents and in which they were uncertain of their own places. These were the roots of the anger, resentment, and self-recrimination that found expression in the discourse of pain and the broken body, and of its ambivalence.

In other words, the modern American Catholic cult of pain and suffering cannot simply be attributed to the European heritage, although it certainly had an ancient resonance. This was not peasant fatalism reborn in the industrial working class: the parents and grandparents of the people writing about how wonderful it was to suffer cancer without recourse to painkillers had come to America to escape pain, after all, not to make a fetish of it. American Catholics of the second and third generation improvised an ethic of suffering and pain out of elements available in their tradition, in conscious and unconscious response to their contemporary circumstances. What they made lent an aura of spiritual heroism to the frustrations and setbacks they experienced in moving, with guilt and uncertainty, out of the ethnic enclaves, and it assured them of their moral superiority over the culture they were ambivalently striving toward. The constant refrain that pain mocked the pretensions of the world transformed their resentment of the people who appeared to be more successful than they were (among whom they were not sure of finding the place they desired) into a satisfying reaffirmation of traditional Catholic values.

The discourse of pain was similar in this regard to that of ethnicity in American Catholic communities of the 1930s (and later).[58] Both were made here, not inherited; both were produced through the constitution of necessary others—racial or cultural, in one case, the depraved, malingering sick person in the other—against which one's own identity and that of the community could be secured and affirmed. Finally, both ethnic nostalgia and the ethos of suffering and pain articulated the complex and ambivalent feelings that erupted out of the changing social circumstances of American Catholics in these years, when the immigrants' children found themselves pulled in different directions by memory and desire, parents and spouses, Catholic and American values. Denial and displacement gave to each discourse its rigidity and harshness.

"You can get up and go get yourself a glass of water," Sally was saying to me in a tense, hoarse voice, "whenever you want. You can get up and walk out of here today, but I can't!" He waved his arm in the direction of the front door.

First the stories of friends hidden in back rooms, and now this. Sally had never been so angry with me before. In between his accusations and challenges my uncle took deep breaths and held himself rigidly against the back of his chair with his long arms, looking away from me, shaking his head.

A new holy figure had recently entered Sal's customary pantheon of saints: Blessed Margaret of Castello.[59] Sal kept an image of her propped up on his messy, cluttered desk alongside holy cards of Saint Francis and Saint Anthony and pictures of his girlfriend, his nieces and nephews, and himself with various camp counselors and UCP staff. I'd never heard of her before or seen her image anywhere else. The holy card showed a small, bent figure leaning on a rough, wooden staff. Her eyes were closed and her feet were turned in. A pamphlet from Margaret's shrine in Philadelphia describes her as "A PATRON OF THE UNWANTED . . . A SAINT FOR OUR TIMES . . . BLIND . . . CRIPPLED . . . HUNCHBACKED . . . DWARF."

Sal had heard about Margaret at one of the First Saturday gatherings he still attended occasionally; a Dominican priest talked to the group about her. "If she'd been born today," Sally said to me, "she'd'a been an abortion." Margaret's father was Captain of the People of the Umbrian city-state of Metola. His thirteenth-century victory over the neighboring Republic of Gubbio had brought him great fame and wealth. The captain hoped that his first child would be a son to carry on the family's name and increase its glory, but his wife had given birth instead to a tiny girl, blind and horribly misshapen, in 1287. The bitterly disappointed couple hid the infant away in the castle, refusing even to give her a name. A gentle servingwoman called the baby "Margarita." The child was not only blind, she had a twisted foot and a hunchback. She was also a dwarf.

Sally interrupted himself. "She wouldn't have been born today," he said again, "she would have been an abortion." I didn't quite understand what Sally meant by this, but later I learned that Margaret's devout say that modern technology would have allowed her wealthy parents to discover

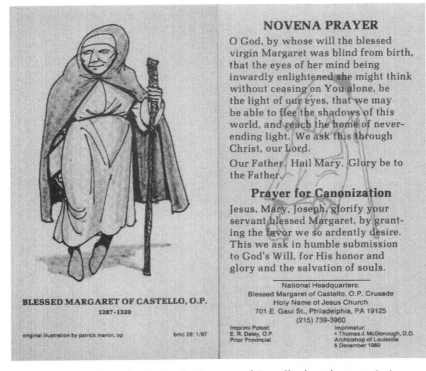

NOVENA PRAYER

O God, by whose will the blessed virgin Margaret was blind from birth, that the eyes of her mind being inwardly enlightened she might think without ceasing on You alone, be the light of our eyes, that we may be able to flee the shadows of this world, and reach the home of never-ending light. We ask this through Christ, our Lord.

Our Father. Hail Mary. Glory be to the Father.

Prayer for Canonization

Jesus, Mary, Joseph, glorify your servant blessed Margaret, by granting the favor we so ardently desire. This we ask in humble submission to God's Will, for His honor and glory and the salvation of souls.

National Headquarters:
Blessed Margaret of Castello, O.P. Crusade
Holy Name of Jesus Church
701 E. Gaul St., Philadelphia, PA 19125
(215) 739-3960

Imprimi Potest:
E. R. Daley, O.P.
Prior Provincial

Imprimatur:
+ Thomas J. McDonough, D.D.
Archbishop of Louisville
5 December 1980

BLESSED MARGARET OF CASTELLO, O.P.
1287-1320

original illustration by patrick martin, op   bmc 29: 1/87

Figure 3. Holy card of Blessed Margaret of Castello, based on a painting conceived and commissioned by Nora AlaFriz, Philippines, that hangs in Margaret's shrine in Louisville, Ky.

her congenital conditions in the womb and that legalized abortion would have permitted them to kill her. For this reason "little Margaret," as her devout call her, has been proposed as the patron saint of the unborn and unwanted and of the antiabortion movement.[60] Sally was starting to get agitated, and the mood of the conversation was growing darker.

When Margaret was six years old, her father, terrified that the lively child would wander out of the castle's shadows and be seen by someone, to the disgrace of his name, had her walled up in a room. The girl was fed through a small window. She remained in this cell for seven years, and it was here that Margaret, cheerful and forgiving even in these circumstances, according to her biographers, began experiencing Jesus' presence in an unusually vivid way. She fasted continually from the age of seven on and mortified her flesh by wearing a hairshirt to increase her discomfort in the cell, which was hot in the summer and freezing in the winter. (It was also here that Margaret, as an adolescent, began struggling with temptations against her purity, as most popular biographies of her say. Sally must have known about this, although he didn't mention it to me.)

Sal paused again, this time to tell me about his friends who'd been hidden in the back rooms of their families' apartments. "May the gates of Calvary close behind you!" the crazy old woman had screamed at my grandmother.

When she was thirteen years old, Margaret was taken by her mother to the nearby town of Città di Castello and abandoned there in a church. Her devout vividly imagine the little girl groping her way along the cold walls of the sanctuary, calling out for her mother, with the church bells marking the hours of the day's passing as she gradually realizes what has happened to her. Margaret lived on the streets for a while, begging for her food, until the townspeople became aware of her sanctity and took her into their homes. She eventually entered a Dominican order of lay-women and died in 1320, when she was thirty-three years old.

"You know what I like about her?" my uncle asked me at the end of the story. "I like it that there's somebody up there"—he glanced heaven-ward—"like us." He was smiling, and the way he rolled his eyes up re-minded me of the looks he'd given me when Aldo was teasing him about girls.

"Don't you think," I asked him, trusting the calm that seemed to have returned between us, "that Saint Francis and Saint Anthony can know what you feel, since they're saints?"

This was when Salvatore began shouting about water and the front door. I'd never know—nor would Saint Francis or Saint Anthony—what it was like to be crippled.

One of the pictures on his desk showed Sally with a beautiful young woman from the South Bronx named Silvia, a counselor at the UCP sum-mer camp whom my uncle was crazy about. Sometimes Silvia came by the home to visit him in the winter. He said that once, when Silvia's little sister had been hit by a car, he and Silvia had prayed together to Blessed Margaret to heal the girl. She did.

"But I never asked her to make me walk," he snapped.

Finally, I had to leave. I got up, kissed my uncle on the top of his head like I always did, and then—just as he said I would—I walked out. The last thing my uncle said about Blessed Margaret was, "She has a little bit of all the things we have."

Margaret's case for canonization has been unaccountably stalled for de-cades.[61] She has performed all the necessary miracles, there is evidence of a continuous cult, and she has a skilled advocate from the Dominican order who appears to be sincerely interested in seeing her made patroness of "the handicapped." But six hundred years after her death, Margaret has still not been elevated to the ranks of the saints. Perhaps not everyone is happy with the idea of "someone like us" in heaven.[62]

The devotional ethos of suffering and pain failed actual sick people. It deepened the silence already threatening persons in pain with its constant injunctions to be quiet, denying them even the dignity of crying out in distress or unhappiness. It intensified the isolation and claustrophobia of the sick. Devotional writers castigated sick people for asking to be positioned more comfortably on beds that such writers liked to see as miniature calvaries rather than as the lumpy, lonely places of human suffering they actually were. The ethos confronted the sick with an image of the suffering Christ and then, in a perverse inverted Christology, told them that this image mocked any suffering of theirs: Did Jesus ask for a pillow on the Cross? Furthermore, by making pain a challenge, or test, of spiritual capacity, devotional culture added a layer of guilt and recrimination to the experience of bodily disease, as it proclaimed that most humans would fail this test. The ethos denied the social, communal, and psychological consequences of illness.[63]

Not surprisingly, given all this, few priests undertook ministry among the sick as their main work, and even visiting hospitals was not always a high priority among parish clergy, as the periodic admonitions in clerical journals suggest.[64] The parish clergy of the time held hospital chaplains in contempt (many still do), as the chaplains were well aware. In a typical lament, a former chaplain complained in 1937 that most parish priests "seem to have the foolish idea that a chaplain is a kind of second-rater, and that the very fact that he is stationed in the hospital is enough to guarantee that he has some failing which labels him 'unfit for real work.' "[65] Often enough, these suspicions were well founded. The Catholic hospital chaplaincy has been a scandal until relatively recently, having been the place to assign—and to hide—priests with emotional or physical troubles of their own, particularly alcoholism, and the dumping ground for men who could not make it in the high-pressure, big-business, hearty male world of the American parish.[66] As late as 1965, when the National Association of Catholic Chaplains was founded, men (and women, although their spiritual work in the hospitals was generally accorded more respect from the first) who had chosen the hospital ministry as their vocation were complaining that they were forced by local church authorities to accept "a semi-invalid or problem personality" on their increasingly professional staffs.[67]

The rapid shift and reorganization of health care from the home to the hospital in the first three decades of the last century posed a daunting challenge to an already overburdened church, and the inadequacy of spiritual care for the sick can be at least partly attributed to this broader development. But American Catholics succeeded in building a network of modern, technologically sophisticated hospitals of their own; Catholic doctors and nurses were trained well in denominational schools; Catholic hospital professionals in the United States were up-to-date and well informed on matters ranging from the latest surgical equipment to the best cafeteria designs, as the publications of the American Catholic Hospital Association show. The church was also capable of providing—and of treating as heroes—military chaplains in several wars. All of this contrasts sharply with the dismal level of pastoral care for the sick and suggests that the latter reflected the impact of the ambivalent ethos of suffering and pain rather than simply the economic or social state of the community.

The ethos also shaped the culture's stance toward religious healing. Healings had taken place at American shrines before the twentieth century, and charismatic healers, usually members of religious orders who scrupulously muted their own place in the thaumaturgic event in deference to ecclesiastical authority, were not unknown in the community before the widely publicized revival of faith healing among Catholics in the 1970s.[68] But Catholic culture was cautious and suspicious of popular healing of all sorts. The traditional curative arts of Irish and of southern European and eastern European women were mostly lost within a generation of their immigration to this country, under the combined pressures of their children's assimilation to the world of modern medicine and the clergy's denunciations of "superstition" and "magic."[69] After the revival of faith healing among American Protestants in the early part of the century, and its subsequent association with flamboyant and disreputable characters, many American Catholics sought to distance themselves from what they saw as an example of Protestantism's tendency toward excess and anarchy. Insecure enough in their middle-class status, Catholics had no desire to get out on anyone else's margin, and faith healing was definitely out on the American margins.[70]

But it was the romance of pain itself that made it so complicated for Catholics to hope for healings of any sort. Their yearnings were supposed to be pointed in the opposite direction, toward a deeper, sustained engagement with the promise and loveliness of "pain" (as opposed to the distress and loneliness of pain). Devotional culture taught that to alleviate pain was to deny the Cross; to seek relief was understandable, perhaps, but still an instance of human selfishness, a denial of the soul's superiority to the body and a rejection of the opportunity for saintliness. In a meditation published in *Catholic World* in 1929, a very sick woman warned others in similar distress that to be healed meant that "you might lose the shining thread of Him" in a misplaced quest for happiness, "only to discover that you had it once when you were bedridden, poor, and alone."[71] Some Catholics opposed painkillers and anesthetics even for the most extreme distress on the grounds that they interfered with an experience intended by God for the good of the afflicted person and intruded upon the intimacy with him available only to those in pain. Father Jerome Dukette celebrated a man, "quite crippled with arthritis," who, after traveling all the way to the Shrine of Saint Anne de Beaupré in hopes of a cure, decided—on the very steps of the shrine—that his suffering was a grace after all and turned away. Thirteen years later, according to Father Dukette, this man (still deformed) came back to the shrine to tell Saint Anne that he was "grateful [to her] for not curing me" because "healthy, I stood a chance of damning myself, [whereas] I prefer to crawl up to Heaven on hands and knees than to run off to Hell on two good legs."[72] The Dominican theologian Bede Jarrett told a story with a similar theme:

> I remember a woman once in a parish where I worked, down in terribly poor streets. I remember her dying of cancer—a terrible cancer, that type of cancer that is all pain. One day she said to me, "Need I take morphia? The doctor wants me to. Need I?" "No," said I, "there's no need to; but why not?" "I think it would be better for me not to. You remember my boy?" Yes, I knew and remembered all about her boy. "It would be better for me not to because then I could offer all my sufferings for him. I'd love to make an offering of them. I can, can't I? That is the teaching of our faith?" What could I answer except that this was indeed our faith. She died in very great agony but wonderfully happy. The worse her pains grew, the happier she became.[73]

What other answer, indeed? Healing would shut off the spiritual dynamo of pain, squandering its exploitable energy. It would be like turning off Niagara Falls.[74]

Everyone agreed that Joey was a saint. Joey was one of Sal's roommates at the home, a short, stocky Italian American man from the Bronx, with a tonsure of wooly brown hair ringing his huge head. His plump thighs strained the cloth of his pants and his wide hips filled the wheelchair, and he always rested his thick arms snugly at his sides. The nurses teased him about his weight, pinching his cheeks and kissing his head (how my uncle would have loved this, for reasons other than Joey did); the orderlies giggled and poked him while they shaved him in the early mornings. No one could resist touching Joey, stroking his hair, patting his round belly. Joey was a devout Yankees fan. On hot summer afternoons and evenings, he sat in front of the enormous window in his room, watching the cars stream by on the Concourse below, nestling his ear against the small transistor radio he held tightly in his hand. There'd almost always be one or two orderlies sitting on the bed beside him, bending close to hear the play-by-play or just staring out the window at the pigeons on the adjacent rooftops while Joey sat rapt in the game. When he wasn't listening to the Yankees or visiting with his mother, who came to the home almost every day, bringing food in foil-covered Pyrex dishes, Joey stared at the clock on his bureau. He was mesmerized by the sweeping second hand. Everyone who came into the room teased him about this.

During one of the summers I worked at the home, I was sunk in a terrible depression because I was having trouble taking my leave of the old neighborhood to go away to college. Unfamiliar with these feelings, I was terrified that I was going crazy; as I went about my chores on the floors or in the garden of the home, my skin prickled with anxiety. Occasionally, the terror was so intense that I raced in panic down the hallways—or so it seemed to me—or hid away in the darkest corners of the boiler room. My green janitor's uniform was always damp with sweat or rain. It never stopped raining that summer. The northern blocks of the Grand Concourse dissolved in the steady drizzle and in the gray steam rising from the hot, wet concrete. My supervisor ran out of jobs for me to do, so we avoided each other on those long wet days. I hid out in Sal's room, listened to the pecking of Jimmy's typing, or watched the clock with Joey.

Sometimes Joey rested his head on my shoulder, and I held his strong hand. He seemed content to have me sitting next to him, and I needed the comfort he provided me. I never told Joey my problems (although I imagined that he knew them anyway). I'd ask how the Yanks were doing or tease him about the clock, but Joey never said much to me. When I came into the room (terror-stricken and forlorn, as I imagine now), he'd smile and pat the arm of his chair, inviting me to sit next to him. I was always on the edge of tears there beside Joey in the cool, humid room, with the smells of the wet streets coming in the windows. Joey patted my hand. My uncle, working at the edge of his bed on a heap of papers or coming in from sitting on the porch with his girlfriend, shook his head sarcastically at me and, pointing to Joey, twirled a bony finger at his temple, letting me know what he thought of Joey, his clock, and me.

Sally will be eighty years old soon. About ten years ago, something obscure and terrible happened to his digestive system, and now his diet is limited almost completely to liquids. He weighs about seventy pounds. He smokes a pack of cigarettes a day, down from his former three. He keeps a leather bag tucked into his chair at his hip, filled with matches, coins, cigarettes, and the chewed and broken stumps of countless cigarette holders. Joey has been dead for a long time.

My uncle was born in the early years of the twentieth century at the beginning of a period of intense devotional creativity and improvisation in American Catholic culture, when the community was working to

transform European spiritual idioms into forms that addressed and reflected the experiences, needs, and fears of the second and third generations in their American lives. The ethos of suffering and pain was central
to this work, for reasons I have already discussed, and Sal—along with
people afflicted by cancer, migraines, pneumonia, and other physical troubles—had no choice but to live within it and contend with it, making
what they could of the ethos and of themselves within in it.

The discourse of pain generally, and of the holy cripple specifically,
offers historians a lens on some inner dimensions of American Catholic
culture in the middle of the twentieth century, if the crafting of that discourse is understood as a practice situated in the social circumstances of
the various communities at the time and not simply as a reflection of
perennial Catholic theology. The children of immigrants, in transition
from one way of life to another, constructed for themselves an ethos that
proclaimed pain (not hard work, ambition, or a desire for success) as a
road to the greatest achievement (which was sanctity, not a bigger apartment, a new car, or a good job). They clung to an image of themselves
as sufferers while their circumstances steadily improved, which in turn
allowed them to transform their envy and uneasiness into judgment on
the social world they aspired to when those circumstances did not im-
prove quickly enough. The elaboration of the ethos in the last century
gave suburban Catholic culture a distinct tone.

Living within this story, however, had many consequences for the everyday experience of the sick and handicapped, who were pivotal to its construction. These consequences were not all bad, as Sal's history shows:
because others said his body made him special, closer to heaven than they
were, those who could walk out the door paid more attention to him than
they might have otherwise and did nice things for him. They organized
outings for him, visited him, made sure that some of his needs were met.
The handicapped had a distinct place in American Catholic imaginations
and public life. Because of this story, the world of Catholic devotionalism
was seen as Sal's natural domain. He has always been a devout man (what
else could he be in this culture?). He says the rosary daily, surrounds himself with images of the saints, and plans to be buried in the robes of the
Third Order of St. Francis. Sal made a home (and a future grave) for
himself in these idioms; through them, he could find comfort, consolation,
and meaning for himself. In the prayer books tightly wrapped with rubber
bands and jammed into a duffel bag fixed to the back of his chair, Sal had
access to an intimate language for discovering, making, and naming his
desires, fears, and hopes, and a language in which to address them to
powerful figures who, he was told, would be listening closely to him.
Devotionalism also gave Sal a set of practices—making the sign of the
cross, fingering his beads, touching holy water, and so on—through which

he could embody the prayers he was saying. It was in this world that he found Margaret of Castello.

But Sal also had to contend with the covert and unacknowledged implications and consequences of the discourse of the holy cripple. This spiritual fantasy was elaborated out of a disjuncture. Ambulatory Catholics expected the handicapped to respond to the circumstances of their lives in ways that they knew they would not be capable of themselves were they trapped in a chair, strapped to a bed, unable to eat by themselves or get themselves a drink of water. Cripples were "better," which really meant that the cripples were not like us—so the discourse of the holy cripple turned people like Sal, Jimmy, and Joey into inhuman others whose inner lives were radically unlike everyone else's, and ultimately unrecognizable. First it made them into others—and then devotional culture celebrated them for this otherness and difference, which was called holiness.

But in its insistence on the innocence, nearness to heaven, purity of heart, and resilient cheerfulness of handicapped people, the fantasy drained away the lived reality of their days. It was the spiritual equivalent of the back rooms into which Sal's friends were tucked. It obscured the anger and resentment of handicapped persons, their struggles to overcome the physical limitations that mattered to them and their frustrations when they could not. It denied them the full range of human desires and hopes, including those for love, mastery, and independence. It hid their dismay at the condescension and good intentions of the volunteers who spoke to them in loud voices and simple words. Holiness ensured the absence of the other. As Sal put it, it created the impression that the handicapped person came from "another planet."

The discourse of the holy cripple accomplished this, furthermore, because it obscured the unequal relationships between those who could walk out the door and those who could not. The pretense of the discourse was that the latter were better than the rest of us—holier, more noble, more cheerful, better spirited. As Margaret Lehr concluded in *Ave Maria*, "Many of us [who can walk] are moral failures, while you almost invariably hear it said of the handicapped, 'My, isn't he wonderful! Always cheerful—always overcoming obstacles and surprising people with his achievements.' "[75] But the power of those of us who could walk out the door over those who could not was evident in the fact that *we* were the ones defining—and limiting—*their* inner lives for them. Their holiness was the practice of our power, and woe to the cripples who would not conform to our prescription. Then "many of us" would taunt them like the man who came up behind Sally on that morning the bus was late, or tell them to shut up, or write them off as complainers and stop taking their distress seriously.

Thus emptied of all but their holiness and innocence, cripples became blank slates for the articulation and vicarious experience of desire. Holiness became the space into which all kinds of unacknowledged needs and impulses could be driven, an exercise of fantasy that was unimpeded by the resistant facts of the other's actual experience, since this did not exist. Holiness became a compelling and productive psychic zone for everyone but the "cripples" it was defining. Aldo's fantasies emerged ineluctably from within the narrative of holiness: once the emptiness of the holy cripple had been opened up, the cripple-with-the-big-penis was sure to fill it. Aldo's were not the only fantasies, though, nor were all the desires articulated through the handicapped sexual. "The physically sound," according to Lehr, "often turn to the afflicted for strength—for moral courage," and so they—we—did.

The cruelty of the discourse of the holy cripple is fully evident in a 1950 "Letter to Shut-Ins" by Thomas A. Lahey, C.S.C., in *Ave Maria*.[76] "This letter is written to you as one of God's favorite children," Lahey begins. He assures his "dear suffering shut-in" and his "dear fortunate shut-in" that he understands what their lives are like.[77] "The music of the theater, the laughter of the banquet table, the natural and normal consolations which come from human relationships—all these are denied you. No matter how helpful those around you try to be, the inevitable fact confronts you that during most of your life you will have to put up with the four walls of your room and the somewhat impersonal companionship which your books and radio can furnish." This will not be easy, Father Lahey concedes. "I do not have to tell you how slowly the clock will tick under such circumstances, and how agonizing will be some of the hours that follow."[78] He attributes such distress, though, to "your own natural weaknesses," not to the awful loneliness of life within those four walls; if his shut-ins are miserable, Lahey wants them to know that it is a sign of their corruption.

But "suffering would not be suffering" if it were not so miserable and painful. So Lahey urges his shut-ins not to try to relieve their distress, since "it is the very fact of your suffering which has marked you out as one of the favorite children of God." Are there any consolations? Of course: "Sealed up as he is from the direct sense-appeals of various earthly attractions," the shut-in is freer of temptation, more likely to look to heaven for satisfaction. Lahey closes by warning the fortunate unfortunates not to squander their time on earth. Join the Franciscans' Apostolate of the Way of the Cross, he encourages them, through which they will receive "free and without any obligation" a crucifix "so indulgenced" that by holding it and saying certain prayers the shut-in can release an untold number of souls from purgatory. Stuck within their own rooms, cripples get to be the liberators of the dead. "Since those indulgences can be received over and over almost without end, you can spend your wakeful hours in helping to deliver not only hundreds but thousands of those poor souls who are pining for release . . . a wonderful missionary project you will admit."[79]

Father Lahey's "Letter to Shut-Ins" was not idiosyncratic; letters like this were a popular feature of American Catholic devotional discourse. Under the guise of compassion and understanding, their authors defined what they imagined and wanted the cripples' lives to be. Their accounts were prescriptive, pretending to be descriptive. While Sally and his girl-friends were in fact dancing and eating together, holding hands and kiss-ing, and hearing the music of the theater at UCP, the devotional press was telling us and them that they did not laugh or enjoy uproarious company and did not feel any human bond, let alone engage in sex, romance, danc-ing. But Father Lahey and the others did not want their beloved shut-ins to live like the rest of us, to enjoy what we enjoy (and the sound of his satisfaction can be heard in the prose), "the music of the theater, the laughter of the banquet table." Rather, they wanted them to be holy. When you get to heaven, Father Lahey assured his readers in conclusion, you will find millions of souls freed from purgatory by your prayers wait-ing to thank you.

I hope that when Sally gets to the heaven he imagines he finds Blessed Margaret waiting to wheel him quickly away from these grateful souls—who think that their heaven was secured by his (and her) isolation and denial on earth—to a place where there are others like him.

Sal discovered Margaret in the devotional world, and he prayed to her and other saints in the idioms of devotionalism, which is just what Father Lahey told him to do with himself. But Father Lahey did not understand that there were enough ruptures, fissures, and contradictions in this world for my uncle and the others to find ways within it of living against it. Catholic devotionalism offered a complex field of expression and experi-ence, polysemous and internally contradictory. These were flexible idi-oms, subject to improvisation. This world afforded many guises and voices, some of them (at least) at odds with the narrative of the holy cripple promulgated elsewhere in the same devotional culture.

I cannot say much about Sal's relationship with Margaret of Castello, since we had only the one, difficult (for me) conversation about her, but I do know that in this conversation, Margaret served as the "articulatory pivot" through which Sal was able to express his emotions.[80] She permitted Sally to uncover the fact of hiddenness: the details of her story created a context in which he could rage against his own sense of isolation and abandonment. The refrain "She would have been an abortion" may have echoed his own anger and anxiety. I do not fully understand how satisfying and empowering it can be to discover oneself reflected in heaven—to see someone up there like me, to see not simply my actual experience embodied in the narrative of a person understood to be close to God now, but my hidden fears and anger as well, or to see my sense of myself as a special, noteworthy person reflected in the adulation given to someone like me. We will have to take Sal's word for this. But as Sally told me, while he was talking about Margaret, there was a lot I did not understand about his experience.

Through the crippled saint, Sally momentarily breached the otherness constituted for him by the same devotional culture that gave him Margaret. He asked—demanded—through her that I imagine myself in his place—did I know what it was like to be unable to walk out the door?—and that I think about his experience as he lived it, not as I fantasized it. By his work of appropriation within a tradition complex enough to allow for such discrepancies, Sal inverted the meaning of holiness: Margaret's holiness became a sign of his own presence. If there were someone up in heaven like him, Sal taught me, then people like him could be recognized on earth. In heaven and on earth, Margaret subverts the narrative of the holy cripple, and this may be why she will not be admitted into the ranks of the saints.

Holiness itself turns out to be a peculiarly unstable cultural construction. Because it emerged out of desire and denial, it seemed to mutate almost organically into its opposite, as Aldo's relentless fantasizing shows. Even though they were themselves a reflex of the emptying discourse of holiness, Aldo's fantasies exposed, through the endlessly, compulsively reiterated image of the large phallus, precisely what holiness was meant to deny: that Sal, like the rest of us, was motivated and inspired by powerful, fully human needs, desires, and hopes. They certainly affirmed that he was a person, present, not absent, and that he would in fact seek the "natural and normal consolations which come from human relationships" that Father Lahey wanted to deny him. Thankfully, Sal, Jimmy, and the others had their own ways of doing so and ultimately did not need Aldo's obsessions to live against Father Lahey's denials.

My uncle is desire and will incarnated now. His flesh has shrunk back to the bone; he looks like a dark, knotted piece of leather. He sits in his chair breathing smoke, the cigarette holder clamped in his teeth. Many times in the last ten years my mother and father have been summoned to the residence late at night with the word that Sal was close to death, and each time Sal has fought his way back. Saint Francis's shroud may be waiting for him, but Sal is not slipping easily into it; holding onto his rosary, he is still fighting the story that was written for him out of the needs of ambulatory Catholics. He is not cheerful, compliant, or uncomplaining. He resists what others want from him, perversely (as everyone else sees it) putting up obstacles to what others want to do for (or, as he sees it, to) him. He is not offering up his suffering for anyone. Jerry Filan's God is not going to get him.

Joey died at just the age when men of his generation with cerebral palsy were expected to die.

A terrible storm hit New York on a recent summer's night when Sal was scheduled to go down to the UCP. The trees outside on Mosholu Parkway were bent to the ground by the wind, and rain poured from a black sky. My father happened to be at the residence that night on some errand and, thinking that my uncle would be frightened by the storm, went looking for him. Sal wasn't in his room or the corridors of his floor, not in the chapel or the lounge. My father finally found him waiting at the front door, all dressed up to go out, a wide, colorful tie completely covering his thin chest. An old black raincoat was crushed between his stiff legs.

"It's the middle of a hurricane," my father yelled at Sally. "What are you doing? You don't really think you're going out in this tonight, do you?"

An iron table was blown off one of the upper porches and came crashing into the street outside.

"Ahhhh," my uncle said, "it's not that bad."

"The highway's closed," my father said, laughing in his fury at Sal's stubbornness. "Are you kidding? No one's gonna drive in this!"

"Go see when the bus is coming," Sally commanded. Then he turned back to face the front door, ready to go out.

Chapter Two

THE MANY NAMES OF THE MOTHER OF GOD

Secular histories are usually produced by ignoring the signs
of these presences. Such histories represent a meeting of two
systems of thought, one in which the world is ultimately,
that is, in the final analysis, disenchanted, and the other
in which humans are not the only meaningful agents.
Dipesh Chakrabarty, Provincializing Europe: Postcolonial
Thought and Historical Difference

ONE OF THE MOST common images of Mary in the United States
in the modern era has been the dashboard Madonna, slender
statuettes of the Virgin set under the curved glass canopy of automobile windshields. The Blessed Mother protected drivers and passengers
from the hazards of the highways that were taking the children and grandchildren of immigrants away from the old ethnic enclaves out to the new
suburbs ringing the industrial cities of the Northeast and Midwest and
rising up in the western deserts. These were usually glow-in-the-dark fig-
urines: late at night, in cars parked on city streets or suburban driveways,
Mary shone with the light she captured during the day from the sun and
from streetlamps in the early twilight.[1]

It is impossible to tell a simple story about the Virgin Mary. She cannot
be held in place by a single attribute—sorrow or delight, purity or compassion—or held accountable for a single social consequence—liberation
or oppression, solidarity or fracture. She is not innocent. Her sorrow, for
example, has been a source of great consolation to women in their grief
but also a means of disciplining them to understand pain and self-abnega-
tion as their destinies. Mary stands for peace and for divisiveness. She is
not solely the creation of theologians or of the masses, and she belongs
completely neither to her devout nor to culture. The Blessed Mother
averts her eyes in most images, a conventional sign of her modesty and
virginity but also an indication that she has very serious things on her
mind. Her poise is inseparable from her power. She is always refracted
through the prism of the needs and fears of the people who approach her,
and so she is a protean and unstable figure. Because of this instability of
meaning, Mary can be the occasion of serious cultural and psychological

distress, which in turn provokes more determined efforts to fix her in place. But she continually frustrates these agendas.

The Madonna cannot be fixed to museum walls, either, cannot be made into an object of aesthetic contemplation (as this came to be defined in modern Western culture). It is impossible to stand back and simply look at images of the Virgin Mary, certainly for most Catholics, but for others too. She subverts the distance that museums enjoin on viewers and alters the practice of looking itself. "When we see a painting," art historian David Freedberg writes about contemporary orientations to art, "we speak of it in terms of color, composition, expression, and the means of conveying things like space and movement. . . . We refuse, or refuse to admit, those elements of response that are more openly evinced by people who are less schooled" in this way of seeing. We do not try to stroke art or kiss it; if we did, museum guards would rush over to reimpose the obligatory distance. We can look at paintings and sculptures in the formal way Freedberg describes because we do not mistake—as some would put it—the representation of a thing with the thing itself. The thing is not *there*; the sign of it is. Icons of Mary, on the other hand, which Freedberg introduces as paradigmatic instances of another experience of the visual, fuse "image and prototype." Responses to them are "predicated on the perception that what is represented on an image is actually present, or present in it."[2]

Devotional images are media of presence and they are used to act upon the world, upon others and upon oneself. Such media include holy cards, prayer beads, relics, statues and images, blessed oils and waters, and the many different things pilgrims bring home from distant shrines. These objects are believed to hold the power of the holy figure (or of the faraway place, Lourdes, for instance, or Knock) and to make it present. "Unlike objects created for disinterested or 'aesthetic' contemplation," historian and theorist of religious art David Morgan writes, "popular iconography is thoroughly 'interested,' 'engaged,' functional and extrinsically purposive."[3] Media of presence are efficacious and they serve as points of encounter—between humans, for example, when one person gives a holy card to another for whom he or she cares and who is in need, and between humans and scared figures. Pilgrims travel great distances to representations of Mary that are believed to heal, and then they plead, argue, and bargain with them, bring them gifts, make them promises. Haitian vodou practitioners write their requests for help in thick pencil strokes on the plaster robes of various representations of the Virgin Mary, as the Mother of Sorrows, for example, or the Madonna of Mount Carmel, who are the Catholic faces of powerful African female spirits, in churches in Miami and New York City. Mary is taken out onto the waves by fishermen to bring them good catches and to protect them from shipwreck, by farmers into dry fields so that the Mother of God can see the cracked earth and send soaking rain, and by city dwellers through the streets of neighborhoods, to mark off religious and ethnic boundaries and to guard the people living within them.[4] Encounters with images of the Virgin are encounters with presence. The whole range of emotion and behavior that is possible when persons are present to each other in one place characterizes these encounters too.

Things taken from shrines bring the healing powers associated with these places—out there on the sacred landscape (even if it is only in the next town or in the church down the street)—into the everyday spaces of sickness, into hospitals, sickrooms, into doctors' offices and to the places where people wait to hear the results of tests from laboratories, which like the shrines are also out there on the landscape, away from home. Once the holy figure becomes present by means of the object in the room, in the hand of a friend or left on a bedside table, circumstances change. Relationships may be reconfigured, expectations and emotions transformed, political dynamics altered. Hospitals are not the same places afterwards. A medal of the Virgin Mary pinned to a humiliating surgical gown or a statue of her propped by a bed table intersects and interrupts the medical space with other meanings and possibilities. In the company of the Virgin Mary, men and women have found the voice to challenge their doctors, to live with or against distressing diagnoses, and to act upon the alien, disorienting, impersonal space of the modern hospital in such a way as to make it more comfortable for themselves.

Frustrated petitioners sometimes inflict their disappointment on the images of uncooperative or dilatory holy figures, turning the face of a statue toward the wall, for instance, or moving it to a lesser position in a home shrine. But no one treats the Blessed Mother like this because she is so beloved, and so feared. There is a genre of Catholic joke with many variations of which the recurring punch line is a voice from heaven challenging Jesus, "Is that any way to treat your mother?"—knocking him down a peg—and this spirit generally prevails among Mary's devout, who love and honor her but are also wary of her power.

So whatever artists, patrons, and curators intend—and they intend many things, including devotion—Mary is *there* in representations of her. Responses to images and three-dimensional objects that are motivated by desire, need, love, or fear are not "premodern" as opposed to "modern." Such a distinction imposes a mandatory sequence onto history, in which the premodern *must* eventually yield to the modern. Mary's power and presence endured well into the modern era and in the most modern nations, subverting this authoritative temporal grid. The precise relationship between the devotional way of experiencing objects and the way that denies or ignores presence is a matter of historical and cultural study; the two ways of experiencing exist together and inflect each other, today as in the Middle Ages. They are not as distinct as those on either side who are dedicated to maintaining the boundaries between them hope they are. It is not a question of premodern, modern, and postmodern, but of different ways of being in the world at the same time.

It is also a question for local and historical analysis how these divergent ways of seeing—one formal and aesthetic, premised on the absence of the thing represented; the other devotional and instrumental, predicated on presence—are implicated in social power. What is happening politically when particular social or cultural regimes of authority seek to deny the presence experienced in sacred objects (invariably on the grounds of a struggle against "superstition," atavism, or popular misuse), or when representatives of one religious world hold in contempt the power of presence in things cherished by members of another religious world, or when religious authorities seek to uproot the experience of sacred presence among their own people? Eruptions of iconoclastic violence are efforts to foreclose the power of presence in things or to limit the access of particular communities or individuals to that power, to make sure that poor people or dark people or people from despised ethnic groups cannot reach that power. Political regimes may obliterate presence in one set of objects and images in order to transfer it, by force, terror, or torture onto other objects and images, and elites allow the experience of presence by particular persons and then turn around and claim it for themselves, as white Americans have done through the centuries in relation to Native Americans and African Americans.[5] Ecclesiastical institutions try to control the traffic in presence-bearing objects. Devotional experience, including the intimate handling of sacred objects, may be discounted, branded infantile or even insane, especially when it is associated with women. But presence persists.

American Catholicism in the latter third of the twentieth century offers a case study of the confusion, at least, but also the anger and despair that may be provoked by conflict over media of presence. Catholic theologians and church leaders embarked in this period on a major rethinking of Mary's place in the church, a piece of the wider reconsideration of the mission and identity of Catholicism in the modern world that culminated in discussions at the Second Vatican Council. Mary's presence had been most real and pervasive before the period of devotional reform associated with the new theology and ecclesiology, and so not surprisingly she became the focus of intense debate, uncertainty, and resistance. Both those who favored rethinking people's relationship with the sacred and those who found the old ways still meaningful and comforting, clearly believed that if the matter of Mary could be settled, if Mary's insistent and ubiquitous presence were either minimized or affirmed, then the major issues confronting modern Catholic culture might be resolved.

Marian devotions had been central to the making and sustaining of the social fabric of working-class and rural Catholic communities in the United States. People in Catholic city neighborhoods marched out into the streets behind images of the Mother of God on Mary's major feast days, a practice that had served to signal the Catholic identity of urban spaces as it blessed them. Rural Catholics took turns hosting rosary nights, farm families gathering in each other's homes around a statue of the Virgin that was carried from one farm to another throughout the year. Weekly Tuesday night novenas in honor of the Virgin were well-attended events in Catholic communities. Each year in May—Mary's month—thousands of uniformed Catholic schoolchildren circled the grounds of their churches and schools to celebrate the Mother of God. Catholic youngsters were literally made to become prayers to Mary in the practice of the "living rosary" when instead of beads, children—one child stepping forward as the congregation intoned each "Hail Mary"—served to mark the sequence of prayers. At the end of the devotion a rosary of little children stood facing the community.

But now, in the 1960s, Catholic leaders were concerned that the Virgin's compelling place in the devotional imaginations of ordinary people had come to overshadow her son. Pope John XXIII warned Roman clergy against the tendency "to cultivate certain excessive devotional practices, even with respect to devotion to the Madonna."[6] Liturgical reformers maintained that the extensive popular practice of Mary's cult distracted people from the encounter with Jesus in the sacrament of the Eucharist that was the heart of the church's life. It had been common practice for people to say the rosary silently during mass instead of paying attention to the sacrifice on the altar, and for many reformers in the 1960s this in particular captured what was most wrong about Catholic popular piety. Catholics committed to ecumenical dialogue feared that devotion to Mary stood as the most formidable obstacle to Christian unity. The contemporary response to all this was to refigure Mary's place in the church: theologians and liturgists presented her now as the model of Christian obedience, humility, and service, the exemplum of the church's mission and identity on earth, and efforts were made to wean Catholics from Marian devotional practices. The impulse was to move from the devotional (associated with the premodern) to the moral (sign of a more mature church, in the language of the times). The custom of saying the rosary beside the open coffin on the last night of a wake was discouraged, replaced by a liturgically oriented service of Scripture reading and prayer.

These religious changes took place amid a broad revolution in Catholic social experience in the United States. The old inner city ethnic enclaves

Figure 4. May procession, St. Mark's Church, Dorchester, Mass., 1963. The young woman in the center, an eighth grader surrounded by smaller children, was designated "Queen of the Saints." (Photo courtesy of Paul J. Connell.)

had begun to disappear. Younger American Catholics were more educated than ever before, the result among other things of the G.I. Bill and of higher expectations of teaching sisters since the 1920s. The generation of nuns that faced the baby-boom classrooms was the best-educated in American Catholic history. Catholics in the United States were becoming a suburban people. Women first and then men were entering the postindustrial, consumer, white-collar and service economy and workforce and the professions in ever-greater numbers. Catholics watched these things happening to themselves, moreover, acutely conscious of the kind of moment they had come into: as one of the many Catholic sociologists writing at the time put it (the presence of trained Catholic sociologists commenting on unfolding events was a distinctive feature of the Catholic sixties), "the contemporary Catholic family is more likely to belong to the middle class [and] to adopt middle class aspirations and values, including zeal for suburbia." This is a little exaggeration: the Catholic working class was not growing but it did not disappear, some of the old neighborhoods hung on into the 1970s and 1980s (albeit with steadily declining and aging populations and in many cases the closing of their churches), and there were regional and ethic variations in the specific timing of all this. But clearly huge changes were under way, in church and in social experience: the religious transformations emblematic of Catholic upheaval in these years—among others the end of the Latin Mass, the passing of novenas and rosaries as idioms of community prayer, and the lifting of the Friday meat prohibition—took place in a community undergoing broad reorientations in the ways it lived, and it is impossible to separate religious and social change or to separate Mary's destiny from that of the older men and women in Catholic communities.[7]

Catholics experienced these changes on the most intimate levels, in their bodies and in their consciences, at church and in their homes: in the unfamiliar postures and sounds at the new Mass, for instance, in the newly permissible taste of meat on their tongues on Fridays, in the suddenly visible bodies of nuns, in the geographical distance from grandparents in the old neighborhoods. Catholics were encountering novel corporal experiences in many areas of life—in the transition from manual labor and farming to office work, from large families to smaller ones, from tiny city dwellings to larger suburban homes, from a complete lack of privacy to a newfound separateness. The body was at the center of the working class and farming worlds: Catholic bodies in city neighborhoods and on farms were physically present, even overpresent, to each other, bodies touching in close quarters, the body at work, the body in pain, the broken body of God in church, God taken out into the streets for Corpus Christi processions. Catholic memories recorded in the 1960s and 1970s very often refer to the smallness of childhood homes and the lack of privacy. Children were prepared, as we will see in the next chapter, to take heroic steps to save God's body from threatened churches. But now new bodies, new ways of being in the world were called for, new postures and attitudes; changes in the different areas of corporal experience—at work, at home, in church, in the streets, in schools, and so on—resonated with each other.[8]

I will return to this period again in chapter 5, when I consider how Catholics in the 1960s came to imagine the relationship between the present and the past—between who they were now in relation to who they had been—and the implications of this for Catholic memory and history. Here the point is that as the working-class Catholic body gave way in the 1960s to the Catholic middle-class body, city neighborhoods and farms to suburbs, among the grandchildren and great-grandchildren of the European immigrants who came to the United States at the turn of the century, so the power of corporal presence—of God's body and the bodies of the saints and of God's mother—began to diminish. Newly middle-class Catholics searched for other ways of imagining and engaging the sacred than those of their grandparents and parents, more consonant with their experience and needs, new ways of acting toward a reimagined sacred. The fate of the Catholic body and the fate of the Catholic sacred were entwined, in other words: as things on earth changed, so did the connections between earth and heaven. Such transformations on heaven and earth do not necessarily happen in tandem, however, and in the 1960s, in Catholic communities and institutions around the United States, the interplay of sacred and social, heaven and earth, in the American Catholic sixties became tumultuous.

Catholic sacred culture before the 1960s was above all a culture of embodiment, of *presence* in bodies and things. God was present on the altar, in the Communion wafers, on people's tongues, in the sign of the cross. The most potent and obvious bearer of presence in American Catholicism, the most pervasive medium of the embodiment of sacred presence in bodies and things, and the clearest sign of Catholic difference from modern culture was devotionalism, that array of practices, objects, liquids, images, ceremonies, and gestures by which Catholics engaged the presence of God and the saints in the spaces and times of everyday life. Devotional media constituted the sense world of pre-Conciliar Catholicism, its smells, textures, tastes, and sounds, and formed the very way Catholic bodies existed and moved, the poise and bearing of these bodies, a distinctly Catholic kinetics, inside church and outside, in schools, playgrounds, and workplaces, on city streets and in rural communities. The Virgin Mary and the saints were present in various representations of them, in the body saying the rosary, in the sound of the memorized Hail Mary and the feel of its thrumming in the body. There was power in rosaries, in oils, and in prayer cards. Not surprisingly, then, the Mother of God and the saints became the focus of the most intense cultural work in the transitional era.

It is neither to defend nor to challenge the reorientations of the era to note that advocates of the new postures toward, and imaginings of, the sacred failed to understand that presence is not quickly dismissed, that objects that for a long time had held the presence of Mary and the saints could not be easily emptied of their power or attraction. How do I know that they did not understand this? Because they did so little to prepare ordinary Catholics for the changes—people looking back on these years from the perspective of the present invariably remember how surprised they were when all of sudden the altar was turned around, new movements were required in church, *they could eat meat on Fridays*!!! One day the saints disappeared, the rosaries stopped, the novenas ended, just like that. This provoked resistance and confusion, and in turn this resistance in the parishes to the new agenda heightened the resolve of its advocates. The result was a season of iconoclasm in the American church, more or less severe and traumatic depending on local circumstances. Old devotions were derided as infantile, childish, or as exotic imports from Catholic Europe, alien and inappropriate in the American context. The dominant register of talk about the saints and devotionalism in the 1960s among Catholic writers who saw themselves on the side of the modernizing church was a biting sardonic humor filled with mockery and contempt. Commenting on the new spirit that frowned on saying the rosary during Mass, Leo J. Trese, writing in the devotional periodical *Sign* in 1965, asked, "Is Mary to be exiled from the sanctuary . . . like a senile grandmother hidden in the back bedroom when company comes?" All that's left of Holy Rosary Month, another writer in the same periodical commented derisively, again in 1965, is "a sprinkling of senior citizens." Statues of the Virgin (and of the saints) were discarded, long-established devotional customs suspended. Mary's presence, in the minds of some, had declined—or should be declining—into senescence. Careful local studies of how this period of change was experienced, enacted, and remembered in parishes around the country remain to be done, but in most churches the saints and the Virgin Mary, who had looked down on generations of faithful, were removed, in some cases simply discarded, sometimes stored away in dirty church basements or in storage areas behind the altars.[9]

As the decade proceeded, conflict over presence became more and more bitter because presence was not going to be easily uprooted, either in religious practice or in people's imaginations. Sacrilege suddenly emerged as a popular genre of Catholic expression in the United States. Catholics were not alone in this in the 1960s, of course—impatient Black radicals lampooning the language of African American religion mocked Martin Luther King Jr. as "de Lawd," and Yippies nominated a pig for president, to cite two of countless examples—but Catholic sacrilege had its own sources, style, and force and its own motivations and ends. The idioms of desecration varied but the targets were the obvious bearers of sacred presence in the community. Nuns had been formidable guardians of the older Catholic way of life and among the most visible representatives of the otherness of Catholic religiosity, and so it was perhaps inevitable that changes in Catholic ways of living would lead to the recasting of nuns' bodies (the occlusion of which had signaled their transcendence of earthly realities in the past that was now being denied). Male writers (sometimes women too) detailed in crude and misogynist ways the bodily functions and sexuality of women religious. But most often desecration was directed toward the saints: in comic books, novels, and memoirs, and even in the pages of the old devotional periodicals, the sacred world of the immediate past was recast as a grim, pornographic, sadistic realm, or else as ridiculous, otiose, and silly.[10]

An example of what I am talking about here that draws together both the reforming and the sacrilegious impulses is a 1965 fantasy published by an industrial-belt priest named Stanley M. Grabowski in *Priest* magazine. "Ours is an old city parish," Father Grabowski tells his readers (who were other priests), "with many older people living in outdated homes. Everytime [*sic*] I have to make a visit to some of these homes with their menageries of statues I tremble with fear of losing control and giving in to this urge to break those horrible representations." The "urge to destroy . . . haunts me," Father Grabowski confesses. The saints are everywhere in this outdated world. "An old man, in his eighties, has four crucifixes of varied sizes, at least a dozen holy pictures and three large statues on a single wall of his bedroom." Going away on vacation offers no escape. "At the beach last summer I experienced something less than an urge to destroy whenever I saw anyone of the bathers loaded down with a half-a-dozen medals strung on a chain around his neck." "Recently I thought that this iconoclastic impulse would get out of control when I was at a wedding reception," Father Grabowski goes on. "At the head table reserved for the bridal party and the priest . . . there was a 24-inch statue of Our Lady of Fatima serving as a centerpiece directly in front of the bride and groom." Father Grabowski manages to restrain himself and leaves the reception early.

What does Father Grabowski want? He wants his parishioners to experience religious icons as *art*, to develop the necessary critical skills of appreciation. He specifically does not want them to experience such icons—of the Virgin and the saints—as *presence*, to kiss them, talk to them, punish them. What way was this to behave in the modern world? Old, older, outdated: these were the temporal coordinates of sacred presence. Father Grabowski wanted his parishioners to become modern.[11]

The irony of sacrilege is that it announces in its very ferocity the enduring power of that which it seeks to destroy or uproot. The iconoclasm of the Catholic sixties paradoxically signaled the Virgin's enduring power and presence. For sure, many Catholics would no longer find devotion to Mary compelling, and her presence faded in their experience. But devotion to the Mother of God persisted in American Catholicism—among older people, among the children and grandchildren of the midcentury generations who rediscovered Mary in the 1980s and 1990s, among long-resident Mexican American Catholics and newcomers from Mexico and Central and South America, and even among those who imagined otherwise in the mid-1960s but found themselves, in later moments of crisis, calling on the Virgin as they had been taught to do as children. The 1980s witnessed a surprising resurgence in Marian apparitions, around the world and across the United States, surprising from the perspective of those who thought that the time of Mary's literal presence was over. The modern present—what is possible in and characteristic of the modern world—is not singular; middle-class Catholicism, for all its different disciplines and expectations, at home and work, continued to be inflected by the power of presence that had so deeply shaped Catholic imaginations. Reformers made the mistake common among champions of the modern: they assumed that the story they were telling was the only one.

The Virgin Mary transforms looking into a devotional activity. The space between image and viewer—carefully monitored in museums, more open and accessible in churches and shrines—becomes an imaginative opening for need, fantasy, desire, like the space between the faces and bodies of children and those of their caregivers. Devotional space is constituted by the presence of the Madonna and the presence of her devout to each other, by the desires and needs of the devout, and by Mary's invitation to them to come to her with the promise that she will recognize their needs.[12]

In 1999–2000, curators at the Davis Museum of Wellesley College in Massachusetts organized "Divine Mirrors: The Virgin Mary in the Visual Arts," an exhibition of images in the museum's collection. A notebook was made available to visitors for recording their impressions about the exhibit. The comments of some visitors illustrate the way that Mary transforms the act of looking. One visitor painstakingly wrote out the Hail Mary: looking had become praying. Another visitor, drawing on the iconographic traditions associated with Marian apparitions in the nineteenth and twentieth centuries (and powerfully reiterated in recent decades), sketched out in ink an image of Mary standing forth in a halo of bright light. In the experience of this visitor, all representations of Mary—including the (apparently) static and aesthetic ones in the exhibition—are apparitional. Someone else left a white, glow-in-the-dark rosary, made from the same material as the dashboard Madonnas, on a bench in a curtained area that had been set aside from the rest of this exhibition as a little "chapel," further marking the area as sacred space (and perhaps issuing a warning to anyone who failed to treat it as such, because rosaries, as we will see, can be distinctly mean implements too). The fact is that images of Mary will be venerated. Roman women seeking assistance with difficult pregnancies, for example, have surrounded Jacopo Sansovino's *Madonna del Parto* in the church of Sant' Agostino with burning candles, and they have worn away her foot by their kisses and touch. A work of art thus becomes a medium of presence.[13]

There are different ways of seeing and different reasons for wanting and having things. Cultural critic Walter Benjamin speculated in a famous essay that the advancing technology for mechanical reproduction of works of art would dissipate the powerful and compelling aura that attached to originals. The diffusion of Mary's image does not follow this logic. She is as present everywhere as she is anywhere. American Catholics seek cures at "reproductions" of the Lourdes grotto built on church grounds across the United States, confident that the Virgin is as present in these reproductions as she is in southern France. They take from these sites "Lourdes water" that comes from city reservoirs, not from the spring that miraculously bubbled up at Bernadette's feet. This experience of presence in the reproduction occurs even when the resemblance between the "original" and the "copy" is utterly attenuated. Images of Our Lady of Guadalupe on refrigerator magnets, T-shirts, and holy cards—and on the skins of *cholos* (gang members)—can be bearers of the presence of the *Virgencita* (as Guadalupe is affectionately known) as much as the miraculous imprint on Juan Diego's *tilma*. There is still special merit in journeying to the sites where Mary is said to have visited. But her presence is not exhausted at them. Rather, she is repetitively present, generously and lovingly so, as her devout see it.[14] The Blessed Mother does not have strong feelings about what constitutes appropriate or inappropriate venues for her visits, either.

In the interplay of persons and things, generally, one thing is sometimes used to displace another, in which case the presence of the one may become the sign of the absence of the other. This is how philosopher and critic Susan Stewart understands souvenirs: as the "traces of authentic experience" that gesture elsewhere to what is not there. By definition, Stewart says, souvenirs are objects taken out of their original contexts and away from the sites of their production, and they come to stand for otherwise inaccessible places, times, experiences. She writes, "The possession of the metonymic object is a kind of dispossession in that the presence of the object all the more radically speaks to its status as a mere substitution and to its subsequent distance from the self."[15] Souvenirs are about absence.

The Blessed Mother's devout take things away with them from Marian shrines; there is a huge international market in Marian souvenirs. The devout display these objects, cherish them, and give them to people they love or care about (or into whose lives they wish to insert themselves). But these are not souvenirs in the way that Stewart defines them, and, again, like the Madonna's presence in works of art, the use of Marian souvenirs challenges us to reconsider fundamental notions—in this case, how we understand people's relationships with objects taken from one place and brought to another. More broadly, we are asked to reconsider the modernist imposition of absence everywhere, and the insistence on absence, or lack, as the necessary origin of desire. Marian souvenirs connect moments and sites of experience—here and there, now and then, the place of Mary's special presence and here, at home. They are conduits of power. Such objects cannot be understood apart from the phenomenology of presence. What makes them desirable and valued, the reason that people want to give and receive them, is the experience, in and through these objects, of presence.

But what is presence? What accounts for Mary's thereness?

One response is that presence is a psychological effect. The Virgin Mary exists in relationships: in the relationships of men, women, and children with her, and in her involvement in complicated relational triangles stretching between heaven and earth—between husbands and wives, for example, or parents and children, among members of religious orders, between clergy and laity, between believers and nonbelievers (as was the case in France in the early nineteenth century, for example, where the apparitions at Lourdes were taken up into the fierce debates between modernists and traditionalists). Mary is called on to mediate family disputes, to judge behavior, and to listen to the most intimate sorrows and fears. This is the interpersonal ground on which Mary arises and this is what makes her presence real and emotionally resonant. In individuals' and communities' experience of her, the Virgin draws deeply on the whole history of relationships, living and dead, present and absent. She borrows from and contributes to memories, needs, fantasies, hopes, and fears, as her dashboard statues borrow their light from other sources. To tell the story of any person's bond with Mary, it is necessary to recount the story of all his or her relationships, from childhood to adulthood, and to locate Mary in her dynamic place among them. The Marian devotional world is an interpersonally crowded one.[16]

Relationships with Mary are never lived apart from the circumstances of particular times and places, however. There is a debate among scholars of Marian apparitions—those occasions when humans claim to have been visited and directly addressed by the Virgin—about the relative worth of social or psychological approaches to the phenomena. The distinction has more to do with academic boundaries and anxieties than with Mary's place in people's experience, however. Mary cannot be found solely in psychological analyses of any single believer's (or even community's) experience of her because Mary and her devout alike find their being in culture. How her devout approach the Blessed Mother, the languages that give shape and limit to the prayers they bring to her and the fantasies they have of her, the memories she evokes, the patterns of family dynamics into which she enters, the disciplinary uses to which she is put, the desires that are thinkable and not in her sight, the emergence of new needs and possibilities—all of this is constituted and constrained by culture and history. Mary is a cultural figure not simply in the sense that she "reflects" cultural idioms or social dynamics (although she does) or that the idioms or lineaments of Marian piety are inherited generationally (which they are). She is a cultural figure in that she enters the intricacies of a culture, becomes part of its webs and meanings, limitations, structures, and possibilities. She contributes to making and sustaining culture, and reinventing it, at the same time that she herself is made and sustained by culture, in dynamic exchanges with her devout.[17]

This is not a matter of culture *or* self, cultural implication *or* cultural transcendence. Mary lives in the imaginations of men, women, and children, at that point where people take hold of the world around them, in the idioms they have inherited, found, and invented. She does not belong completely either to culture or to self, but to the spaces where the two are most intimately entangled. The Blessed Mother tends to make her most dramatic, public appearances—in southern France in 1858, for example, the Saarland in 1876, Portugal in 1917, in the Basque country in 1931—when social, political, and economic transformations disrupt the customary ways people have been connected to each other and to the social world. She appears amid broken bonds or bonds that are changing one way or another. She may assist men and women to accept the circumstances of their lives, to resist them, or, most often, to find some way of living between the desirable and the ordained, within the possibilities of the given.[18]

Given the deep social and psychological etiology of Mary's presence, she is not always a benign figure. She may touch the most primitive fears in her devout, their terrors of abandonment or rejection. Her children bring the most insistent needs to her—and there is always the threat that Mary will refuse or ignore them. Or her children may fail to satisfy her. Mary's dangerousness surfaces in certain features of Marian lore and in aspects of her apparitional messages. There is a southern Italian tradition, for example, which holds that the Madonna will wound those who do not respond adequately to her demands for attention. Mary warns her visionaries of dire consequences to humankind if her calls to repentance are not heeded. Ignore me, and you will suffer, she says. Apparitional sites become psychological playgrounds, where the most intimate desires, needs, and fears are put in play; this kind of complicated imaginative activity inevitably provokes uncertainty, dread, confusion, and panic. "The Devil . . . comes to Oliveto almost as often as the Madonna," anthropologist Paolo Apolito writes of a contemporary apparition site outside Naples, Italy—Oliveto Citra, where the Madonna began appearing in 1985. "The two figures sometimes seem to alternate on the stage of the transcendent in a kind of two-sided game." I was told by a gas station attendant in the town of Knock, where Mary appeared in 1879, on a visit to Ireland in 1975, that "here is where the transcendent broke into time." Such tectonic shifts in the relationship of the planes of the natural and the supernatural are eruptive and destabilizing. There is, says Apolito, "a kind of vertigo from the temptation of the transcendent." Describing an incident in which visionaries suddenly lost any interpretive grip on what they were seeing, Apolito writes, "All was left suspended between ordinary perception and the possibility that all of a sudden something might emerge from the depths of the unspoken, breaking out of the accustomed surface of things, creating an opening that might suck the everyday order into metahistorical reality."[19]

Because Mary exists relationally, it is impossible to read out from theology or iconography the quality of people's experience of her or to anticipate its social implications. Devotional writers may have evoked a sorrowing, submissive Mary against the desires and aspirations of young women; indeed, there is such a disciplinary literature of Marian piety and poetry, written by men and women, lay and religious, clearly intended to constrain women's imaginations, desires, and behavior. But all this tells us very little about Mary's place in real women's lives. Mary's perpetual virginity may have been intended to authorize an ideal of sexless and obedient womanhood and to shame living women for their desires, but the American adolescents who belonged to the Children of Mary and other devotional sodalities in the middle years of the last century dated each other's brothers and called on the Blessed Mother to help them find work, regardless of what devotional literature stipulated. (The statue of our Lady of Fatima that so exercised Father Grabowski was part of the festivities of a young couple's wedding, and what most annoyed the priest was the pleasure the bride's mother was taking in the color and fabric of the Virgin's gown.) Praying to Mary is not an activity that is easily controlled by others, or ever completely controlled.[20]

While the meanings of Mary are not exhausted by theology or ecclesiastical iconography and while there are often serious discrepancies between the moralizing intentions of clerical proponents of Mary's cult and the prayers of her female devout, it is not the case that there are two completely distinct worlds of Marian devotion, official and popular, one disciplinary, the other emancipatory. Contemporary theologians in the United

Figure 5. An antiabortion protester holding up rosaries and plastic fetuses outside a medical clinic in Buffalo, New York, April 1992. (© Peter Blakely/ Corbis Saba)

States, Latin America, and Africa have developed a doctrine of Mary as champion of the oppressed; on the other hand, "popular" expressions of Marian piety in the United States today include harsh and abusive tactics by self-declared soldiers in Mary's armies against young women and their families entering or leaving abortion clinics, such as aggressively brandishing rosaries in women's faces. (Not since the Reformation has the rosary been so regularly implicated in vicious social conflict as it has been in the American struggle over abortion.) Priests and nuns participate in all forms of Marian devotionalism, including ones not officially sanctioned by the church; theological discussions about Mary build on and authorize popular understanding and practice. It was the decision of the "Queen of the Castle Committee," which represented the concerns and authority of the church in Oliveto Citra, to accept the claim of local boys to have seen the Madonna that unleashed the popular imagination there, which soon enough was seeing, in addition to the Madonna, bleeding stones and "strange and inexplicable fiery snakes in the shape of the number six." It is another dimension of Mary's protean nature that she completely confounds any attempt to stabilize the categories of popular and elite.[21]

Mary was the clearest sign of Catholic difference in the United States. One of the reasons that American Catholics carried rosaries in their pockets until recently was so that in the event of an accident their religious identities would be immediately recognized and a priest (not a minister or rabbi) called for them. But Mary's relationship to Catholic identity and difference—between Catholics and other Americans, as well as among the various Catholic ethnic communities—is complicated.

Mary is enthroned in the Basilica of the National Shrine of the Immaculate Conception in Washington, D.C., as the patroness of the United States. The cornerstone of this immense temple, which integrates elements of the Byzantine tradition with American architecture, was blessed in 1920 by James Cardinal Gibbons, the archbishop of Baltimore. Some years earlier, in 1887, Gibbons, who was one of the leading figures of late-nineteenth-century American Catholicism—and the one most responsible for negotiating between Vatican perceptions and American ways—had delivered a powerful sermon in another Marian temple, the Roman church of Santa Maria in Trastevere, in which he proclaimed his love of the United States and its political institutions, especially for the separation of church and state. "Our country has liberty without license," Gibbons proudly declared, "authority without despotism. . . . [O]ur nation is strong, and her strength lies, under Providence, in the majesty and supremacy of the law, in the loyalty of her citizens to that law, and in the affection of our people for their free institutions." Mary's presence in the nation's capital city represented the unity of *American* Catholics, sanctioning their patriotism and loyalty to the nation. This is Mary as an American citizen.[22]

Among earlier generations of American Protestants, however, fearful that Catholic immigrants were plotting to take over the country, Catholic devotion to the Blessed Mother provoked great bitterness and alarm. The Virgin was the sign of what was threatening and inassimilable in Catholicism, most profoundly un-American (although, ironically, it was precisely as the avatar of Catholic otherness, evoking ancient times and distant places, that the Virgin also became the object of desire among elite critics of industrialism, consumerism, and modernity). From the perspective of this fear, Mary was the anticitizen, a decadent European queen out of place in the New World democracy. Catholicism was perversely feminized, anti-Catholics maintained, dominated by a woman who usurped Jesus' rightful prominence. Pornographic anti-Catholic literature offered Americans fascinated by the Catholic other a compelling account of dark, wet interiors (convents, monasteries, crypts, and ruins) presided over by obscene, lascivious priests who ravished innocent virgins—just as the pope threatened to ravish the innocent United States. The bitter taste of this is still with older Catholics.[23]

"Thank you," a visitor who identified herself as "an Active Legion of Mary Member," wrote in the "Divine Mirrors" exhibition comment book, "to Wellesley College (a bastion of WASP Boston civility) for recognizing the contributions of a poor young ethnic minority (pretty much single) mother." This begins a long communication with a number of interleaved messages. With whose contribution is this woman concerned? With Mary's? With her own? Perhaps she is thinking about the contributions of Catholics—"a poor young ethnic minority"—to democracy in the United States (an important theme in a tradition of American Catholic political thought to which Gibbons belonged). The writer's own cultural vulnerability becomes clear in the next sentence. "By showing this exhibit you are validating the existence of the Blessed Mother." But why does Mary require validation by an American college? Even to imagine this is to disclose the deepest uncertainty about the value of one's own culture in the eyes of others who are believed to hold the authority to validate and invalidate it. It is not surprising that such a disturbing revelation should be followed immediately by a protective hostility. "Perhaps this will assist to bridge the class gap between the students of your fine (real or perceived) institution and the members of surrounding communities who haven't had the same types of privileges. Thank you." *Real or perceived.* Things are not always as they seem. Fine institutions like Wellesley may not really be as good as they are held to be, groups as mistrusted as Catholics may not be as bad as others say they are. This woman's Madonna glows with the captured light of three centuries of anti-Catholicism.[24]

Mary has not been an uncomplicated symbol of unity among American Catholics either, however. Different immigrant and migrant groups brought regional and national representations of the Virgin with them to the ethnic enclaves of American cities, including southern Italy's Madonna del Carmine; Mexicans' Nuestra Senora Santa Maria de Guadalupe; la Caridad, who is the patroness of Cuba; and the Polish Black Madonna of Czestochowa. These dark-skinned Madonnas existed alongside "American" images of the Blessed Mother—"American" here meaning those either not associated with any particular ethnic group (such as the Sorrowful Mother or Our Lady of Perpetual Help, both of whom had hugely popular novenas in their honor in the twentieth century) or those who attracted universal devotion (Our Lady of Lourdes, for instance). Nationally and regionally identified Madonnas contributed to sustaining immigrant and migrant affective ties to the old countries, serving in some cases as pivots of enduring political and social aspirations for the homelands. Annual feast day celebrations in honor of these Madonnas were occasions for making the worlds their respective devout had come from present again in the American environment: in the gaze of the Madonna, the familiar sense world of the old countries—smells, the taste of remembered food and drink on the tongue, the music of childhood, and so on— were re-created, or created anew according to the exigencies of immigrant memories. The ethnic Madonnas evoked absent relatives (just as shrines in their honor recalled absent places), especially absent women (which was particularly important and complicated in those periods of immigration when men preceded their female kin to the new world, sometimes by years). By their faithfulness to the Madonna, immigrants and migrants could demonstrate to the community—and to themselves—their enduring compliance with the expectations and norms of the old societies, even as the circumstances of their lives made such faithfulness extremely difficult, if not impossible.[25]

At the same time, Marian devotions assisted (and continue to assist) migrants in coming to terms with the reality of their departures and its implications. Our Lady of the Americas, for example, who has been appearing to the visionary Estela Ruiz in South Phoenix, Arizona, since the early 1980s, has helped the Ruiz family, and many of their neighbors and friends, negotiate the tension between the values with which they were raised in Mexican households (and which they are eager to pass on to their children and grandchildren, in some fashion) and their success and ambitions in the American economy (which depended on other qualities, such as competitiveness, a single-minded focus on business affairs, and so on).[26]

The immigrant and migrant Madonnas also stood at the intersection of generations. Men and women whose lives were shaped in one place (or in the movement from one place to another) took their children, born or raised in the United States, into the shrines of the ethnic Madonnas, and these became pilgrimages to ideal versions of the moral and religious worlds of their childhoods in those other places. "This is how we lived in Mexico!" "This is what life was like in Naples!" Such moments could be tense and uncomfortable for young people because the cultures of European and Latin American villages were recast on these occasions in such a way as to chastise youngsters for their lives in the new country. Calling on the Madonna to be their witness, immigrant and migrant parents held their offspring accountable to ways of living that were not only irrelevant to the youngsters but that had been abandoned by the immigrants themselves. Younger people were thus asked to assume roles in their parents' inner struggles with guilt, memory, and loss, and, not surprisingly, many of them came to despise such devotions, ridiculed them, or resisted participating in them—until they themselves were older, that is, when the Madonna assisted them, in turn, in demonstrating their own faithfulness and dedication to their aging parents and grandparents and when they made pilgrimages of memory with their children to the Madonnas in the old neighborhoods.

At the end of novenas in honor of the Blessed Mother, in October or May or on her major feast days, people knelt to chant her litany. At the altar, priests, dressed in the heavy brocaded robes used for the service of Benediction and flanked by altar boys swinging smoking thurifers, intoned a long list of Mary's titles. In response to each the congregation sang, "Pray for us." Mary's names unfolded—Mother most pure (*pray for us*) . . . Mother most chaste (*pray for us*) . . . Mother inviolate (*pray for us*) . . . Mother most amiable . . . Virgin most prudent . . . Gate of Heaven . . . Morning star . . . Health of the sick . . . Queen of Angels, Queen of Patriarchs, Queen of Prophets . . . on and on and on. There were litanies for other figures too, but none as solemn and eloquent. The Marian litanies expressed social and psychological realities. Mary is not easily named. She requires long lists of names and attributes—pure, chaste, inviolate, undefiled, amiable, admirable, prudent, venerable, renowned, powerful, merciful, faithful—succeeding each other, in many voices, accumulating.[27]

There was also a Marian prayer called the Memorare, which read in part, "Remember, O most gracious Virgin Mary, that never was it known that any one who fled to thy protection, sought thy intercession, was left unaided. Inspired by this confidence, I fly unto thee, O Virgin of Virgins, my mother!"[28] The Mother of God denied no one her compassion.

Catholics were once taught imaginatively to conjure up scenes from the lives of Mary and Jesus, in great detail, while they tolled the beads of their rosaries. These were called "mysteries," in the sense of signs of God's truth in history, and there were fifteen of them: five Joyful Mysteries (the Annunciation, the Visitation, the Nativity, the Presentation, and Finding in the Temple); five Sorrowful Mysteries (Agony in the Garden, Scourging at the Pillar, Crowning with Thorns, Carrying of the Cross, and the Crucifixion); and five Glorious Mysteries (Resurrection of Christ, Ascension of Christ, Descent of the Holy Ghost, Assumption of the Blessed Virgin Mary, and the Crowning of the Blessed Virgin Mary). These moments constituted as well a catalogue of the narrative subjects of much of Western Christian religious art. Such imagery was there to assist people in the work of imagining their way into the narrative of salvation history, aiding the inner eye to reconstruct the landscape of the sacred world.[29] This was one juncture between art and devotion (although still not what Father Grabowski was hoping for).

Such devotional imaginings were meant to be emotionally vivid: one of the attitudes to be developed by this practice was empathy for Mary's experience. So Catholics imagined the Blessed Mother's delight in her infant boy, although they appreciated that this joy was shadowed from the start by the Virgin's foreknowledge of Jesus' necessary fate. (What parent cannot identify with this sorrow?) They rushed into the temple with her when she finds the boy Jesus, who had wandered away, to be, mysteriously, about his father's business, recognizing that, like any parent, Mary would have been feeling simultaneously relief and annoyance. They were encouraged especially to imagine and to sympathize with Mary's great sorrow on Calvary. The murmuring of the repetitive prayers, the presence of others praying alongside oneself, and the feel of the beads across one's fingers rendered the interior processes of the imagination corporal and moved Mary into the body.

So Mary became everyone's contemporary. Her kinship with John the Baptist's mother, Elizabeth, located the Blessed Mother in the recognizable context of family ties. The mysteries told the story of Mary's movement through the life course, subject to all the vicissitudes and sorrow of human finitude. She aged, she knew loss and loneliness, her hair whitened. Mary has never been held, at least not in popular experience (or in artistic representation) to a single life moment. She was not always, only, the young, slender, beautiful mother. Rather, the Blessed Mother accompanied her devout through the succession of the mysteries, joyful and sorrowful, of their own lives. By imagining Mary's history with the emotional discernment born of their own experience, her devout understood and affirmed that Mary recognized the anxiety, loss, and promise of what was happening to them. She had experienced all these things herself. Through the recitation of the mysteries, the Blessed Mother and her devout became recognizable to each other. This was their shared book of years, the lived equivalent of the monastic Book of Hours.

Her devout knew what Mary looked like, therefore. She was familiar to them from contemplative practice and from the conventions of devotional art. The Madonna's image has taken shape, again and again, in the ongoing interplay of art, devotion, and experience, in the everyday lives and practice of Catholics. One consequence of this is that among the criteria the devout use in assessing different representations of her is whether or not they know her as she is depicted, whether they recognize her. Some images of Mary are disappointing; this is not what she looks like, the devout think. All Marian art is, in this sense, realistic, more like photography than painting. The image on the wall is inevitably viewed through the lens of the image within.[30]

On several occasions over the last century in the United States a portrayal of the Blessed Mother in art has offended and outraged some of her devout, who have vigorously protested what they viewed as sacrilege. Sometimes Mary's defenders have demanded that the troubling image be banned or censored. An example of such a controversy was the tumult over the painting titled *Holy Virgin Mary* by Nigerian artist Chris Ofili that appeared in the "Sensations" exhibition organized by London's Royal Academy and presented at the Brooklyn Museum in 1999. Ofili's use of small quantities of elephant dung in the preparation of the work incensed some Catholics, who considered the proximity of the Blessed Mother to little piles of animal feces a defilement of her.[31] (But, as other, more earthbound Catholics might point out, what about the oxen and asses in the Bethlehem stable? I will return to this alternative perspective in a moment.)

This was not the first time New York Catholics—or some of them—were convulsed by outrage on Mary's behalf. An even more intense furor greeted the 1950 American premiere of Roberto Rossellini's film *The Miracle*.[32] The movie told the story of an unstable young Italian woman who believes that the child she bears after a liaison with a stranger, whom she takes to be Saint Joseph, is the infant Jesus. New York's Francis Cardinal Spellman angrily asserted, in a letter read from the city's pulpits on 7 January 1951, that Rossellini had offered "a vicious insult to Italian womanhood." Any number of social and cultural issues came into play in this incident, including the eagerness of American Catholics to display themselves, in the early years of the Cold War, as the last dependable defenders of morality against the threatening onslaught of world Communism. (Other Catholics, such as the editors of the liberal journal *Commonweal*, defended both the artistic merit of the movie and people's rights to come to their own judgments about it.) The religious source of the scandal (although this can never be completely separated out from other factors) was outrage at what was seen as the degradation of the Madonna by her association with human sinfulness, madness, and shame. Such of-fense seems completely out of place, however, in relation to a holy figure who is regularly begged in the prayer addressed to her daily by millions of Catholics to "pray for us sinners / now and at the hour of our death." Many people die in their beds; many others die in truly awful places and in terrible ways. Catholics believed that Mary would be present even at the most dreadful of them. This was affirmed, described, and elaborated in fiction, pious literature, poetry, and prayer, and especially in the leg-ends and tales Catholics told each other about the Blessed Mother. There was no place, no circumstance, so degraded that Mary would not enter it to comfort the lost and the afflicted, especially if they had once loved her and had, in some way, even if only the most secret, remained faithful to her.[33]

When the transcendent breaks into time, as Mary does regularly, the transcendent is bound to get dirty. Mary may have been free of sin, but her robes got stained with the mud and blood of Calvary. This is not a theological affirmation (or it is not as such that I make this comment here); this is how Catholics once and not too long ago imagined and talked about the Blessed Mother. Devotional practice had elaborated a story of the Blessed Mother as knowing shame, humiliation, and suffer-ing. As the Legion of Mary visitor to Wellesley's "Divine Mirrors" exhibi-tion puts it, reflecting such popular traditions about the Blessed Mother, Mary was "pretty much [a] single mother," stunned, as Catholics were encouraged to imagine devotionally, by the enormity of what had hap-pened to her and feeling at least a transitory disgrace at an unexpected pregnancy of uncertain paternity.[34] Stories are told today that Our Lady of Guadalupe comes in the middle of the night to distract guards along the border between the United States and Mexico, allowing migrants to slip past them undetected. How does she capture the attention of these rough men so late at night?[35]

"Am I not your Mother?" she asked him in his language, Nahuatl. "Are you not in the folds of my mantle, in the crossing of my arms?" She ap-peared first in 1531 to the man named Cuauhtlatohuac—He Who Speaks Like an Eagle—but known since his baptism as Juan Diego on the hill of Tepeyacac where the mother-goddess Tonantzin had been worshipped by his people, and she appears today on bolo ties, playing cards, tattooed on the skins of *cholos* in East L.A. and South Phoenix, on belts, pillows, towels, cigar boxes, lampshades, "among horns honking, ambulances running, children crying, all the people groaning and dancing and making love," in the struggles of farmworkers, in the places of the sick and dying, carved in soup bones, and in ravines on the border between Mexico and the United States. She is—in a litany that joins ancient and modern names

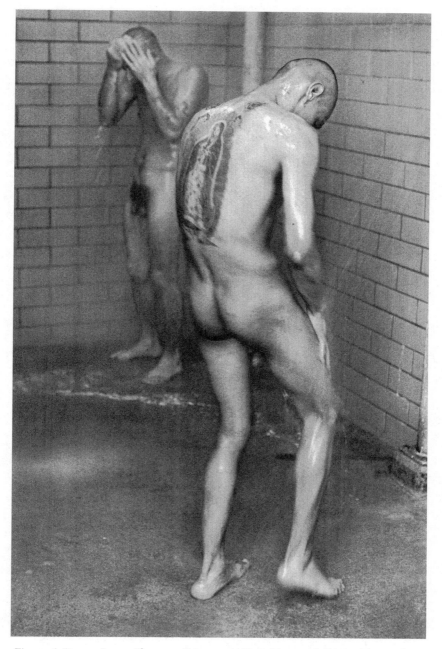

Figure 6. Danny Lyon, *Showers, Diagnostic Unit, Texas*, 1969/70, gelatin silver print from the *Conversations with the Dead* series. (Courtesy of Magnum Photos.)

for her—Tequatlanopeuh (She Whose Origins Were in the Rocky Summit), Tllecuauhtlaupeuh (She Who Comes Flying from the Light Like an Eagle of Fire), Tequantlaxopeuh (She Who Banishes Those That Ate Us), Coatlaxopeuh (She Who Crushed the Serpent's Head), Mother of Mexico, Mother of Orphans, Our Lady of Tepeyac, *la Santa Patrona de los mexicanos*, Empress of the Americas, Mother of the True God, Mother of the Giver of Life, Mother of the Lord of Near and Far, Mother of the Lord of Heaven and Earth, Mother Who Never Turns Her Back, Sister in Suffering, Subversive Virgin, Undocumented Virgin, *la tele Virgen*, "the sustainer of life, the one who protects us against danger, the one who comforts our sorrows," she who "understands everything," Our Lady of the Cannery Workers, Vessel of the Indigenous Spirit, *Madrecita, la madre querida, la Morenita, la Diosa*, Guadalupe-Tonantzin, *la Virgencita, la Virgencita tan bella*, the Virgin of Guadalupe.[36]

Of all the images of the Virgin in the *Divine Mirrors* exhibition, the one that touched me most deeply, in part because it was the one that seemed truest to the popular history of Marian devotions, was the tattoo of Our Lady of Guadalupe on the showering prisoner's naked back in American photographer Danny Lyon's *Showers, Diagnostic Unit, Texas*. Guadalupe is a national symbol, but her presence is more intimate here. It is a common practice among Latino gang members to put Guadalupe on their skins to protect them from violence and common also for their mothers to grieve to *la Morenita* when their sons die. We cannot assume anything about the experience of the man in Lyons's photograph because he comes to us without a story, but it would be good to know if Guadalupe's touch on his back comforted him, whether it reminded him of his mother or of the skin of his lovers, whether Guadalupe indeed kept harm away, and what he made of the moments when she failed him.

The excitement caused by the Virgin's apparitions may distract from the fact that, among her devout, the Blessed Mother is always there, amid the daily circumstances of their lives. This is not a benign reality; presence, however it is understood, is not easily or finally located on one side, the positive side, of a set of discrete moral categories—helpful/hurtful, reassuring/frightening, good/bad, and so on. Recall here the rosary held in the faces of shaken young women outside of abortion clinics or the proliferation of mischievous devils at Oliva Citra. Presence changes things, alters experience, reconfigures relationships, necessitates new maps for familiar landscapes. Presence is known by what happens, what becomes possible, what is foreclosed, in the space between the faces of the devout and the face of the Virgin, present to each other, in art, prayer, and history.

Chapter Three

MATERIAL CHILDREN: MAKING GOD'S PRESENCE REAL FOR CATHOLIC BOYS AND GIRLS AND FOR THE ADULTS IN RELATION TO THEM

> He could not choose to deny his father, even less his father's beliefs. These have become as material to him as the stucco-over-chicken-wire from which these houses are made.
> *D. J. Waldie*, Holy Land: A Suburban Memoir

IN THE LAST CHAPTER I asked what accounted for people's experience of Mary's presence in their lives. Presence is central to the study of lived Catholic practice—the study of Catholicism in everyday life is about the mutual engagement of men, women, children, and holy figures present to each other. But presence is a human experience; how sacred presences become real in particular times and places is a question. That is what I begin with here. How do religious beliefs become material? How do the gods and other special beings—and, more broadly, how does the world, visible and invisible, as the world is said to be within a particular religious culture—become as real to people as their bodies, as substantially *there* as the homes they inhabit, or "as the stucco-over-chicken-wire from which these houses are made?" Anthropologist Clifford Geertz's influential 1973 definition proposed that religion is "a system of symbols which acts to establish powerful, pervasive, and long-lasting moods and motivations in men by formulating conceptions of a general order of existence and clothing these conceptions with such an aura of factuality that the moods and motivations seem uniquely realistic." Geertz was primarily concerned with the cognitive realness of religion and its emotional and intellectual viability. Religions offer and substantiate accounts of the world that render the chaos and pain of experience meaningful and tolerable. But Geertz's reference to religion's capacity to clothe—to give material substance, fabric, and texture to—a culture's vision of the way things are suggests another account of religion. Religion is the practice of making the invisible visible, of concretizing the order of the universe, the nature of human life and its destiny, and the various dimensions and possibilities of human interiority itself, as these are understood in various cultures at

different times, in order to render them visible and tangible, present to
the senses in the circumstances of everyday life. Once made material, the
invisible can be negotiated and bargained with, touched and kissed, made
to bear human anger and disappointment, as we have seen in men and
women's relationships with the saints. But the question remains: how
does this happen?[1]

Religious cultures offer multiple media for materializing the sacred. There
are images, statues, beads, ritual objects, smells, visions, colors, foods
and tastes, vestments, oils, and waters. The invisible often becomes visible as faces, in heaven (in the face of Blessed Margaret of Castello looking
at my uncle Sal) and on earth (in the face of a woman who keeps an
image of the Sacred Heart of Jesus on her bedroom dresser and teaches
her grandchildren how to pray to this holy figure and who is forever associated in their minds with the suffering savior). Religious rituals, with
their movements, smells, sounds, and things, are privileged sites for rendering religious worlds present in the movements of bodies in space and
time as well.[2]

Things do not exhaust the materiality of religion, however, and rituals—particularly major performances in control of religious authorities—
work more or less successfully to limit materialization and to bind presence. It is true that people find ways of having private experiences of
presence within authorized and controlled ritual time and space that are
sometimes tolerated, sometimes not. But there is a difference between
Christ's presence on the altar during the sacrifice of the Mass and the
Mother of God standing on a Basque hillside. The two are not unrelated,
nor is this a simple matter of elite or official religion versus popular or
vernacular religion; such boundaries are never absolute, as we have seen
in previous chapters. But ritual is only one venue for the constitution of
a religion's realness. Rituals are occasional events. How the realness of
the world as enacted in ritual is carried over into ongoing everyday life
remains a problem for religious theory. So ritual is not a sufficient answer
to the problem of presence.

The materialization of religious worlds includes a process that might be
called the corporalization of the sacred. I mean by this the practice of
rendering the invisible visible by constituting it as an experience in a
body—in one's own body or in someone else's body—so that the experiencing body itself becomes the bearer of presence for oneself and for others. The following example will help clarify what I mean by the materialization or corporalization of the sacred as an experience evoked, produced,
or occasioned in bodies. In an article addressed to Catholic parents and
educators in December 1937, a teaching sister from Detroit's Marygrove
College asked her readers how the truths of Advent and Christmas—

"Christmas is Jesus' birthday. Jesus is God. He made you and me and everybody . . . Jesus will bless us and make us happy with Him"—could be made real to children. These abstract theological notions, Sister Mary warned, make no sense to youngsters unless somehow accompanied by "concrete experiences."[3]

The "spiritual," Sister says again, must be "made concrete," and the way she proposes to do this is by having children make a crib for baby Jesus. At first it seems Sister is concerned to teach children by means of the *things* they actually manipulate, but her plans are more complicated than this. The boundaries between matter (the crib and its figures, straw, and animals), experience (the child's inner apprehension of the realness of Christmas), and the sacred get erased in Sister's discussion of the project. The crib must be a thing, she says, a box or a basket that "will actually be the crib in which the statue or picture of the Infant will be placed on Christmas morning," but the crib "must actually be spiritual, that is, made of prayers and acts of love and sacrifice." Actually spiritual, actually material: these are not separate in the way Sister is thinking about this classroom work.

Between the truth of Christmas and the box that stands for that truth is the child's body, and it is mostly with this that Sister is concerned. It is in the child's flesh that Christmas will be made real, tangible, and accessible. "Eating things the child does not like could make the straw," Sister advises, "being obedient the coverlet, being nice to others when playing with others, the pillow." Saying morning prayers *devoutly*, by which Sister means with a particularly attentive and focused attitude of body and mind, brings the image of the Blessed Mother to the crib; devoutly reciting bedtime prayers summons Saint Joseph to the manger. "Special acts of love—telling Jesus he loves Him, asking Him to come on Christmas and be happy in our home, telling our Lady he loves her, giving a picture or statue a kiss, saying a prayer during the day—these could be special trimmings around the Crib in the form of flowers or snow or anything else which would show the child that he is waiting for the Blessed Babe." The child "lives the same life as ever, but he conquers himself and does all now in the power of the Infant King." Sister means real things by coverlet, snow, flowers, and so on—the appropriate posture or attitude in the child's body leads to the literal placement of additional things on the crib—and she means what is happening in children's imaginations and bodies.[4]

Where is the materiality of religion here? Where is presence? In the crib or in the taste in the child's mouth as she eats foods she does not like? In the straw or in the postures the child must assume for the privilege of putting the straw in the crib, in the statues or in the special acts of love that give the child permission to arrange the holy family there? Religious

materiality or presence here is not things but practice. Sister Mary's intentions are clearly directed to making spiritual realities concrete in children's experience. The objects involved are media of a much larger materializing ambition. The Catholic word for the instruction of children in the
faith was *formation*, but "instruction" is too pallid a word for what this
process aimed at and "formation" was not a matter simply of shaping the
intellect. What was formed in formation was the realness and presence of
the sacred in the bodies and imaginations of children.

Sister's ambitions become especially clear in her discussion of how to
treat time. Children live in an endless present, she says; the notion of
time's passing has very little meaning for them. This cognitive limitation
creates a special problem when it comes to Advent, a season of anticipation that requires some notion of time. Otherwise, how can a child look
forward to Jesus' birth? The challenge, as Sister construes it, is to materialize time: she recommends that parents draw a vertical line across each
day of a special calendar to signify that a child has said his or her morning
prayer, a horizontal line for evening prayer, and in this way "each day as
it passes will . . . be marked with the cross . . . and time will come to have
a real meaning" to the child. Invisible minutes and hours acquire a solidity
borrowed from the corporal experience of children, who before they
know how to tell time will have known time's moral and cosmic significance in their bodies, in their praying limbs.[5]

This is what Sister and I mean by "concrete experiences" of the sacred.

The bodies of others may become the vehicles for the materialization of
the sacred. This was especially true in the psychologically and religiously
fluid domain of Catholic devotionalism. In this religious world, the bodies
so used were, first of all, those of the saints. It was from the cult of saints
and relics (which included matter taken from or put in contact with saints'
bodies) that this orientation toward the sacred experienced in bodies was
developed and popularized in Catholic cultures. A relic is explicitly an
object of power taken away from the body of a holy person, either a piece
of that body itself or something touched to it. Then, too, all corporal
realizations of the sacred are mimeses of the presence of the divine in the
body of Christ and of Christ's body present in the host during the sacrifice
of the Mass.[6]

But the sacred could be present in the bodies of living persons too. The
experience of persons with disabilities in their solitude and pain (as their
experience was constructed in the discourse of the holy cripple) was made
the site for encounters with the sacred by others who were not disabled.
Just as pain may be alienated from the bodies of those in pain and made
to substantiate the realness of things separate from them—this is the logic

of torture, as philosopher Elaine Scarry has pointed out—so too may sacred presence. Often enough (certainly in Catholic devotionalism but in other religious contexts as well) religion is the feelings, acts, and experiences of some people as these are imagined, imposed on them, and then taken from them by other people. Not all bodies serve this purpose, moreover, but bodies marked in some way within particular social worlds by special kinds of difference. As we saw, the bodies of the "handicapped," constructed as bodies-in-pain by the nonhandicapped, became media of presence, a political and religious transubstantiation that did not necessarily help the "handicapped" live better lives.[7]

One such medium of religious materialization—for rendering the invisible visible and present—of special importance for religious practitioners is children. Adults tell themselves (urgently and usually fearfully) that they must pass their religious beliefs and values on to their children. To this end they organize catechism classes, Sunday school programs, afterschool religious instruction, special children's rituals, and so on. The fear is that without such instruction children will be bereft and alienated on the deepest levels; in the story that adults tell about this exchange, children need religion for their own benefit.

But this is not all there is to this. Children represent among other things the future of the faith standing there in front of oneself; at stake are the very existence, duration, and durability of a particular religious world. Children lacking the capacity to experience Advent, as Sister Mary feared, meant that a substantial portion of the Catholic population (its *entire* future population) did not share a major religious season with everyone else. Children signal the vulnerability and contingency of a particular religious world and of religion itself, and in exchanges between adults and children about sacred matters the religious world is in play. On no other occasion except perhaps in times of physical pain and loss is the fictive quality of religion—the fact that religious meanings are made and sustained by humans—so intimately and unavoidably apprehended as when adults attempt to realize the meaningfulness of their religious worlds in their children. This is why discussions of children's religious lives are fraught with such great fear, sometimes sorrow, and sometimes ferocity, among adults, especially in times of social change or dislocation.[8]

The apparently commonsensical and straightforward nature of this enterprise—we want to pass our beliefs on to our children—naturalizes or normalizes a far more complex relationship. Children's bodies, rationalities, imaginations, and desires have all been privileged media for giving substance to religious meaning, for making the sacred present and material, not only *for* children but *through* them too, for adults in relation to them. The child addressed in religious settings and the religious world that is represented to this child are constituted in relation to each other. This is the dialectic of what is usually misnamed "children's religion."

The work of substantiating the interiority of the faith is how Elaine Scarry interprets the biblical story of the sacrifice of Isaac. As the narrative slowly unfolds in excruciating detail—father and son build the altar, gather wood for the fire, Abraham binds Isaac—Scarry says, "we encounter the rhythm of substantiation, more and more emphatic presentation and re-presentation of the body to confer the force and power of the material world on the noumenal and unselfsubstantiating." The danger to Isaac is the risk taken, Scarry observes, "*to make* an already existing God more immediately apprehensible, *to remake* of an unapprehensible God an apprehensible One." The story of Abraham and Isaac "does not merely describe the rigors of belief, what is required of belief, but the structure of belief itself, the taking of one's insides and giving them over to something wholly outside oneself"—God—"as Abraham agrees to sacrifice the interior of his and Sarah's bodies, and to participate in that surrender."[9]

Children are uniquely available to stand for the interiority of a culture and to offer embodied access to the inchoate possibilities of the culture's imaginary futures. But the "interior" of Abraham's body is a grown child with his own feelings and perceptions. Isaac is a boy who understands that he is about to be killed. Child sacrifice is not self-immolation but the murder of a separate human being whose identity is not exhausted by his or her status as son or daughter nor as a sign of the future of the social world. It is this fluidity—if not the actual erasure of the boundaries—between the body of the child and the interiority of the adult engaging the child in a religious setting that makes possible the materialization of a sacred reality through the bodies, minds, and imaginations of children.[10]

"Children" and "cripples" share certain characteristics that when looked at together can help us understand why some bodies and not others become privileged sites of sacred presence in Catholic culture. Both "child" and "cripple" are apparently natural or given categories, self-evident identities, but both designations are fundamentally constituted by culture. "Cripples" and "children" are what culture makes of particular biological or physiological circumstances. Young people and persons with disabilities are assessed against and imagined in relation to normative models of what they are not—adults in the case of children, persons without disabilities in the case of those with them—so that they wind up being defined by absence or by what they lack. So defining them works to authorize and privilege those who possess the missing qualities—again, adults and persons without physical disabilities. Persons with disabilities and children (in this case without the marks indicating cultural constructs) are more or less dependent on others, more or less needful of some very basic things (as my uncle Sal angrily reminded me). (Of course, all people are needful of others, but one of the tasks of the discourses of the holy cripple and of the innocent child is to deny this.) They might need assistance with movement (getting from here to there), with getting dressed and undressed, or with basic body care. This makes them vulnerable to others, and this vulnerability can lead these others to fantasies of power and possession, as we have seen. This same physical vulnerability is true of children too.

Both children and people with disabilities, moreover, are experienced as uncanny, distinctly alien, even though they live closely among us. Their struggles with language and speech, for instance, or their problems of coordination mark them off as different. What sociologist of childhood Chris Jenks says of childhood is true, as was evident in chapter 1, of persons with disabilities as well. "Simply stated," Jenks writes, "the child is familiar to us and yet strange, he or she inhabits our world and yet seems to answer to another, he or she is essentially of ourselves and yet appears to display a systematically different order of being."[11] Finally, both "children" and "cripples" (once constituted as such) become objects of the desires of others. Vulnerable, physically and emotionally, the foci of tremendous cultural attention and work, emptied (in the fantasies of others) of their own agency and capacity, "children" and "cripples" become the repositories of need and desire, including religious need and desire. Once they are defined by absence, "children" like "cripples" can become the space into which desires and needs may be chased and found.

The innocent, empty, and so desirable child has been an important feature of modern Catholic culture since the end of the eighteenth century. Roman Catholics around the world in the modern era believed themselves to be living in the "age of Mary," the final era before Christ's cataclysmic return in triumph and judgment. The Marian age was heralded by the Mother of God's interventions at sites of grave intellectual and political contest between the church and the modern world. But the time can just as well be called the "age of children," because at LaSalette, Lourdes, and Fatima, at Marpingen in Germany's northern Saarland, on the Basque hillside at Ezkioga, at Garabandal, and then at Medjugorje, Mary appeared most often to children. It was the sight of children in ecstatic communication with the invisible figure of the Virgin and the sound of their childish voices speaking her messages of consolation and warning that so captured the imaginations of proponents of the apparitions (and of defenders of the church) and so incited the anger and contempt of detractors of the apparitions (and of the church's antagonists). That Mary

Figure 7. The three child visionaries of Fatima—Lucia Dos Santos (*center*), Jacinta (*left*), and Franciso Marto (*right*). (© Reuters/Corbis.)

chose to reveal herself to little children was taken by devout as proof of the validity of the events—because how could innocent children deceive anyone—and by critics as proof of the church's intolerable and decadent corruption of the minds and hearts of simple people.[12]

The age of children had its pope, Giuseppe Sarto, Pius X, who took a number of initiatives to bring youngsters into full participation in the life of the church. It had been a deeply rooted custom throughout Europe prior to this time to wait until children were eleven or twelve, often as old as fourteen, before allowing them to make their first Communions. It was thought that younger children could not understand the eucharistic mystery. Even young children in imminent danger of death were denied the sacrament in some countries. It was also common to let an interval of a year pass between a child's first Communion and his or her taking the host again. Pius X was committed to increasing the frequency of Communion among adults, but he was particularly interested in bringing children to the altar. In a series of decrees and instructions the pope lowered the age of first Communion and urged children to receive often. Nor did Pius think that children should wait until they were seven, the traditional age of reason, for this. According to a story that circulated widely in the international Catholic press, an English visitor who brought his four-year-old son with him to a private papal audience happened to mention that the boy hoped to make his first Communion in a few years. Pius turned to the child and asked him two questions: "Whom do you receive in Holy Communion?" and "Who is Jesus Christ?" The boy answered both correctly and Pius instructed his father to "bring him to my Mass tomorrow morning and I will give him Holy Communion myself." Pius also improved and standardized catechetical instruction for children throughout Italy and promoted devotion to the child Jesus.[13]

Childhood—or "childhood," meaning the qualities presumed by adults to belong to children—became the model of adult faith in the age of children. In an allocution in 1929 on Saint Theresa of the Little Flower (whose autobiography was a major document of this culture of child spirituality), Pope Benedict XV summed up the ethos of the age, "In spiritual childhood is the secret of sanctity for all the faithful of the Catholic world." A charismatic woman named Soledad de la Torre Ricaurte founded in Spain an association of priests dedicated to boyish innocence who called themselves "Sacerdotes Ninos" (child-priests). In the manual she wrote for them in 1920, which was approved by diocesan authorities, La Soledad addressed her priests in baby talk and encouraged them to talk to Jesus in this way too when they visited his playhouse, as she called the sanctuary. The boy saint, Guy de Fontgalland, who died in 1925 at the age of twelve, captured the imaginations of Catholics throughout Europe and North America and became the object of special devotion among priests. In a pamphlet published in the late 1920s for American Catholic youngsters, Chicago priest Raymond J. O'Brien wrote that Guy enjoyed a special intimacy with the "Little Jesus" whose living presence Guy could feel under his hand in his own beating heart after receiving Communion, an image of considerable erotic and spiritual resonance. So thoroughly had Catholicism been identified with the cult of childhood in the age of children that anti-Catholics singled this aspect of Catholic culture out for particular contempt and derision.[14]

The church and the modern world were at war with each other. Rumors of the murder of priests and nuns and the despoiling of church property terrorized Catholics all over Europe, from the age of revolutions to the conflicts of the mid–twentieth century. Philosophers challenged Europeans to liberate themselves from intellectual thralldom to the church and to come of age intellectually and religiously. For cultural critics from Voltaire to Freud it was contemptible for adults to maintain a childlike dependence on God and church. *Infantile* became a term of rich moral and religious opprobrium in political, philosophical, and psychological literatures. Rome in turn called on the faithful to practice a simple devotional piety in the face of the distress and complexity of modernity, the more securely to locate Catholic populations under its authority. And it was the explicit hope of Pius X and of the popes that came after him as well as of religious educators in the United States and Europe to restore the integrity of the church by forming children in a deep and well-instructed faith.

American Catholics created a distinctive culture of childhood in the twentieth century. The bishops meeting at the Third Plenary Council in Baltimore in 1884 stopped just short of *requiring* parents to send their children to parochial school under pain of sin, but they gravely urged this, and so until the mid-1960s it was an American Catholic obsession to build and maintain elementary schools. Children who went to parochial elementary school grew up in the precincts of the church and in the closest daily relationship with priests and brothers and especially with nuns. (The number of children in Catholic elementary and high schools varied by geographical region, by ethnic community, and at different times between the 1890s and the 1960s, but always constituted a substantial percentage of the school-age population, and this increased sharply in the middle years of the twentieth century.) Whatever desires, intentions, or dreams drew these adults into the religious life in the first place, their most insistent responsibility and challenge in the twentieth century was to supervise the religious formation of children. Considerably more than half of all women religious in the United States were serving as teachers by 1930. To be a nun until the 1960s mostly meant to be inescapably bound to children. Nuns shepherded thousands of children to daily or weekly mass, and priests spent a good part of their Saturdays listening to children confess "sins" the youngsters had carefully and anxiously rehearsed (usually without knowing what the words meant).[15]

Catholics expected a great deal from their children religiously, on earth and in between earth and heaven (as intercessors for the souls in purgatory, for instance, or special petitioners for graces on earth). They prided themselves on offering children direct access to the sacred, not what they imagined as the scaled-down, make-believe, Sunday school version of Christianity given Protestant children. Other Christians may have kept their children out of sacred space, but Catholic boys and girls played special roles in the church's liturgical life. They were assigned substantial religious responsibilities and duties. Altar boys, who were privileged to stand in close proximity to the tabernacle where adult women religious could not go (as clerical magazines regularly pointed out), were essential to the church's sacramental life. Mass could not be said without them, and if by chance no boy showed up, then an adult male who had once been an altar boy stepped in and reenacted his childhood role in the sight of the congregation.[16] The status and responsibility of the altar boy lasted a lifetime. Children were to know and to be able to defend the doctrines of the church against the many detractors adults warned them that they

Figure 8. The interiors of churches were unimaginable without the presence of altar boys. This view of the altar inside Chicago's Holy Name Cathedral was taken in 1929. (Photo courtesy of Chicago Daily News negatives collection, Chicago Historical Society.)

would inevitably encounter, to the death if necessary—and thousands of
Catholic children in the United States came to believe on some level of
their imaginations that this might very well be asked of them one day (an
instance of a distinctly American Catholic countercivics). "We teachers,
by the grace of God," a teaching sister in Armstrong, Wisconsin, summoned her colleagues in 1953, "have been selected as marshals in direct-
ing and guiding the smallest of God's soldiers in the part they are to play
in winning the world for Christ. It will mean a tremendous battle." Children were encouraged to develop devotional routines, to carry rosaries in
their pockets when they were out playing, to take on additional disciplines
of penance and sacrifice beyond those required by the church, to aspire
to sanctity on the model of the holy child-heroes held out to them, and
to choose a saint for personal prayer and petition. Children and adolescents were taught to think with the intricate logic of Catholic moral theology so that they became practiced casuists themselves, adept at parsing
degrees of culpability and exoneration. Catholic teenagers in the postwar
years were not simply concerned with what they could and could not
do sexually in an absolute sense but with the flexibility of sexual boundaries and with the circumstances and conditions that made for greater or
lesser permission or prohibition. Even the Friday meat prohibition was
subject to moral speculation. What if you ordered meat before midnight
prior to a day of abstinence but ate it afterwards? What about artificial
meat substitutes?[17]

American Catholics invested their children with tremendous religious
hopes too. Catholic leaders early in the century looked to children to
instruct immigrant parents and other adult relatives in the faith, charging
youngsters with the responsibility of bringing their families to Sunday
mass, showing grown-ups how to worship and how to support the church
in the way that American Catholics were expected to do. In an immigrant
and migrant church, children would teach their parents how to comport
themselves as Americans and as *American* Catholics. Catholic commentators maintained in the anxious years just after the period of immigration
had ended in 1924 that children represented the great hope of the church.
Children alone might bridge "the gulf which now separates the people
and the priest," a prominent educator claimed in an address to the National Catholic Educational Association in 1930. Adult religious may
have felt trapped by "those armies of children," as one exasperated and
overwhelmed priest described the scene in his parish in 1936, and later in
the century, in the 1970s, adults wondered whether the long preoccupation with children had not only been worth it but even healthy. In the years
in between, however, and in a way that was not true of the eighteenth or
nineteenth century, Catholicism in the United States was made and sus-

Figure 9. American Catholic vocational ambitions literally made material on girls' bodies, circa 1940s. While Catholic children were encouraged to dress in clerical garb during celebrations of Vocation and Mission Sundays, some children fashioned habits out of bedsheets at home. (Photo courtesy of the Archdiocese of Chicago's Joseph Bernadin Archives and Records Center.)

tained in the relationship between adults and children in the spaces of the sacred and in the everyday routines they shared.[18]

Nuns were determined to instill a passionate prayer life in children and to form their limbs in the appropriate devotional postures. Very young children were encouraged not only to imagine themselves as priests and nuns but also actually to make themselves into little religious. Catholic retailers sold miniature replicas of the complex garb of various religious orders for dress-up play. Until the middle of the century, Catholic boys and girls entered the religious life barely out of puberty, deciding their religious vocations at the age of ten or eleven. Religious play was seriously consequential in this environment: a child's games could be taken as an indication of if not an actual commitment to religious vocation. Children were asked to have at least a memorized grasp of the intricacies of Thomist theology. Sanctifying grace, an article in the popular periodical *Junior Catholic Messenger* casually reminded its readers in 1943, is the "superlife of the soul," deeming it reminder enough for children who had first learned this theology in the simplified but still quite demanding question-and-answer drills of catechism class. Immigrant communities retained old-world customs that assigned children special roles in sacred performance. Children welcomed the poor to Saint Joseph's altars among New Orleans Italian Americans, for example, and helped feed the strangers who had come to eat.[19]

Children and adults watched one another very closely in Catholic culture, perhaps inevitably so given their daily involvement with each other. Adults responsible for preparing altar boys for liturgical duties constantly reminded their charges that the congregation was able to *see* them at the altar. Altar boys were virtually defined by the fact of their visibility, as objects of public scrutiny. "Perhaps you saw my boys on Christmas," the mother of two altar boys exclaimed in *Ave Maria* in 1948, emphasizing the visual. Servers were described as uniquely held in the gaze of eyes on heaven and earth. The boys themselves were aware of this. The true altar boy, a writer for the *Clergy Review* noted in May 1940, "likes to be seen wearing the uniform of the sanctuary and is proudly conscious of the admiration of relations and friends when they are given a close-up view on such occasions as processions." "The eyes of the world are on you at all times," a priest named David Rosage wrote in a manual for altar boys in 1952. "Your manner of walking to the altar, your conduct during Mass, the way you guard your eyes, and the many actions you perform while serving Mass will teach the people a valuable lesson on the sacredness of the most important action in their whole lives—the Holy Sacrifice of the Mass." The first thing a boy sees as he sets foot in the sanctuary, a priest wrote in the *Catholic Educator* in 1948, is "the misty glance of Mary in her blue niche" upon him.[20]

What was emphatically true for altar boys was also so for children generally. Little children at mass were told that Jesus was watching them from the altar. They could see for themselves the nuns in the aisles taking note of their behavior for later review. "You knew every kid in school," a woman who grew up in New Orleans in the 1940s told me, her voice dragging out the sentence, "because you'd watch them go to Communion and you'd watch them come back." Catholic communities gathered regularly for religious ceremonies, such as the crowning of Mary in May, first Communions, or living rosaries (described in the last chapter) in which adults watched children interacting with the sacred (like the spectators at Lourdes and Fatima, the archetypal modern instances of the sacred captured for adults in children's experience of it). Saturday afternoon confessions were an agony for children who were painfully aware that their movements after leaving the confessional box were being closely scrutinized by their peers for signs of what they had just confessed. To emerge from the booth to the staring faces of your friends, teachers, and family members after the priest had yelled at you—which happened often

Figure 10. Two girls dressed as Our Lady of Fatima during celebrations at the shrine in May 2001. (Photo courtesy of Corbis.)

enough—was an experience of deep shame. "If you said anything kind of wrong," a seventy-one-year-old Mexican American man described his childhood church in Tyrone, Arizona, for me, the pastor "would yell at you and then the rest of the people would know that you did something wrong." He learned to say no to all the priest's questions about what he had done that week, and at the end of the confession he added all these lies to his list of sins. "That was a way of getting around it."[21]

Children looked back too. They kept a sharp eye out for every stray wisp of a nun's hair or glimpse of her skin. Adult Catholic memories today record children's acute awareness of nuns' bodies and smell. A forty-six-year-old Mexican American woman who grew up in Phoenix and went to Catholic school there remembered her sixth-grade teacher, Sister Vivian Marie, as "very pretty body-wise, she was a very pretty woman." When sisters began abbreviating their religious garb in the 1960s, this woman recalled, Sister Vivian Marie "started having the skirt coming up to here, kind of A-line, like a jumper, and you could see she had a figure. And you know, I'm growing up, I'm a young girl, and I'm going 'Damn, she looks good for a nun.' And she had a real nice face and she had her hair cropped and kind of tousled. . . . She had a real pretty shape, wasn't fat at all . . . bottle-shaped legs and everything. You notice this, 'God, a nun has legs.' " Boys and girls both, perhaps for different reasons, looked very closely at nuns' bodies. Children and adults watching each other and watching each other watch them—this was the world of midcentury Catholicism in the United States.[22]

But it was not a simple matter to bring this many children—"these armies of children"—into the domain of the sacred, to invest them with such profound religious hopes, or to make them objects of such sustained religious desiring. There has always been a deep ambivalence in Western Christian culture about the spiritual and moral status of children, akin to ambivalence about the sick. Saint Augustine in the fourth century (reflecting on the troubles of his own childhood) thought that children were naturally depraved. Other theologians believed that children were good only because they lacked the physical capacities and opportunities for sin; still others found children angelic and naturally innocent. Christian conceptions of childhood throughout the Middle Ages "oscillate[d] between extremes," church historian Janet L. Nelson writes, "because children's behaviour was taken to indicate good or bad supernatural power: on the one hand, lack of control suggested diabolical influence, on the other, weakness and unpretentiousness suggested access to the divine." In either case a child was taken to be a "channel, vessel, sign of power beyond him/herself." Pius X told an audience of four hundred French children in April 1912, in the Sistine Chapel, that every day their guardian angels beheld God's face in "the souls of these little ones where God is

reflected as in the mirror of their innocence, their splendor, their purity."
Although the attitude evident in the pope's comment was more prevalent
in the modern era than among Augustine's or medieval theologians, the
old ambivalence did not disappear. Wherever there is innocence in Catholic imaginings, evil is not far away.[23]

The doubleness of children in midcentury Catholic adult imaginations is
most clearly evident in the ambiguity and instability of the figure of the
altar boy. Adult men (including priests) who had once been altar boys
themselves and altar boys' mothers together created a warm and evocative
genre of stories that cast altar boys at least as little heroes but more as
miniature saints. Altar boy stories were as sensual as those describing
the physical distress of cripples. "Someone once termed altar-boys 'little
priests in minor orders,' " the man who evoked Mary's misty blue gaze
on boys wrote in 1948, and he went on to offer this loving and tender
portrait of altar boys: "He knows the still of a church at six o'clock on
winter mornings—the touch of cold silver from the chalice and paten, the
chill rustle of gold cloth in a vesting drawer. . . . He knows the struggle
of puffing on charcoal lumps held in wire forceps over a flickering candle
by numb fingers as well as the early morning summer bird's song, and the
fresh fragrance of June roses that hover about the tabernacle door. . . .
The censer gives off more pungent ribbons of smoke, the mosaics above
the altar burn more fiercely in the candle flame-rings, and Mary smiles
. . . his world is suddenly made whole." This was the romance of the altar
boy. So precious and special was the boy at the altar, close to the tabernacle, that he became strangely unrecognizable even to his own mother. One
woman turned to verse (in 1945) to describe this feeling about her son:
"His childish head bowed low in prayer, / Candlelight falling on his hair, /
As though he were somehow divine: / I wonder if this child is mine." The
altar boy captured in a striking way the uncanniness of children.[24] (Just
as Isaac's destiny was the expression of his father's faith, so when a priest
or nun looked at an altar boy and imagined him yearning to be a priest—
a priest in the making—they were expressing *their* desires, not his. This
could become a real problem for boys who had to resist, sometimes
fiercely, what others were determined to make of their lives.)

But the uncanny is dangerous, and a narrative of the bad altar boy
shadowed the romantic view. Everyone knows that the boys who become
acolytes are "the most irreverent lads in the parish," a priest claimed in
the clerical trade journal *Homiletic and Pastoral Review* in 1938. These
"casscocked little hooligans" are bad enough to "break a priest's heart."
"The altar-boy problem" was a common topic in clerical journals. Sometimes it was called the "altar-boy evil." Priests described themselves as
being at the mercy of boys run amuck at the altar. Servers holding the

long, trailing cope worn by celebrants during benediction fell behind and dragged the priest back "as a driver would a restive horse," a writer complained in the Benedictine liturgical review *Orate Fratres* in 1943, or else they raced ahead and pulled the priest forward "as if he were reluctant to proceed." Priests found themselves caught in an altar boy tug-of-war in full sight of congregations. Boys competed with each other to see who could hold the priest's vestments up the highest, turning sacred occasions into playground competitions. Some boys only showed up for mass if they were paid. It was not unheard of, priests complained, for boys to trap young bridegrooms in the sacristy and demand a ransom before letting him rejoin the wedding party.[25]

The real danger of the uncanny altar boy was ritual disruption. Boys represented a threat to the solemnity of the mass. Father George P. Johnson writing in the *Ecclesiastical Review* in 1932 admonished his fellow clergy that "the altar-boy problem is one that requires careful study, zealous effort, and systematic treatment" because it has "such a tremendous influence upon the dignified execution of our liturgical ceremonies." Altar boys subverted the majesty of the mass, Father Johnson wrote, by their slovenliness, their unkempt bodies and bad posture, and their filthy shoes. This was all distracting "disedification" for the faithful. Father Johnson was particularly worried about the tendency of untrained acolytes to "perform the ceremonies according to their own judgment." He reminded readers that "we have all, at some time or another, marveled at the originality in ceremony manifested by the ill-instructed boy serving at the altar." The dirty bodies and unpredictable behavior of altar boys in ritual space represented the profanation of the sacred and the transgression of ritual order. "Familiarity breeds contempt," Father Johnson warned. Bad altar boys encouraged "disrespect even for the most sacred of places, the sanctuary."[26]

Tensions between boys and priests at the altar were so common and so vexing that in 1941 the widely read clerical journal *Ecclesiastical Review* published an extraordinary fantasy by a Philadelphia priest named Edward J. McTague called "To an Unknown Altar Boy."[27] McTague's fantasy opens with a somber description of the funeral of an altar boy: a lovely day, relatives sobbing, and then at the undertaker's signal a gravedigger "touched a lever and the little coffin slipped smoothly into the grave." This was a "gruesome case," Father McTague says grimly. The twelve-year-old boy was brutally slain. The unnamed victim had been a faithful acolyte, a "tractable and docile pupil," who "crept from his warm and comfortable bed to serve an early Mass, plowing through the snow and sleet while the city lights were still sputtering and the milkman was going his rounds." But the boy had one fault: he simply could not properly memorize the Latin prayers. So one day in the middle of mass as the boy was mangling the Confiteor ("*Beato Maria semper Virgine, beata Michael the Archangel, beata Johnny the Baptist . . .*") the priest at the altar "seized [him] by the ears and dragged him down a back stairway and into the street. There he conducted him to a lonely spot beyond church property, where he stamped on him most vigorously, snapping every bone in the child's head," killing him. The deed done, the priest feels no remorse; the district attorney decides that this is a case of justifiable homicide; the boy's parents accept their loss "with resignation." On the altar boy's tombstone the priest who killed him writes, "Dear Altar Boys take my advice / And know your stuff or pay the price: / Don't mix, if you desire to live, / The dative and accusative." "I like it," the murderer-priest sighs, "I think it's quite fetching."

This all may be a dream. Father McTague himself cannot quite decide how he wants to frame his dreadful fantasy. But here it is: in 1941 in a highly regarded periodical for his fellow clergymen a priest published a lurid and graphic tale of another priest stomping an altar boy to death. Father McTague was confident that other priests would find this funny. The essay made it past the priests who edited the periodical. The article is unapologetic—at the end, the killer gets to enjoy his breakfast. Father McTague writes with real delight (in the same voice, indeed, that other priests celebrated the joys of the shut-in life at the same time in American Catholic history). Clearly, all was not well in this culture between priests and children, Bing Crosby notwithstanding.

Children's bodies generally, their comportment not only in the spaces of the sacred but also in the streets and alleys around the churches, were the subject of persistent concern among Catholic educators and commentators in the years just before and after the Second World War. At first this was simply generational change between Europe and the United States: Italian American teenage girls, for example, did not carry themselves in the way their Sicilian or Neapolitan mothers or aunts did or their older sisters. Changes in Catholic life throughout the middle years of the century entailed new figurations of the lived bodies of children and adolescents, of their actual physical experiences in the spaces and relationships of their everyday lives, in what youngsters expected of their bodies in terms of pleasure and pain. Among the first places that social transformations in the community were registered was in children's bodies; with each new sign of change registered here, there was distress, disorientation, and anxiety. The altar-boy evil commotion was one instance of a wider preoccupation with children's corporality and its dangers.[28]

Go to church some Sunday and look down from the choir loft on your former or present pupils, Sister Mary Consilia of the Dominican House of Studies in Washington, D.C., bleakly urged her fellow educators in

1938 in a lament typical of the times, and you will see "half-genuflections by tight-skirted girls who can't bend any lower; fingering of curls, collars, eye-lashes, anything and everything but not of rosaries; eyes congregation bound, not altar-riveted." Those few girls who do go to Communion treat the walk to the altar rail as a fashion show; the others just sit there carefully keeping "their silk-stockinged knees" off "the hard rough wood of the kneeling bench." The boys are no better. "Their elbows, probably, are stretched out on the forms before them, and not infrequently throughout the Mass their heads are pillowed upon them. Is the posture respectful? Is it suitable for the presence of divine royalty?"[29]

How then to make the sacred real and concrete (in Sister Mary's terms) to this generation of Catholic children and adolescents, whose American bodies provoked such anxiety (and rage) among their parents, teachers, and pastors, whose bodies caused disruption at the altar and in the pew, who held themselves in such apparent disrespect and disdain for the sacred world that adults knew and who thereby seemed to undermine the very authority and stability of that world? How to make the sacred real in such disruptive bodies? "Please don't make Jesus stoop too low" by misbehaving in church, a popular writer for children, Father Gerald Brennan, begged his readers in 1939. It is striking that the culture had come to this pass where children could humiliate Jesus. This was a religious world made and sustained in the ongoing relationships between adults and children (in sight of each other)—and one party to this bond had begun to be very anxious about the risk posed by the other to their common world. Whether or not Catholic adolescents were really doing these things, whether they had become so threatening and disruptive, is an open question; what is important here for the moment is that this is how adults represented them. That American Catholicism should have reached this point was perhaps inevitable as a result of the bishops' 1884 decision, which insured that religious professionals and children would be spending so much time together.[30]

The adults whose responsibility it was to form children's religious imaginations and understandings and to order children's bodies in the appropriate postures—whose responsibility it was to form children in the faith—developed many techniques for rendering the sacred corporally present. I want to talk about three of them: the disciplining of children's bodies at mass, the practice of memorizing prayer, and the promotion among children by adults of the cult of the guardian angel.

"The liturgy provides unformed minds with a most direct access to God and the things of God," an American Franciscan, Brendan Mitchell, told a symposium on "the Teaching of the Liturgy in Elementary Schools" in 1939, because it is at mass that children meet God directly "in His varied,

lovable, and colorful life amongst us." So children must be encouraged,
Father Mitchell and the other conference participants agreed, to participate "intimately in the liturgy" and "to live the liturgy." It is even possible, Father Mitchell went on, that the most intense spiritual engagement
with the meaning of the Mass came when one was a child. At this tender
stage, the little ones felt they were "actually sharing in something very
real," whereas later in adolescence and young adulthood "there is often
the prejudice that liturgical practice is merely a sort of spiritual play-act-
ing." Father Mitchell was expressing an adult fantasy of innocent childhood spirituality; his comments served to create a sharp line between
childhood and adolescence and to constitute the latter as spiritually cor-
rupt or deficient. But the reality of younger children's mass attendance
was not quite like this, as Father Mitchell and his colleagues—who fretted
constantly about how best to make the Latin Mass even a little more
accessible to children—well knew.[31]

Although patterns and frequency of church attendance varied among
Catholic schools and between children who went to parochial schools and
Catholic children in public schools, children of Catholic families spent a
tremendous amount of time in church and a tremendous amount of time
at mass from the 1930s to the 1960s in communities around the country.
In addition to mandatory Sunday mass attendance, some children went
to daily mass with their classmates, others on Fridays and special holy
days. Children went to church to say the rosary, to practice for public
events, to make the stations of the cross in Lent with their classmates, to
go to confession, to worship the Blessed Sacrament, for Tuesday night
novenas, for funerals and weddings. Children who did not attend Catholic school went to mass less often than those who did, but they still went;
in some places, public school authorities made it possible for Catholics
to get out of school to get to church for holy days. The spacious parish
grounds of the last century—including rectories, convents, school buildings, outdoor shrines—and the big churches that rose over farm communities and city neighborhoods made inviting spaces for playing too. So
Catholic children spent a lot of time in and around church.

For all this and for all the familiarity it bred, Father Mitchell's goal of
"intimate participation" in the liturgy was not to be easily achieved. The
structure of the mass in these years was not particularly welcoming to
children. The priest's back was turned to the congregation, and while he
murmured the Latin inaudibly (except to the altar boys) people prayed
silently in the pews. Children could figure out what the priest was doing
only from the little red drawings of liturgical rubrics in their missals if
they had them, but otherwise they were compelled to sit absolutely still.
Catholic children of all ages were capable of reverent attendance at mass
and they certainly understood the seriousness and majesty of the liturgy.

One clear indication of youngster's recognition of the centrality of the mass to Catholic life was the fact that playing mass was a regular pastime among them. But the structure of the liturgy and the rules mandated for it were such that children at mass—very large groups of children sitting together—were also routinely restless, distracted, and bored. If they were expected by their parents or teachers to receive Communion, as they would have been on Sundays, First Fridays, and other special occasions, children were also dizzy and nauseated because they had been fasting since midnight as church law required. That Catholics did not make any special concessions to children's needs when it came to sacred participation is especially evident in the seriousness with which the midnight fast was presented to them. "It would be a great sin to receive Holy Communion after we had swallowed even a little bit of food and drink," the *Junior Catholic Messenger* warned its readers in 1944 in a regularly reiterated admonition, "even a crumb of food or a drop of water would break the fast." Catholic children on their way to mass learned to brush their teeth very carefully.[32] (Sisters sometimes covered the drinking fountains around the church and school before mass so children would not go unthinkingly for water.)

Some Catholic educators tried to make the mass a little more approachable for young people by playing through liturgical movements on little model altars in their classrooms or by putting cutouts of the priest at various moments of the celebration on classroom bulletin boards. Children were encouraged to play mass at home using (if they could afford it) make-believe mass kits sold by Catholic retailers or else household objects (if they could not.) Candy Necco wafers were popular Communion hosts among children all over the country. The great educator Maria Montessori published *The Mass Explained to Children* in 1932, one of many such manuals that took youngsters through the doctrine and movements of the sacrament. A "children's mass" was introduced in a Manhattan parish early in the twentieth century with some special features designed to help children participate more fully, such as a question-and-answer sermon and periodic explanations of ritual movements. But the idea of a children's mass never really caught on. For most of the century "children's mass" referred simply to the one Sunday mass all parochial school children were required to attend together, sitting with each other (apart from their parents). Catholic liturgical understanding and custom did not permit much innovation. So the mass remained a challenging religious exercise for children for most of the century and a religious challenge to their teachers too.[33]

Children experienced an acute hyperphysicality in church. Some vomited at the first whiff of incense. "I got sick all the time in church," a woman who grew up in rural central Nebraska in the 1940s told me, describing the experience of many Catholic children around the country at the time, "because it was long, and especially during Benediction I had to sit down." ("Probably the smell too," her husband, who grew up in the same area, added, "the incense smell." Adults describing their childhoods in the church often recall difficulties with the smells of incense on empty stomachs.) Others fainted so predictably that their mothers waited in the back of the church to be on hand when this happened. To enter the precincts of the sacred meant that children had come into a space where their bodies were overpresent to themselves, perhaps even treacherous, and where devotion meant the most demanding and frequently futile self-restraint under the eyes of the sisters, the priests, and of God really there on the altar. Adult religious insisted over and over with grave threats that children be absolutely silent in church; the capacity to remain still was sometimes offered as the standard for determining when a very young child might be taken to mass. They enjoined a strict physical discipline on their charges that only intensified children's preoccupations with their bodies.[34]

Children were given precisely detailed instructions about how to arrange themselves before the altar. When receiving Communion, readers of the *Junior Catholic Messenger* were told in 1943, "we should keep our eyes cast down. Our hands should be joined, the inside of one hand against the inside of the other, right thumb over left. The joined hands should point upward . . . [After receiving] we draw back our tongue slowly, and swallow the Sacred Host as soon as we can." "When you receive Holy Communion," another article coached, "hold up your head—but not too high. Put out your tongue—but not too far. Swallow soon—but not too soon." Genuflecting at the pew, "the right knee touches the floor, near the left heel," the torso and head are kept straight, eyes fixed on the tabernacle. Speaking for these cohorts of Catholic school children, the Mexican American woman cited earlier (on the shapely bodies of nuns) described her childhood mass attendance: "The nuns were very strict, you couldn't slouch, you didn't dare cough, because you'd get it. And you had to hold your hands folded this way, pointing to heaven." "You didn't dare turn around," the woman who got sick in church told me, you didn't dare "look around."[35]

The *Junior Catholic Messenger* began a long-running illustrated series in January 1940 on "manners in church" to call attention to the many different ways children failed to control themselves in the sanctuary. A different behavior was identified each week, illustrated by a funny little drawing, and anatomized for readers. The editors seemed determined to develop a vocabulary of corporal transgression in order to fix the discipline of self-control in children's memories and bodies. Henceforth children would know exactly how they were failing in church because the

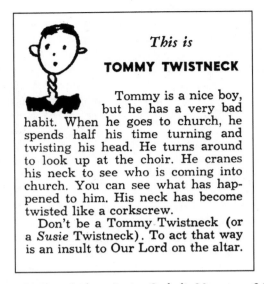

This is

TOMMY TWISTNECK

Tommy is a nice boy, but he has a very bad habit. When he goes to church, he spends half his time turning and twisting his head. He turns around to look up at the choir. He cranes his neck to see who is coming into church. You can see what has happened to him. His neck has become twisted like a corkscrew.

Don't be a Tommy Twistneck (or a *Susie* Twistneck). To act that way is an insult to Our Lord on the altar.

Figure 11. Tommy Twistneck, from *Junior Catholic Messenger*, 24 January, 1940

elusive movements of their disordered bodies would have been lifted from the confused wriggle of shifting, struggling, squirming, and stretching limbs and recast into a precise disciplinary vocabulary. So we meet "Tommy Twistneck" (who looks everywhere but toward the altar during mass), "Harry-In-A-Hurry" (who rushes out of church "while the priest is still on the altar"), and "Halfway Harry O'Kneel" (who "half sits and half kneels in the pew"). There is "Whispering Willie," "Vestibule Charlie" (who stands just outside the sanctuary as long as possible before mass), "Turnabout Mary," "Mummo the Clam" (who never prays aloud), "Danny Divebomber" (who is distracted by every insect that comes into church), "Philip Flip" (who rustles through the pages of his missal during mass just to "hear them swish when everything is quiet"), "Don Drop-It" (who "spends most of his time under the pews picking up his collection money and prayer book")—and on and on and on. The threat of (or the adult fear of) destruction and profanation by children's physicality surfaced more explicitly in the figures of "Timmy the Termite" (who chewed on the pew in front of him), "Wilfred Waster" (who tore up collection envelopes and scattered confetti all over the floor), and "Bertie Bumper" (who incessantly kicked the pew in front).[36]

Such involvement with the bodies of children in church was necessary because God's body was there too. Christ is literally present on the altar during mass, in Catholic understanding, a reality that Catholics lived out in many ways—by venerating the host, for example, or being extremely

Manners in Church

Wilfrid Waster

Wilfrid is the first to snatch special collection envelopes when they are passed out. But Wilfrid does not use the envelopes properly. He tears them up and strews the paper on the floor. This is very wasteful. It is also very bad manners. Be sure that *you* are not like **Wilfrid Waster.**—R.V.

Figure 12. Wilfred Waster, from *Junior Catholic Messenger,* 10 September, 1943

diligent with the fragments of hosts broken during the liturgy. The affirmation of Christ's real presence on the altar was what made Catholics different from Protestants. It was of the greatest urgency that children develop a vivid and visceral apprehension of the realness of the real presence, and tremendous effort went into this, to insure that children knew it in their bodies and imaginations. But it was not a simple or easy matter to make this doctrine apprehensible to younger minds and hearts because the notion that God "has made Himself into a little white host," as one educator expressed the cognitive challenge, was strange and elusive.[37] God's real presence on the altar was a regular topic in Catholic children's literature, endlessly reiterated in stories, legends of the saints, poems, and nonfiction adventure tales. Always in these stories, a child or some figure meant to capture the child's imagination (like a pirate or a knight) reacts in a direct and immediate way to Jesus' presence in the tabernacle; the children in the stories are called on to make a bodily sacrifice of some sort on behalf of the real presence. Little John, in a 1942 *Junior Catholic Messenger* tale, risks his life by returning to a flooded church after the rest of the town has fled to higher ground because he does not want God to be lonely or afraid in the tabernacle.[38] In such stories, the real presence

Figure 13. Timmy the Termite, from *Junior Catholic Messenger*, 22 May, 1943

was embodied in the actions of children who were willing to sacrifice themselves for it.

I discussed the issue of how the nuns communicated to children the realness of Jesus' presence in the host with a group of women in their early seventies who had grown up in New Orleans. How did the nuns do this, I asked, and the women burst out laughing and began talking excitedly over each other. "Don't let it touch your teeth!" "Don't brush your teeth!" One of the women, who had been raised in a French community just outside New Orleans, said, "We always knelt down to receive Communion, never went up there with our hands." While she was speaking, another woman who came from an Italian American neighborhood in the city exclaimed, "Oh, we'd die if it touched our teeth!" Someone else added, "Even if we got sick, and threw up, the nun could not be able to clean up that host, only the priest could clean up that host." They all agreed with one woman's comment that it was "too much . . . almost" the way the nuns insisted on this. "Oh, don't let it touch your teeth, they'd scare you, like you were doing something bad, like you were committing a sin."[39]

By means of such strenuous effort—by dint of prohibitions, fasting, constant admonitions (to the point of terror) against allowing one's teeth to touch the host, by disciplinary self-preoccupation, physical discomfort and the resulting dynamics of losing control and struggling to retain or regain composure—the body of God and the bodies of children were aligned. The one became real in the experience of the other, in children's bodies, for themselves and for the community. In the sacred world adults and children made together, the essential but most elusive interiority of the faith—the deep apprehension of the realness of God's presence on the altar—was substantiated and realized for children at mass and for the adults supervising them there by means of the close and ceaseless disciplining of children's restless bodies. Whether children dreaded or resented this or were proud of their physical abilities in church—and many children not only did not find all this onerous but actually delighted in their capacity to maintain the discipline and posture demanded of them, and many children loved going to mass, their imaginations captured by its mystery and splendor and pleased to share in the community's distinguishing sign of recognizing God's real presence on the altar—it was in their bodies that children were made to know the realness of God.

Catholic children were encouraged to pray constantly—aloud with their classmates at regular times, at home before meals and at bedtime, silently to themselves as they sat at their desks, when they walked home in the afternoons, or while they played. When you step out the door to join your friends, the *Junior Catholic Messenger* typically urged, say to yourself "Jesus, Mary, and Joseph, bless us now and at the hour of our death" because the dangers awaiting children could never be foreseen and a child's death (as Catholic children were told over and over) was always possible. Occasions of temptation—when "we feel like getting angry," for example, or when we refuse to play with unpopular children—should be met with "pious ejaculations," short, simple expressions of desire for God. Children were encouraged to write down lists of the prayers they had said or were promising to say and to give them away as gifts.[40]

But how to teach children to pray? How to make prayer a regular part of a child's life? The generation of Catholic educators that emerged in the 1930s and 1940s and went to teachers' colleges in these years tended to dismiss "rote memorization" as a way of inculcating a rich prayer life. At meetings and in their professional journals, religion teachers proposed instead more psychologically appropriate (as they understood this according to the educational psychology of their time), enjoyable, and aesthetically appealing methods of teaching children to chat informally with God about their daily concerns and to awaken in them a desire for the lovely things of the faith. There was even a new interest in this period in the psychological well-being of religion teachers because the idea had taken hold that only positive, emotionally stable, and happy people should be introducing the faith to children.[41] As was the case with discussions of the children's mass, however, the innovative ideas of religious educational theorists did not always find their way into local practice. The most widely used method of teaching prayer to children for most of the twentieth century was to have them memorize formal prayers, and this remained the primary way that Catholics prayed until the 1960s. The culture offered little sanction for religious improvisation among children, and memorization allowed teachers authoritatively and hierarchically to impose on children acceptable, normative, invariant forms of prayerful speech. So memorization persisted along with the newer emphases. American Catholic children's experience of praying in the twentieth century was shaped by the coexistence in their schools and released-time classes (for children not attending parochial school) of these discrepant pedagogical and spiritual orientations.

The result on one level was a confusing ethos of prayer. Students participated in prayer memorization contests, competing with their peers for the most perfectly memorized and perfectly enunciated recitation, but they were also told that the prayers they had memorized under strict classroom discipline were to be spoken passionately from the heart. A School Sister of Notre Dame urged parents in 1933 to teach their offspring to love the rosary (a memorized and repetitive prayer) by uncovering its beauty for them. This would be a gift of inestimable "temporal and spiritual advantage" to children, but only if the rosary were said "devoutly[,] not only with the lips, but from the heart."[42] Loving the beauty of the rosary— but also knowing and practicing the necessary postures of the body and attitudes of the mind and the memorized sounds. On another level, this double attitude toward children's prayers and of prayer pedagogy—disciplinary and passionate—created a powerful instrument for forming (in the richest sense of the word) praying children. The challenge for children and the adults in relation to them became how to set fire to long, formal prayers in archaic English competitively memorized. This became the goal of Catholic educators, priests, and nuns.

One way that children's desires in prayer were enflamed and focused was by having them pray for relief for the "poor souls" in purgatory. These lost beings, shadowy figures in the space between heaven and earth, served as conduits between the enduring practices of memorization and the newer emphasis on religious feeling. "Children must be taught how they can come to the assistance of the holy souls," Notre Dame sister Angela Merici wrote in 1930, which she recommended doing by appealing to their sense of compassion and natural affection for their families. "Children readily sympathize with those who suffer, and if they are taught in their tender years to be charitable toward their departed relatives and friends, who are tortured in the flames of purgatory, they will acquire the habit of practicing charity toward all the holy souls." Other spiritual counselors drew the connection between the souls in purgatory and the lives of earthly children even closer to home and to children's deepest anxieties. In "The Forgotten Soul," a short piece of fiction published in the *Junior Catholic Messenger* in 1935, twelve-year-old Charles dies and goes to purgatory, where he meets the soul of his father, who preceded him in death by six years and who now accuses his son, "why didn't you pray for me—you, whom I loved so much and for whom I worked so hard." Unable any longer to help his father, Charles finds himself in the same forlorn circumstances, and the moral of the story is clear: "Charles had forgotten his father and others had forgotten him."[43] An intimate sense of cosmic reciprocity together with a deep fear of the dreadful consequences of failing to meet one's obligations toward the poor souls was meant to instill in children a passion for prayer.

Charles's story needs to be set in the wider frame of Catholic moral instruction for elementary school children. Catholic teachers repeatedly stressed to children that good deeds would be rewarded in some direct, usually material way—by getting a toy a child may have wanted, for example, or finally winning acceptance by friends—and bad deeds just as materially punished. Catholic school children came in this way to inhabit a moral world of endless personal implication in which thoughts and intentions were deeds that could harm and destroy as well as empower (although empowerment never operated apart from the background of fear). It was as if adults believed that children could be formed as moral agents by stimulating their imaginations with visions of cosmic grandiosity and of the materiality of moral recompense. Morality was imaginatively linked in this way with power and powerlessness: children were certainly agents of this cosmic world but they were utterly vulnerable in it as well—indeed, their agency made them vulnerable. The moral world of Catholic children was a tangle of reciprocal bonds that connected their feelings and intentions (as well as their behaviors) in a direct and consequential way to the fate of other persons, living and dead. The souls in purgatory *needed* children on earth—"they are waiting and crying out to you," Father Brennan told his little readers—and their needs impelled children to pray.[44] The aim of having children pray passionately throughout their days and the belief pressed on them that their prayers were efficacious worked to create an atmosphere of moral and cosmic accountability and responsibility among children. Catholic children bore burdens. This in turn produced an edge of moral anxiety for adults to exacerbate and exploit. Catholic children did not live in constant terror. They developed a sense of gravity and generosity about their responsibilities that could enrich their moral lives and deepen their connection to their social world. But there was a real connection among prayer, responsibility, and anxiety, and children knew and acted out in their bodies a tense cosmic drama of prayer and redemption.

So Catholic children understood that what happened in their bodies and imaginations was very powerful and could affect the well-being of others on earth and in the spaces of the afterlife. For example, Catholic popular custom held that on All Souls Day (November 2) immediate release could be secured for souls in purgatory by a special indulgence granted church visits on this holy day. It was a common practice among children to step into church, say a prayer, step immediately back outside (thus completing one indulgenced visit), step back in, say another prayer, and out again (another visit), throughout the morning, with the expectation that for each "visit" powerful indulgences were secured and souls freed. Children imagined on these days that they could literally see the movement of souls up toward heaven as the result of their actions on earth.[45]

Given how important children's praying was to adults in the community it is not surprising that religious educators were forever devising strategies for ensuring that children prayed. This usually meant action upon children's bodies. Have children place their shoes beneath their beds at night, Father Henry Sullivan, a leading educator, proposed in 1937, "so that they will have to go down on their knees to obtain them the next morning." Exactly how children prayed and especially how they arranged their bodies at prayer were carefully monitored. "Father Brown," a regular contributor to the *Junior Catholic Messenger* in the 1940s, incessantly admonished children to pray with the right physical composure. "Prayers are often said too fast," he scolded in a typical column. "The words run together. The same program is sent too often. God gets tired of hearing, 'Give me, give me!' He wishes to hear something else. Not enough broadcasts are made. God cannot be expected to be satisfied with only a few programs." Among the behaviors "Manners in Church" warned against was "Dick the Dreamer," who "may *look* as if he is praying, but God on the altar knows he isn't." Another was "Windmill Willie": "Splash go his fingers into the holy water font. Zip—goes his hand to his forehead, his breast and shoulders. The holy water flies through the air."[46]

Prayer—praying in school, praying in church, and praying at home—served as another medium for making and substantiating the religious world adults and children constituted and inhabited together. The goal of Catholic prayer pedagogy and practice in its ideal expression (as this was articulated in countless earnest and passionate articles by teaching sisters throughout the middle years of the century) was to create children who prayed unceasingly, who experienced the world across the thrumming of prayer in their bodies, and whose praying bodies could be seen by all. Adults watched children at prayer and choreographed their movements and postures. Children's inner worlds, their religious imaginations, and their understanding of the moral bonds among people and between heaven and earth were constituted in the corporal disciplines of prayer pedagogy. Catholic prayer disciplines worked to embody in children the Catholic scheme of cosmic reciprocity and moral accountability. Morality was not a matter of learned rules and sanctions but of the powerfully experienced corporal connections between heaven and earth and among people on earth realized, enacted, embodied in the child *at prayer.* Carefully disciplined to pray in particular ways, children experienced for themselves and for the adults in relation to them the realness of Catholic cosmology and the bonds between domains of the spirit (heaven and purgatory) and the earth, as any adult would have appreciated watching children go in and out of the church doors on the day set aside for the liberation of souls from purgatory. How much more real does the cosmos get than this? Imagine what that must have felt like, to have seen the cosmos embodied in children's movements in and out of church on behalf of legions of invisible needy souls.

Catholic children were taught that their guardian angels prayed with them. It is impossible to exaggerate the importance of the figure of the guardian angel to mid-twentieth-century Catholic children's imaginations and spirituality. The role of angels in representing the faith to children dates to the seventeenth century, when these special beings emerged as protectors of children newly identified as innocent. Angels accompanied vulnerable children on their forays out into the adult world that had been recast as a realm of danger and temptation and a place where children did not belong. (Having grown up in this world, one of the women I have already mentioned from New Orleans told me that to this day, in her older age, she never goes out without putting on an angel pin.) Guardian angels were fundamentally associated with childhood. Catholic teaching maintained that God sent every child an angel at birth to keep him or her company throughout life. Angels were said to be children's most dependable, loyal, and loving companions and protectors, and children were encouraged to speak with their angels, disclose their hearts to them, and to ask them for help as they went about their studies, did their chores, and played with friends.

Angels were everywhere. They appeared on commemorative tokens for the major transitional rituals of childhood—on the hard covers of first Communion missals, for instance—as if literally to accompany the child across these times of change. Images of angels were given children as reward for doing well in school. Angels turned up as characters in children's literature. There were coloring books of guardian angels for preschool children. The point of all this was to "foster greater intimacy between the child and his Guardian Angel," in Sister Angela Merici's words. Children

Figure 14. First communion photo, New York City, ca. 1933.
(Photo courtesy of Cavallaro family.)

made room on their desk chairs so their angels could sit beside them.
They talked with their angels. Adult Catholics today warmly recall their
relationships with their angels as one of the most consoling and comforting aspects of their childhoods, and they recite with obvious pleasure the
little prayer they memorized as children: "Angel of God, my Guardian
dear, / To whom His love commits me here, / Ever this day be at my side /

To light and guard, to rule and guide, / Amen." Angels were among the most important vehicles of communication between adults and children in the common Catholic world they made together.[47]

Although this dimension of the way that guardian angels were imagined and presented to children is lost to contemporary memory, the literature of midcentury Catholic pedagogy makes it clear that children were assured that *some* boys and girls had actually *seen* their guardian angels. This was a privilege reserved for the saints, but very obedient children (saints in their own ways) might be granted such a grace. Elementary school religion teachers generally emphasized the empirical verifiability of sacred phenomena to children, teaching them that invisible holy realities cold be touched, tasted, felt, and seen. Children were encouraged to have such direct sensory experiences of the sacred, and many children desired them intensely, hoping for miracles to happen to them or to experience the presence of sacred figures with their senses. Children yearned to see their angels, then, who seemed to hover just on the edge of visibility.[48]

Because angels became popular in the modern era as the companions of children who were newly understood by the culture to be vulnerable, the angels inevitably bore hints of danger and risk. Stories about angels were always stories about children in peril. A popular Catholic holy card showed an angel leading two very small children across a rickety bridge over a raging torrent just below their little feet, a horrifying vertiginous image. Adults remember this image sixty years later. Stories about angels embodied and articulated the message that children were in real danger in the world and that they needed protection all the time. Children's deaths were inscribed in angel lore. A pamphlet on "stories of the angels," for example, by the popular and prolific writer for youngsters, Father Daniel A. Lord, S.J., invited children to sing a "hymn to the angels" that went in part, "without their protection / So constant and nigh / I could not well live, / I should perish and die." So angels were etched into children's imaginations by an implicit but deeply imbedded threat of physical harm and death, and the realness of angels in children's imaginations was in part the product of this compelling dread.[49]

Because angels went *everywhere* with their little charges (and everywhere here includes the secret places that children might slip off to precisely in order to be free of the adult supervision that was the implicit message of angel stories), they not only saw and heard what children were doing and saying, but in a more immediately and vividly imagined fashion they were *there* right beside children in whatever they were doing. For a child to get into a morally objectionable situation meant that he or she had brought his or her angel into it too. Children were warned that although *they* might forget "how near your angel is," their angels were always attentive to their behaviors and their thoughts—children were meant to know that angels knew what they were thinking and feeling and to understand that the angels knew they knew. The angels brought a particularly intense moral self-reflexivity into children's experience.

But the connection between angels and children in Catholic imaginings was even more intimate than this. Angels did not only see what children were doing and hear their thoughts, they *felt* children's behaviors in their own angelic beings. A child's rudeness or anger caused his angel deep personal distress and sorrow, a child's kindness or generosity made his angel happy. One little girl who was specially privileged to see her angel, as reported in the *Junior Catholic Messenger* in 1937, noticed that when she did something good, her angel smiled, but when she was bad, "the angel would turn sadly away." She was doing this to her angel. She was making her angel feel this way![50]

The angels contributed in this way to the materialization of the moral life in Catholic culture. Children were taught that the good things they did and thought (their pious sentiments, when they resisted temptation, when they helped a friend, and so on) were literally borne up to heaven by their guardian angels, who returned bearing graces and gifts from God. When a child weeps for her sins, Father Brennan wrote, her guardian angel catches one of her tears and carries it to God.[51] By their immediate connection to the child's experience and emotion, the angels bestowed a rich emotional resonance on the moral universe and rendered it imaginatively vivid and present to children. Catholic children were encouraged to experience themselves as being in two domains, natural and supernatural—there was another body out there in the world that knew and felt all the things they did. The angels thus contributed to the dissolution of children's boundaries: the identification between children and angels was so immediate and intimate that children's inner consciousness, their unspoken thoughts and desires were known in their angels' bodies. In this way, then, among their many roles in human experience, the angels guarded against children's autonomy: angel lore cast children as fundamentally in need of constant supervision, moral scrutiny, and accompaniment, a need endorsed by the fear of (or the threat of) harm and death. When children moved over to make room for their angels on the seat next to them in church or in school, they were moving themselves ever more securely into the moral and cosmic world that adults were making for and with them in the media of Catholic devotionalism.

Catholics today like to tell stories about their childhoods that emphasize the absurdity of them, or the brutality, sometimes the wonder and sometimes the silliness of their growing up. The impossibility of accounting for the past in one tonal register (absurdity or awe, brutality or kindness, and so on) reflects the complex and intense nature of Catholic childhood experience in the mid–twentieth century. It also reflects the fact that contemporary Catholic memory straddles the break between the working-class and rural immigrant church and the modern middle-class culture that took shape among Catholics in the United States in the 1960s and 1970s. One of the ends of Catholic religious formation in these years, as I have said, was to create passionate and disciplined children who prayed and made sacrifices, confessed their sins and went to mass, and who inhabited a radically tangible and accessible moral and spiritual universe. The *Junior Catholic Messenger*, which generally tried to appeal to normal American children with its serialized adventure stories and features on sports, interesting new technologies, and funny animals, held out the most rigorous and demanding spiritual standards for its readers. Give yourselves over to the mass, editors urged children in 1943, with the intensity of a burning candle.[52] But all of this was not done for children only. By the disciplining of children's bodies at mass, by forming children's limbs and emotions at prayer, and by drawing children into the circulation, association, and intimacy of bodies, destinies, needs, and feelings between heaven and earth—of the lost souls, of the guardian angels, and of earthly children (although in this world children were never merely earthly)—the world as it was said to be in Catholic doctrine became sensible, affectively alive, emotionally urgent to children and to the adults who labored so hard to represent and to embody this world in children.

Children were not passive in this dynamic. Catholic religious formation would not have been as effective had they been or if the realness of the world presented to them had been merely imposed on them. Children enthusiastically embraced the cult of the guardian angel. They fervently assumed their share of responsibilities for the souls in purgatory. They dressed up as priests and played at saying mass. They struggled with their restless bodies to keep still in church to please Sister and to earn her respect and praise. They got swept up in the beauty of the church buildings and the rituals that took place there. They took their missals to mass and tried to follow along with the distant inaudible priest. They knew in their bodies their bonds to the souls in purgatory, which they experienced as love, guilt, and fear, and they experienced the intimacy with their guardian angels that linked their bodies to these other supernatural ones. Some of this was conscious, but much was also there by discipline, inference, in feelings produced in them by the stories adults told them and in which children were implicated. Bodily apprehensions are not always conscious, but they are real. Catholic reality took hold of children's bodies, was embodied in children's bodies, whether they knew it or not, and their bodies bore the realness of this world, at the same time that children took hold of the world in the idioms given them by their teachers and parents.

A former nun, now in her midseventies, shared with me a memory that illustrates what I mean here by a body awareness that can operate below the level of consciousness. This woman, whom I will call Margaret, became an "activist nun" (her phrase) in the 1960s, rejecting the devotional styles and methods of her childhood faith—rejecting, in other words, the very media I have been describing: memorized prayer, devotion to the saints, her imaginary angelic friend, and so on. This was all in her past. Then one day Margaret found herself trapped during a race riot on the streets of the midwestern city where she was working in social services. She was in real danger and she was frightened for her life. Then, all of a sudden, when her fear was extreme, she heard one of the old prayers she had memorized as a child sounding in her head. She was not "saying" this prayer, Margaret explained to me. The prayer was "echoing in my body." Her childhood prayer was saying her. The disciplined instruction in praying she had received as a child and adolescent, the determination of adults to embody praying in her, had done its work.[53]

The world made real in children's bodies did not always have such a positive enduring presence as one might expect given how prevalent guilt was in its constitution and death and pain in its sanctioning. The following account was sent me by a psychotherapist working in another large midwestern city: "I have listened to hours of disclosure from suffering victims about the damages of pre-Vatican [II] practices. Midlife women still angry at missing their babies' Christenings because they hadn't been churched yet (cleansed of the stains of childbirth). A mother who felt guilty for years that her SIDS baby's death before baptism sent him to limbo . . . Scores of midlife women who have never experienced an orgasm because they were taught that sex was so dirty . . . A woman who had an abortion after a rape and now believes her two subsequent miscarriages are punishments from God." The making of the realness of a religious world is not a benign process; religious reality achieved in children's bodies (and reverberating in the memories of the adults these children become) did not make the world safer for these children, more comforting, or even necessarily more meaningful. It made it real. The consequences of this achievement of sacred realness in children's bodies would only be recognized and known by people like Margaret later in life, for better or worse, as their bodies encountered new experiences and new circumstances.[54]

The lived Catholic body was shaped in exchanges between the emergent generations of American Catholics and the adults in relation to them who sought to enact in young people's bodies and imaginations the world of Catholic meanings and possibilities. These adults had become anxious about this world in the years after the end of immigration and at the beginnings of changes in American Catholic life; they worked fervently to render the interiority of Catholic faith visible and materially substantive for children—and for themselves. Children actively participated with adults in this work of cultural making and remaking. Tommy Twistneck, the guardian angels, and the souls in purgatory awaiting redemption by the movements of children's bodies on Holy Thursdays, the living rosaries and the ways that adults arranged children at prayer—none of this was "children's religion." What was being formed in all this was not children's religious experience but the distinctive quality of modern American Catholicism.

Chapter Four

TWO ASPECTS OF ONE LIFE:
SAINT GEMMA GALGANI AND MY GRANDMOTHER
IN THE WOUND BETWEEN DEVOTION AND
HISTORY, THE NATURAL AND
THE SUPERNATURAL

> This action by which charity grows invisibly among us, entwining
> the living and the dead, is called by the Church the Communion of
> Saints. It is a communion created upon human imperfection,
> created from what we make of our grotesque state.
> *Flannery O'Connor, in an introduction to* A Memoir of Mary Ann,
> *by the Dominican Nuns of Our Lady of Perpetual*
> *Help Home, Atlanta*

> St. Gemma Galgani, Virgin. May 14. St. Gemma Galgani was born
> at Camigliano near Lucca, Italy, on March 12, 1878. At twenty
> years of age, St. Gemma was attacked by tuberculoses of the spine.
> This disease was declared by the doctors to be hopelessly incurable.
> After countless novenas to Saint Gabriel, she was completely cured
> on the first Friday of March, 1899. At this time, apparently free
> from her recent illness, she sought to fulfill her lifelong religious
> vocation with the Passionist nuns, but her application, as previ-
> ously, was rejected. In 1902, she was again stricken once more
> with an illness which was thought to be tuberculoses. The fame of
> her sanctity spread rapidly throughout the world. She was beatified
> by Pope Pius XI on March 14, 1933, and canonized by Pope Pius
> XII on Ascension Day, 1940. Prayer: Hear Us, O God, our Savior,
> so that we who rejoice in the feast of Blessed Gemma, Your Virgin,
> may be taught by the spirit of holy devotion. Amen.
> *Rev. Hugo Hoever, S.O. Cist., ed.,* Lives of the
> Saints for Every Day of the Year

BEFORE WE GO any further here and assuming that most readers will not have heard of the saint from Lucca, Gemma Galgani—she is all but lost to contemporary American Catholicism (although there are many Catholic women in their forties and fifties, sometimes younger, named after her, so the saint endures at least in this nominal way)—I want to note that this little devotional biography, taken in its entirety from a popular mid-twentieth-century American collection of lives of the saints, inexplicably omits any reference to what some might consider the central feature of Saint Gemma's life. On the feast of the Sacred Heart in 1899, when Gemma was twenty-one years old, Jesus appeared to her in a vision and with flames pouring out of the wounds of his Passion marked Gemma's body with the same bloody wounds. For the next two years, every week from Thursday evening to Friday midday, the young woman, who was basically homeless and forced by poverty and illness to live with family or friends, bled heavily from her hands and head and moved in and out of ecstatic visions of Jesus. Then her spiritual director, troubled by Gemma's highly emotional and even flamboyant and histrionic nature (he found her immature and he was irritated by her flirting coyness toward him and toward Jesus) demanded that she ask Jesus to take away the outward signs of his Passion. He did so, but Jesus remained Gemma's beloved and her tormentor, torturing her by threatening to withdraw his love, a prospect she dreaded endlessly in anticipation. Meanwhile, Gemma's relatives and neighbors treated her with contempt and although she eventually found a confidant in a woman named Cecilia Giannini, with whose family she lived toward the end of her life, Gemma was a lonely and troubled soul. She was also caught in the politics between her confessor, Monsignor Giovanni Volpi, a diocesan priest in Lucca, and her spiritual director, Padre Ruoppolo Germano, a Passionist father based in Rome. The former required that she ask Jesus to take away the stigmata; the latter supported Gemma's intense spirituality in part with an eye to the benefits a stigmatic might bring his order by way of fame and prestige.[1]

How could the author of the brief life of Saint Gemma with which I opened this chapter leave out the fact that Gemma was a stigmatic? Any reflection on this is hypothetical, of course, because I have no idea who wrote this sketch, but it is possible that the very thing which from one point of view would seem to make Gemma's life and especially Gemma's tremendous physical and emotional suffering *meaningful* and indeed that which seems to have empowered or ennobled this troubled person—her bleeding in imitation of Christ—is actually a source of disorientation and discomfort for those who encounter her. Or the silence here may not be simply denial but a sign of mystery too. It is even possible that the (hypothetical) uneasiness of this anonymous writer reflects the confusion of Gemma's contemporaries and of Gemma herself, who often (and understandably) seemed overwhelmed by her experience. This suggests again that what happens when "the transcendent breaks into time," in the phrase of the gas station attendant at Knock, is more confounding and unsettling—socially, culturally, psychologically—than "meaning making." It may be that some religious stories are too hard to tell or that at the heart of the telling of them there remains a core of uncertainty and even distress that narrative can only circle but never resolve. And this in turn raises the question of whether or not "meaning-making" is the best way of thinking about religions.

Families tell stories about themselves, in the world of Catholic devotionalism people told stories about the saints, and in the years when the saints were fundamental to Catholic life the two sets of stories regularly intersected so as really to constitute a single genre of popular narrative—a kind of domestic hagiography. It is not enough to say about such narrative overlaps that among mid-twentieth-century American Catholics stories of the saints and family stories reflected one another, as if heaven and earth were mirrors. Rather the two kinds of stories fundamentally shaped and formed each other. Tales about an uncle or a grandmother were cast in hagiographical tropes—this was the great temptation that he fought all his life, she sacrificed her life for her children—and in turn the saints took on the qualities of favorite or frightening, loved and hated relatives. All this is not surprising but is worth emphasizing: the saints and all the ways that people stayed connected to the saints and to the Mother of God—by tucking prayer cards in a wallet or purse, or rushing into a church to light a candle before a favorite holy figure at lunchtime, or setting up a little shrine to a saint in the bedroom or on the dashboard—fundamentally conditioned Catholic imaginations and thus the way Catholics thought and talked about family life. Likewise the exigencies, joys, and complexities of family life fundamentally conditioned the world of the saints. When the saints were taken out of their niches in the 1960s, among the things that changed were the stories Catholics might tell about themselves and the world. This was a radical transformation in Catholic narrative orientation and imaginative resources.[2]

Figures from heaven and earth appeared in each other's stories, as we have seen. Saints were commonly associated in family lore and memory with particular relatives so that stories about the one were inevitably stories about the other too. Luisa, whose devotion to her grandmother's beloved Sacred Heart of Jesus I mentioned in chapter 3, told me that during dreadful and harrowing childhood experiences she brought her terrors and pleas to a statue of the Sacred Heart in a church near her home that reminded her of the image in her grandmother's bedroom. "It was through the Sacred Heart," she told me, "when I went to kneel to him that he told me he was with me. I remember, I think I was about eight years old at that time. He has been with me ever since. . . . I would sit and I would pray, and I would pray, and I would pray like I used to see my grandmother pray." The Sacred Heart and Luisa's grandmother acted together in her life and they remain forever associated with each other in the stories she tells her children and grandchildren. This was generally true in Catholic culture. Among the many ways that the natural and the supernatural were bridged and the communion of saints made and enacted—by prayers for the souls in purgatory, for example, and by devotional acts—one of the most pervasive and existentially consequential was by storytelling. A saint's story was not exhausted by the details of his or her life on earth, just as stories about family members do not stop being told when they die. Hagiography is best understood as a creative process that goes on and on in the circumstances of everyday life, as people add their own experiences of a saint to his or her *vita* and contemporaries get woven into the lives of the saints. Such storytelling was one of the ways the communion of the saints became real in people's experiences and memories.[3]

This particular kind of Catholic story was enormously consequential for everyday lived experience. It was by telling stories about the saints and about family life—*in relation to each other*—that Catholics reflected on their worlds and came to knowledge about themselves (came again and again to different understandings of themselves and their world successively over the times of their lives might be a better way of putting this), about who they were, what was good and what was bad, what they might desire and what was forbidden, how they should behave and how they might love, and what they should endure. Making lives in relation to sacred stories proceeded on both conscious and unconscious levels: the saint was a straightforward model of the good life, and at the same time, in deeper and unnoticed ways, the movements of the most extraordinary desire, pain, and joy in a saint's life opened and oriented those who lived their lives in relation to these narratives to similar and unexpected levels of experience and emotion. It was not an easy or simple matter to live among the saints, as Catholics in the United States (as elsewhere) once did. As we saw in earlier chapters, adults and children can be asked to live in stories told against them (as in the tales of the holy cripple), but storytelling can also be countercultural (as my uncle's stories about Blessed Margaret were). Wherever heaven and earth touch—at a shrine or in a story—the consequences are complicated for people's experience.

What follows tracks the intersection of two sets of stories: hagiographical lore about Saint Gemma Galgani mostly derived from her own autobiographical accounts and from the eyewitness testimonies assembled during the process of her canonization as these tales were retold by American Catholic writers in the middle years of the twentieth century; and stories about my grandmother, Giulia, whose favorite saint Gemma was, and about my family. Some of these latter stories were told to me by others, some were mine to tell. Once my grandmother enters the picture, so do

I, as the boy who heard the stories about her and Gemma Galgani and then as the scholar of religion that boy became. It is the scholar's professional responsibility to interpret and understand religious phenomena, but I have come to recognize how haunted the scholar remains by the experiences of the boy. So this chapter offers yet another instance of in-betweenness—in this case, interpretation proceeding in between the experiences (and anxieties and confusion) of the boy and the intellectual perspectives of the man. (This will be the explicit subject of the next chapter too.) The academic returns at the end, recognizable by his voice, although it is my hope that the process of telling stories that precedes this will in the end have altered that voice.

Gemma's devout (unlike her relatives) did not always see the pain occasioned by the intersection of heaven and earth, which means they did not always fully see Gemma as much as they said they loved her. Writing in the trade journal of the American Catholic Hospital Association, *Hospital Progress*, in 1958, for example, American Jesuit Alphonse M. Schwitalla said that Gemma passed from the ecstasy of Christ's embrace to her supper chores and other mundane responsibilities and back again with as much ease as we pass from one room to another in our homes. God had granted her this grace. Schwitalla, one of the founders of the American Catholic Hospital Association, was promoting Gemma as the patron saint of hospital pharmacies and pharmacists. (Gemma's father, Enrico, was a pharmacist.) From her conversation with the heavenly visitors who came to her, he said, Gemma turned "without effort or strain" to "wash the faces of her younger sisters and brothers" and to set the table, the voices of the angels and saints still in her ears. The lesson of Gemma's easy movement between worlds, Schwitalla concluded, between the natural and the supernatural, is that "the life we live now" and the life to come "are but two aspects of one life." Gemma will protect those whose vocation it is "to supply the materials for the alleviation and cure of human suffering."[4]

But the truth is that the movement between Gemma's two worlds was not as easy as Schwitalla suggests. After Jesus pressed a crown of thorns into her head in July 1900, and "blood flowed freely" from the puncture wounds around her hairline, Gemma sometimes bled at the dinner table, in the midst of her family. "The drops flowed increasingly," one of Gemma's English-language biographers, Father Herbert George Kramer, described such an occasion, "until the blood trickled down her soft cheeks and neck and stained her dress." I imagine Gemma's brothers and sisters and aunts staring quietly down at their half-eaten food, their conversation frozen, as blood streams onto Gemma's dress and the clean white tablecloth. "A sweat of blood flowed from her eyes, nose, mouth, and ears," another of Gemma's English-language biographers wrote of a moment when her stigmata opened unexpectedly, "as well as from the hands."[5]

Gemma sat bleeding at dinner. What was this like for the other people at the table? How about for the *lavatrice* in these middle-class households, the working women who did the laundry and had to clean out the marks of Gemma's sanctity? Gemma's life was not an easy one before she received the stigmata and then it got a lot harder. The space between Gemma's worlds revealed itself in such moments to be an open wound, for all to see. Blood marked the passage from one world to another. Father Schwitalla's interpretation of Gemma's life is not faithful to the stories, in other words. His interpretation rendered her invisible (as did interpretations of the holy cripple or of the innocent child)—or more specifically what he occluded was the pain of heaven and earth's meeting. But the bloody details of the stories challenge such misinterpretations.

My father says that his mother, my grandmother Giulia, loved Gemma Galgani more than any other saint, more than even Saint Francis or Saint Anthony, of whom she asked countless favors, and almost as much as the Blessed Mother, who was my grandmother's lifelong companion. Giulia and Gemma were born in the same region of Italy, in nearby villages on the plains surrounding the walled city of Lucca, in Tuscany, Gemma in 1878, my grandmother exactly twenty years later. They were born in the same month so they shared the same birthstone, "green chalcedony with spots of red jasper," according to one of Gemma's American storytellers, "A Sister of Saint Joseph" (as she is identified on the cover of her school play about Gemma, *The White Flower of the Passion*, published in Boston in 1940 and intended for parochial school children to perform). "Isn't this a funny stone, Gino?" Gemma's beloved youngest sister Julia asks her older brother. "The spots are like blood." "That's why it's called a Bloodstone," another brother, Antonio, answers her. Birthstones hold secrets about those born in the months associated with them, another character adds, and little Julia wonders whether the spots of jasper mean "Gemma is going to be a martyr some day and shed her blood?" Perhaps my grandmother Giulia wondered this too about her own life.[6]

My grandmother died in 1987, eighty-four years after Gemma's death, forty-seven years after her canonization. Such a rapid canonization process is a sign of the power and access of Gemma's Passionist patrons at Rome, among other things.[7] (Gemma's spiritual director, Padre Germano, boasted that "he could bring even Garibaldi to the honors of the altar.") I remember seeing an image of Gemma Galgani in my grandmother's tiny bedroom where I often slept. The holy card impressed me because it was more like a photograph than an icon, a black-and-white picture of a girl bringing the mystery of the saints into my own time. Her face was lifted up, obviously engaged with someone or something just above and beyond the frame of the image and above and beyond this world. That the saint was wearing the same clothes as the people in the photographs in my grandmother's thick red photo album added to the sense of familiarity about her. Gemma's American devout believed that the saint's being "so near to us in time," as one writer put it, made her a figure "we turn to . . . quite naturally as to one who understands our problems and stands ready to help us."[8] "I walked in the same streets she did, I prayed in the same churches," my father said when I told him I was planning to write about him, my grandmother, and Gemma Galgani. Central to how Gemma has been spoken of in my family is this pride of place and thrill of shared origins, making her a patronal figure, at least for my family of Tuscan immigrants, like the many holy figures that accompanied Catholic migrants and immigrants in their journey to the United States.

In the stories told by my family, Gemma was the strongest of my grandmother's ties to heaven. "She loved Gemma," my father says. The connection was so deep that my grandmother kept it close to her heart, not quite secret—there was the photograph, after all, and everyone knew about her devotion to Gemma—but not completely shared either. Silence may be a sign of mystery and some religious stories may be too hard to tell, and there are always things that people want to keep to themselves.

An old green bottle of vermouth, full and corked, stood on the top shelf of the glass-fronted cupboard in the kitchen of the very small apartment my grandmother shared with her younger son (until he got married in his late forties) in the Bronx. The wine was a deep shadow inside the heavy glass, behind the thick gray dust that had collected on the bottle over the years. No one ever touched it.

This was my grandmother's "death bottle." During one of their frequent, bitter arguments, my uncle reached in among the bottles of brandy and brightly colored *liquori* distilled by the monks of a Cistercian monastery in my grandmother's hometown and pulled out the vermouth. "I'll open this," he said to her, brandishing the bottle in her face, "on the day you die, and drink the wine to celebrate." My grandmother sardonically named it *"la bottiglia della morte."* My uncle is a fleshy man. He had been an American marine during the Korean War (another set of family stories described how his best friend's severed head had been tossed into my uncle's machine gun post one cold night by Chinese troops on the contested parallel) and pictures from that time show him lean and taut. But he had put on weight as he aged. When he sat at his mother's table, he leaned over his *pasta sciutta*, surrounding the bowl with his thick arms as though he wanted to hide it close to his chest.

Figure 15. St. Gemma Galgani

My grandmother fretted and fussed behind him. My uncle's brilliantly
white and precisely starched waiter's tunic was folded over the back of a
kitchen chair. My grandmother scrubbed his shirts on an old wooden
washboard she had brought with her to the United States from her mother's house in Italy. Done eating, my uncle stretched back and opened his
heavy arms wide, then brought his palms down hard on either side of the
empty plate with a great crashing noise of silverware and dishes. Survey-
ing the kitchen, he was the master of all this. My grandmother would dry
her hands carefully at just this moment and gently bring him his shirt.

The bottle of vermouth remained in the kitchen, visible on the top shelf
of the cabinet, for many, many years. My grandmother never threw it out
and my uncle never rescinded his threat. My grandmother's eyes must
have rested on that bottle often when she was alone at night, saying her
prayers at the kitchen table, or in the long afternoons of an old woman,
which she spent in the kitchen, wiping, soaking things, cooking. Why
didn't she throw it out? Why didn't she smash the bottle against the side
of her deep kitchen sink and say to her adult son, "This is my house—
leave. I will not be forced by you to look at my own death all day"?

There are a number of ways of understanding the relationships that develop between humans and saints. These holy figures can be taken as
moral exemplars, ideal expressions of how people in a particular social
world ought to live. Hagiography in this context becomes prescriptive.
This is the safest way to imagine the bonds between heaven and earth,
and church authorities generally prefer it. Several of the earliest American
and English-language commentators on Gemma Galgani emphasized
what one called "the heroic virtues of [the] unknown Italian maid" in
their representations of her. The true test of sanctity is not the miraculous,
the readers of *Ave Maria* were reminded in a 1942 article on Gemma, but
"the heroicity [sic] of virtue practiced in everyday life." Leo Proserpio,
S.J., the bishop of Calcutta, in a pious biography of Gemma written
shortly after her canonization, numbered the saint's virtues: humility, obedience, asceticism, "chastening of the flesh," purity, poverty, charity, penance, courage, and endurance. "All pleasures," Bishop Proserpio wrote,
"however small and innocent, were banned from the scheme of life she
had early chalked out for herself." Gemma was represented like a holy
"shut-in," in other words, just as persons with disabilities were represented like Gemma. She remained modest and composed in the face of
her family's anger and of her neighbors' derision. A nun named Gemma
of the Visitation testified to this during the canonization process: "in the
midst of so many humiliations and suffering [Gemma Galgani's] courage
never once failed, but she was calm and serene in soul and in her external
countenance." The saint never complained (according to her American

biographers—history records another story, let me add). "No human ear ever heard her utter a bitter word," an article on Gemma in the *Catholic Charities Review* in 1943 affirmed, "and God Himself must have seen no reproachful thought in her sinless soul."[9]

Gemma's virtue was called on by her English-language devout to witness against the general depravity of the modern world and against the inadequacies of so many Catholics, especially younger ones. The story of Gemma's moral "heroicity" thus took on a disciplinary edge. Gemma's early life, Bishop Proserpio wrote, presents "a striking contrast to the life nowadays led by many Christians" who are "frivolous and dissipated by an excessive love of worldly comforts and pleasures." Sister Consilia's criticism of "tight-skirted girls" who kept their "silk-stockinged knees [off] the hard rough wood of the kneeling bench" could never be made of Gemma. Gemma was marshaled against such girls. "Her bearing was noble and graceful," an American priest, writing at the same time that Sister Consilia was lamenting the moral condition of Catholic girls in the United States, described teenage Gemma, "and though she dressed modestly and simply, and scorned the artificial means with which so many young women try in vain to enhance their appearance, the young Signorina Galgani had a loveliness which charmed everyone." Gemma was the perfect counterpoint and caution to the American Catholic female body.[10]

To make Gemma into a moral model, however, took some doing. Her American devout needed to recast her life story, muting the more troubling dimensions of Gemma's experience and imagination—the blood at the table, her eroticized visions of Jesus, her combat with her spiritual advisors, her rages—that could not be easily mobilized on behalf of a disciplinary narrative of good and bad. Maybe this is why the writer of the little life of Gemma with which I began omitted her stigmata: devotional culture has a way of slipping the bounds of clerical authority, and perhaps this author was afraid of what might happen if he or she put the blood in the story. Gemma was so unstable and so disturbing to church authorities in her own time that she failed more than once to gain admission to a local convent she was desperate to join. But her American biographers never fully explain this, other than to blame Gemma's rejection by the nuns on the poor state of religious life in Italy at the time. Their protective silence on this matter introduces a troubling and destabilizing note of uncertainty into their narratives—after all, why wasn't Gemma admitted to a convent?

Bishop Proserpio cites Padre Germano's judgment that Gemma "had a remarkable simplicity which ran through all her actions. . . . In church, where she spent her hours before the Tabernacle, there was nothing singular in her attitude, not a sigh, not a movement out of common." (This about a woman who demanded her own way and fiercely fought her male

mentors for the legitimacy and authority of her visions.) Others introduced conventional folkloric elements into Gemma's story, reconfiguring
her more recognizably as an Italian fairy princess. Enrico Galgani is described by the author of *The White Flower of the Passion* as "a well-to-
do chemist . . . descended from the family of Blessed John Leonardi."
Gemma's mother, Aurelia, came from "the noble house of Landi." (The
family's means were in fact quite modest and then desperate after Enrico
died.) Edna Beyer, a contributor to American Catholic popular magazines, refers to Aurelia Galgani as "a saintly woman of noble birth" (another exaggeration) and Bishop Proserpio locates her in the lineage of the
holy mothers of saints, comparing her favorably to the mother of the
immensely popular modern Italian saint, Don Giovanni Bosco. Little
Gemma is presented as preternaturally mature, exceptionally generous
and attentive to others, and a great beauty, the most attractive, popular,
and desirable young woman (this is a modern hagiography after all!)
between Lucca and Viareggio and always the life of the party. Missing
from these accounts of Gemma's life and sanctity were her infantile
flirtatiousness, self-absorption, preening, vindictiveness, and immaturity.
Missing too is the blood.[11]

These writers were determined literally to domesticate Gemma. "At the
age of eight years," Father Schwitalla assures his readers, "Gemma had to
take all the housekeeping duties on herself." Gemma managed her father's
business and balanced his books while tenderly nursing him through his
last illness. To make sure that Gemma herself says nothing to contradict
such accounts, her voice is stilled by her hagiographers. She possessed the
virtue of silence to a heroic degree, they said.[12]

But try as they might to remake Gemma into a fairy-tale princess, the
most humble of women, or an ordinary soul, the saint's American devout
finally could not successfully contain her, because what most captured
their imaginations, what most compelled them about Gemma, was her
suffering and pain. This was after all the culture so taken by the darkly
erotic romance of sacred suffering, as we saw in the first chapter. The
culture's fascination with pain subverted the efforts of Gemma's devout
to render her sanctity safe. Narrative details of pain and blood eluded the
constraints of their uneasiness and filled their images of Gemma, keeping
her a troubling figure.

My grandmother lived on the corner of Webster Avenue and Gun Hill
Road in the north Bronx in a tiny apartment on the second floor of a
squat brick building that was literally being shaken apart by the constant
vibration of the traffic that passed beneath her windows all day and all
night. The street-facing wall in her bedroom where she kept Gemma's
image was cracked open and through it you could see and hear the unmuf-

fled cars of the Bronx and the clattering and screeching wheels of the elevated train.

Toward the end of my grandmother's life, this apartment house seemed like a residence for very old and demented widows, still shopping for themselves in the bodegas and Korean markets that had replaced the Jewish delicatessens and Italian groceries in the neighborhood and forever burning pots they had forgotten on their stoves. One after another these women died, until only my grandmother remained, alone in the building with newer, rougher tenants. Prostitutes took over the apartment next door, and across the hall there was a man who every night beat the woman he lived with.

"It's so safe here," my father said to me once, when our visits to my grandmother's place coincided, "of all places on earth, this is the most peaceful." My grandmother was still cooking for her sons (by now her younger son had married and moved away, though he came back every day for lunch) and for her grandsons, but the chicken was bloody and raw, the polenta studded with pebbles of hard, uncooked cornmeal, the garlic and onions burnt black and bitter. "Ah," my father said, standing up and putting his arms around his mother, slumped in her chair at the other end of the table, her face masked by her unkempt and thinning white hair, "*questa e la mia beata mamma*. Who is there like a mother? Here"—his arm swept the small room—"*soltanto qui sono sicuro*."

My grandmother began to hallucinate. She called my father in the middle of the night and pleaded with him to come over and stay with her. Water was pouring into her apartment, she told him, flowing in under the door to the hallway. On other nights she whispered in a shaking voice that a strange man was trying to break into her apartment. She could see his face, masked by shadows, through the peephole in the door. "Please come," she begged my father. "I can hear him in the hallway. He won't let me sleep." Water was dripping from the ceiling, people howling outside her door. My father went and tried to comfort his mother, and himself, in her dry apartment. I never knew for sure whether or not she had really been imagining all this. Was it right to doubt everything she said? The neighborhood had changed; strange men were drawn to the building. Maybe these men were mistaking my grandmother's door for other ones. "They won't leave me alone," my grandmother told me once, toward the end of her time in this place, and I had no idea how to assess the statement. We could barely hear each other over the loud rock music coming from the apartment next door, pounding my grandmother's walls.

My uncle took to speaking in baby talk to his mother in these months. He had just finished his lunch when I arrived one afternoon to bring my baby daughter to see her great-grandmother. "Siddown and have some of this," my uncle shouted, pointing to a greasy *frittata* of eggs, swiss chard, potatoes, and onions. "Looka this, can you believe this, my eighty-five-year-old mother made this lunch for her son?" He reached over and put his arm around my grandmother's waist, drawing her close to him. "*Mamma mia, mamma mia.*" Pulling her face down to his by closing her cheeks in his hands and squeezing them, my uncle began to lecture me over his mother's shoulder. "This is the woman . . . look at her, *guarda, come sei bella, bellina, bellina,* my mommy . . . oooh, do you love me, *mammina?*" My grandmother pushed herself free of him.

"*Oh, mamma mia, non mi lasce!*" He pointed a thick finger at me. "That woman, alone in Boston"—referring now to events of his child-hood, when my grandmother had first come to the United States in the early 1920s with her young husband who died ten years after their arrival—"her husband dead, leaving her with two children. She gave her life for these children. She bent her back with hard work, you think it's easy to sit at a sewing machine for ten, twelve hours a day?" My uncle's hymns to his mother were inevitably accusatory and disciplinary (like the accounts of Gemma's life by her biographers). He assaulted his listeners with his mother's story as he imagined this story. "She sacrificed everything for us." He was inexplicably angry with me now, as if I contested any of this. "She sacrificed everything for us. She never"—this was how the narrative assault always ended—"she never got married again. She never betrayed us."

"She bled from wounds in her hands and feet and side" every Friday, an American priest, Father Sweeney, writes of Gemma; "purple welts and ugly bleeding stripes suddenly covered her whole body . . . her scalp was horribly punctured and blood, matting her hair, oozed down her cheeks and neck." On a visit to Gemma's tomb in 1931, an American pilgrim named Therese Elizabeth Alexander only just resisted pressing Gemma's "white, blood-sprinkled gown" to her lips. Alexander was restrained at the last moment by an impulse of "some great awe." Holding the garment close to herself, Alexander imagined "great drops of blood" raining from Gemma's forehead, "where the crown of thorns pressed close, while her eyes shed tears of blood." "She sweat blood in agonies of pain," the playwright Sister of Saint Joseph described Gemma. "Blood poured forth profusely from punctures all over her head, while terrific headaches prostrated her." So deeply did the wounds of Christ's scourging cut Gemma, Father Kramer told his readers, that on one occasion bone poked through the open flesh. Gemma resembled, in this moment, said Father Kramer, "the Man of Sorrows in Whom all is one wound." She was forever plunged and held in "a veritable ocean of pain," in Bishop Proserpio's words.[13]

My father says my grandmother read one book in her life. This was Gemma's spiritual autobiography. My grandmother either did not like reading or else, perhaps, found it difficult, although she paged through the Italian picture magazines *Gente* and *Oggi* and the newspaper *Il Progresso Italo-Americano*. When he told me this, my father said again that my grandmother was very proud of Gemma and happy that they came from the same Italian province. "They were *paisane*." My father remembers that his mother read passages aloud to him from Gemma's book when he came by to see her and to eat in her kitchen, recounting details from Gemma's life and visions.

The mystery of Gemma's suffering and pain, according to her American biographers, began with her mother's death when Gemma was a little girl, or more specifically, with Gemma's giving God permission to take her mother's life after God had asked her for it on Gemma's confirmation day as the girl knelt praying before the altar. This is how Gemma tells the story herself: "On the 26th of May 1885, I received Confirmation, but weeping, for I feared Mamma would die without taking me with her. I listened to the Mass praying for her; all at once a voice spoke in my heart: 'Do you wish to give Me your Mamma?' 'Yes,' I replied, 'if You take me also.' 'No,' said the voice, 'give your mother to Me willingly. You should stay with your father. But do you give her to Me willingly?' I was obliged to answer, 'Yes.' The Mass finished, I ran home. My God! I looked at my Mamma and wept. I could not help myself." This was the first sign of Gemma's holiness, her English-language hagiographers maintain, the first indication of her special intimacy with heavenly figures. Gemma's life as a saint opens with her "yes" to God's question in the most intimate of settings, "do you give [your mother] to Me willingly?" "It was the first locution," Bishop Proserpio writes of the incident, "the first of those heavenly voices which were to play such an important role in the life of this Virgin Maid of Lucca." The teenage Gemma reminisces in *The White Flower of the Passion* that "this was the beginning."[14]

Aurelia Galgani is represented in some versions of the tale as already dying of consumption when her daughter hears the heavenly voice that dooms her. This permits us to understand the child's fantasy of God's request as a way of contending with the most dreadful fears of abandonment, separation, and powerlessness. But most American accounts omit this detail (which was historically the case: Aurelia was already sick when Gemma consented to her death), making it seem as if a cruel and unpredictable God asks the little girl's consent to the death of her perfectly healthy mother. This is Jerry Filan's God. Americans also thus inadvertently lifted up the Oedipal subtext of the narrative: Gemma wills the death of her beautiful, young, vibrant, and devoted mother and gets to have her father all to herself. As the heavenly voice promises her, "for the present you must remain with your father." Enrico is not the only male beloved Gemma gets exclusive access to by means of this death-trade. "Jesus first spoke to me when I was only seven," Gemma says in *The White Flower of the Passion*. "He told me then of His love." The reason she sacrifices her mother, Gemma says, is "because His love burned in my heart [and] I could not say no. . . . Since then He has shown that His love brooks no creature-love to take [*sic*] first place in my heart." Jesus' love is not easily satisfied in its insistence on exclusivity, Gemma will learn. She is called on next to surrender her brother to death and then her father, meaning that her eventual isolation is the outcome of Jesus' desire for her. Erotic rivalry is one of the ways that heaven and earth are linked in this story. Gemma's sanctity has its origins, then, in the interplay of jealousy, grief, absence, and desire. Her holiness is inseparable from loss. How she loves and how she is loved are fundamentally connected to pain and death.[15]

My father was awakened by neighbors, he remembers, two strange shapes standing beside his bed in the very early morning. It was still dark outside and the apartment was cold. They pushed the drowsy boy's limbs into his clothes and brought him out across the hallway to the apartment next door. He was ten years old. His home was filled with policemen and he heard his mother sobbing and moaning in another room. My father wanted to run back into the apartment but the neighbors held on to him and he watched from inside the grip of the strong old man who lived next door as more and more people arrived. My father's father, a chef at a popular Boston restaurant, had come home late that night. He had carried his heavy, weary body up the three flights of steps to his apartment, but he did not make it all the way. My grandmother was asleep. She never waited up for her husband. The crash in the stairwell jarred her awake.

My grandmother and her sons talked about this moment for the rest of their lives. The terrible crash on the stairs—my grandmother rushed out and found her husband lying on the second floor, his neck at a horrible angle against the bend in the stairway—had the significance of an augury to them and they returned to it over and over again for clues to the meaning of their lives. My grandmother believed to the end of her days that a jealous neighbor, probably a woman, resentful of my grandfather's success and resenting his beautiful wife and sons, whom he loved in an exemplary manner, had killed her husband. While she slept in her big bed, warm beneath the covers, her husband's killer crouched down in the shadows, waiting. I used to wonder, having heard this story so many times, if the man my grandmother saw outside her apartment in the Bronx in her fear and disorientation was not this same figure again, now come for her.

My uncle agreed with his mother. "He was a big man," he always says of his father when he talks about this night at family gatherings, "a big shot. *Tutti l'invidiano.* You shoulda seen people looking at us when we walked down the street together. *Che bella famiglia*! My old man was so proud of us and it showed, *sai,* he walked down the street with his head back. *Bella figura. Tutti li guardavano.* They hated him. They used to talk about him and they got together to kill him."

Two days after my grandfather's funeral, just after the dead man had been laid to rest in the ground, my grandmother tried to kill herself. She was sitting in the darkened third-floor apartment, where the smell of flowers, espresso, and anisette biscuits still lingered from the wake. Her sons, dressed up in suits and ties, sat on the couch in the parlor, watching their mother. She paid no attention to them. They didn't exist for her anymore. My uncle says that his mother sacrificed her life for her sons after the chef's death, but maybe he forgets these long days, which lasted over a year, when his mother's only desire was to join her husband in his tomb. She rocked and moaned in her chair while my ten-year-old father and his six-year-old brother watched her. She couldn't live anymore, she cried, she couldn't survive. Why hadn't God taken her too? Why couldn't they have been killed together? Suddenly, she ran to the window and while her children screamed and pulled on her skirts she parted the curtains, opened the sash, and tried to climb out.

Did she really want to kill herself? My grandmother was a fervent Catholic and she knew that suicide was the worst of all grave sins because there was no chance for confession and absolution. One died in the act of sinning and went straight to hell. Suicides were buried apart in Catholic cemeteries, in sad unhallowed ground. This would have meant eternal separation from her husband, in their graves on earth and in the afterlife. Maybe all she wanted was to be in the ground with her husband. Her sons believed she wanted to kill herself, and they clung to her legs shouting for help. I imagine my uncle staring at his mother's white skin as the windowsill dragged on her heavy skirt. I picture my father with his determined head bent to the task of saving his mother's life. My grandmother's cousin ran in from the next room and pulled her back from the window.

My grandmother declined quickly after this. She refused to eat and wouldn't smile, as if any expression of pleasure would betray her dead husband. In my father's stories of the time, ice cream becomes the central symbol of loss and fear. When the chef was alive, the family used to go out on warm Sunday afternoons, everyone dressed elegantly, to buy gelato. They promenaded through their Somerville neighborhood, my grandmother holding on to her husband's strong arm. "You know, they used to kiss in the street all the time," my uncle once told me. "They were like kids." "Do you think after my father died there was no one wanted to marry her?" my uncle asked, his voice becoming thicker, more aggressive, and angrier. "Are you crazy? Half the men in Boston wanted to marry her." Now the trips to the ice cream parlor stopped. My grandmother would do nothing, tolerate nothing, to relieve her sorrow or her sons' pain. Her grief was amorous. Her sons could not compete with her dead lover. My father still cannot eat ice cream without sadness because it tastes of this time.

So my grandmother raced through the streets in the months after the chef's death, badly dressed, revisiting the places she had enjoyed with her husband on their Sunday strolls. She lost weight. Her once-voluptuous body vanished. Her doctor took my ten-year-old father aside and told him that if he did not take his mother back to Italy right away she'd be dead by the end of the year. She was determined to join her husband, and her sons had to prevent this. They had to win her affections and attention and diminish their father's hold on her. A peculiar kind of struggle was joined.

With her "yes" to God's request that she surrender her mother's life to him, five-year-old Gemma embarked on her "holy and mysterious vocation for suffering." The remainder of her short life would be devoted to the unfolding of her identity as the woman who suffers. What was important to her devout—and to Gemma herself—was not merely the pain itself, for all their obvious fascination with Gemma's blood, but that this suffering was for others. Gemma was a "victim soul." The term first emerged in the late nineteenth century, just around the time Gemma and my grandmother were born, and designated those chosen to take upon themselves the burden of pain in atonement for the sins of others and in "obedient submission" to God's will and in imitation of Christ.[16] Pain was Gemma's gift of love and concern, to Jesus, to the world, and to her devout. "[S]he was called to the apostolate of mystic physical pain," Father Kramer defined Gemma's life, "of burning but never consumed love, of misunderstanding and misrepresentation—the closest approach to the Redeemer's own suffering that has ever been man's privilege." The blood that poured down Gemma's face, the pain in her head and side, the anxiety of demonic attacks, were all signs of Gemma's generous and capacious love. Jesus told her, "I have need of victims and strong victims," and this is what Gemma would be, a strong victim, the strongest of them all. "When the lady of the house fell ill and suffered much," an American priest who was proposing Gemma as patron saint of hospitals wrote in 1940, "Gemma offered herself to God to suffer in her benefactress's stead." The saint bartered her pain for the release of poor souls in purgatory. "There is no doubt," another of the saint's American biographers commented, "that her life is one long story of superhuman sacrifice for others."[17]

Physical suffering and pain are isolating. The person in pain, to borrow a phrase from French philosopher Simone Weil, is hammered into one place, his or her experience constricting to the limits of the body and the space of the sickroom. Pain renders the person in pain powerless in his or her solitude. Not so with Gemma. The saint's suffering located her in a special place in the economy of salvation. Pain put her at the center of the world. "I wish you to be," Jesus said to her in a vision in April 1900, "a victim and that you suffer continually to placate the wrath which my Father has toward sinners, and that you offer yourself to Him as a victim for all sinners." Gemma's suffering allied her with Jesus' Passion. Pain in this way bound Gemma to others, first to Jesus and then, in widening circles, to family, friends, neighbors in Lucca, and the souls in purgatory. "I invite you," Jesus said to Gemma toward the end of her life, "to die on the Cross with me." On Good Friday, 1899, determined to fulfill her desire to join Jesus in his suffering, Gemma tied a well-rope tightly around her waist until it caused her serious pain. The saint's love for Jesus "grew into a devouring thirst for union with Him," in Father Kramer's words, "in His most excruciating anguish." Jesus not only marked Gemma with his wounds, the author of *The White Flower of the Passion* wrote, but "He permitted her to participate in all the sufferings of His Passion." In August 1901, Gemma's blood-sweat became especially intense because, in Bishop Proserpio's words, "she had taken upon herself to atone for the negligences and the sins of priests."[18]

Not all Gemma's sufferings were physical. Family and neighbors, local children, young men in Lucca's narrow streets, garrisoned soldiers—all were a source of torment to her and all were taken up in the drama of her victimhood. Her neighbors mocked her, especially as evidences of her supernatural relationships proliferated. Her immediate family, deeply embarrassed and frightened by Gemma's unusual experiences, reacted with contempt, derision, and at least on one occasion with punitive violence. Gemma's younger sister Angelia taunted her to go into ecstasy for friends she brought home for the spectacle. One of her brothers punched her in the eye. Gemma never protested this treatment or defended herself, enduring it all cheerfully, working "as hard as the meanest servant, humbly obeying everyone, assisting everyone whenever possible."[19]

So Gemma was a "victim of love," immolated by the fires of her passion for Jesus and of his for her. "O Father," Gemma wrote Padre Germano in the last months of her life, "if you could only say in a few days' time: 'Gemma was a victim of love and died of love,' what a blessed death!" Gemma described her experience of pain and prayer as that of a soul wandering "in this paradise of incomprehensible beauty and ineffable truths." Jesus, she said, "is a burning fire. It burns but does not consume, on the contrary, it gives light and warmth and joy, and the more it burns, the more happy and perfect it makes those encircled by its rays, and the more anxious do they become to be burning in His fire."[20]

My father took his mother by the hand a year after the chef's death and led her back to Tuscany. They went to live with my grandmother's aging parents, who fed their daughter infant food again, *pastina* stars with butter and grated cheese and soft eggs. When she was feeling better, my grandmother took up her old chores on the farm again. She carried food in a covered wicker basket out to the men working in the fields of the Cistercian monastery, which my family served as tenant farmers, and she swept the earthen floors of her mother's kitchen. My grandmother had been terrified as a young woman that she would die a spinster and then the chef had come along and made her a bride; now she had come back a widow. Women in the village talked about her as *quella povera donna* and told her story on the riverbanks where they went to pound clothes against the rocks. "She had so much, and now . . ." "Two little boys . . . and now . . ." "A house in America, and now . . ." The unspoken coda to these observations consigned my grandmother to her hard lot, because—and now—she was alone, without her husband, defeated by America and humiliated by having to accept her parents' help. If only she could have had visions of Jesus like Gemma's, my grandmother perhaps would have found some consolation, as Gemma did when she slipped out of the security of family networks after her parents' death. Instead, she rewarded the cruel pity of the women at the rocks with sighs. Sorrow and loss filled her up and obliterated at last all traces of the chef's young wife.

My grandmother had the most expressive range of sighs of anyone I have ever known, and she was always sighing. She sighed at her sewing machine and at the stove. She was still breathing lamentations at the end of her life, sitting in a worn housecoat on a broken recliner in the apartment my uncle had moved into after his marriage some years before, where she was taken in her last months. This was how she remained faithful to her dead husband, forcing her sons to compete with a ghost. The two of them chose different ways of fighting their dead father.

My father imposed a strict silence on himself. He had been dropped back several grades in the local Fascist elementary school because he couldn't read or write Italian, and he obediently squeezed his big boy's body without complaint into a child's small seat every morning until someone took pity on him and brought him a bigger desk from another classroom. At night he sat beside his mother and helped her finish her chores. The women on the rocks called him *l'uomo*, the man of the house, and said he was like a husband to his mother and a father to his brother.

My father quit school in the sixth grade without protest and went to work in a tiny hardware store tucked into one of Lucca's arches, setting off every morning after helping his mother and grandfather feed the animals. This was the end of his dream of becoming a priest or a doctor or a poet, which the nuns in Boston had encouraged. My father loved his grandfather's big, stolid domestic animals, especially the beloved great ox. This animal, which knew the roads home to the farm from the fields, was killed and eaten by Nazi soldiers during the occupation of this part of Italy. Whenever he told us stories about these first years back in Tuscany, my father always got around to the smell and feel of the gentle animals in their fragrant stalls. He respected their stoic submission, fortitude, and calm acceptance of their fate, which were the same virtues the women at the rocks admired in him.

Meanwhile my uncle ran wild through the streets of the village. The women at the rocks called him "whoremaster." He was still in short pants when he began pulling girls into the monks' ditches. He played soccer and stole cigarettes from the café. The village women reported his adventures to my grandmother and she chased him and beat him with a broom handle so that everyone could see she was trying to raise him without a father, but he ran off into the ditches again with welts on his back. The women at the rocks said my father was a saint, his brother a pig.

Suffering, as we have seen, was fundamental to the way that Catholics understood themselves and claimed a place for themselves in American culture just before and after the Second World War. This was a time of the most profound ambivalence in the relationship between Catholics and American culture. As much as they were assimilating to American ways—and indeed because of this—Catholics were intensely concerned to mark and maintain the difference between themselves and other Americans. They accomplished this—or convinced themselves that they were accomplishing this—in large part by establishing, emphasizing, and intensifying the distinctive boundaries of the Catholic *body*. "Americans" (which, in Catholic usage meant American Protestants) applied too much eye makeup. Their faces betrayed the weary fatigue and emptiness that haunted modern culture. Catholic freedom from this culture was signified and maintained by their bodily practice. Catholics (in this idealized comparison) did not wear makeup (this is not what Sister Consilia and others were seeing, of course). Catholic bodies bore the real presence of Jesus Christ taken in the sacrament of the Eucharist. Catholics disapproved of birth control, which other Americans used freely (according to Catholics). By midcentury, Catholic prohibition of artificial contraception had become the single most public marker of the community's difference and—in its own eyes—superiority. The Catholic body so marked and defined was essential, then, to Catholicism's cultural integrity in this period and to its self-representation in American culture.

But Catholics, as much as any other group in the United States, were caught up in mass culture in these years, as influenced by developments in American media, education, entertainment, and technology. Young Catholics participated in the vast new peer culture of adolescents that took shape in the United States, abetted by advertising and educational psychology, in the early twentieth century. Most Catholic young men and women went to American public high schools.[21] Most American Catholics lived in cities or suburbs, furthermore, which put them at the center of the forces of American popular culture that were making for a new national conformity—radio (and later television), fashion, music, advertising, and consumerism. Catholics desired the things offered by American culture as much as any other group, although with a distinctly bad conscience for betraying their difference. So for all the efforts to create and sustain Catholic distinctiveness and the determination among Catholics to embody this difference in a physicality defined in opposition to modernity, Catholics were becoming—their bodies were looking—much like everyone else, as priests and nuns involved with adolescent boys and girls well knew. The integrity of the Catholic body, and so of the Catholic community, was at risk.

Gemma was absorbed into this discourse: Gemma's suffering was borrowed for the criticism and discipline of young Catholic bodies, one instance of a much wider use of the saints—and especially the martyrs—by Catholic educators and commentators as a way of cautioning youngsters, setting boundaries around their behavior, and defining the ideal Catholic self against modernity. It is one of the peculiarities of an international and transhistorical system of signs such as Catholicism that signifiers rooted in one place and time may detach from the specific historical and cultural ground on which they arose and circulate freely, becoming available in very different cultural environments, sometimes acquiring different meanings in the process of translation, and sometimes serving different ends. The pains of Gemma's body were cast by Americans as a rejection of modernity and a reproach to its weakness and cowardice despite all its pretensions to power and sufficiency.

Gemma is a "unique soul in a modern world where men flee from suffering and inconvenience," Mary Fabyan Windeatt wrote in 1940 in a popular magazine published by the Passionist Fathers. "God has thrown this modern-day child in the teeth of a materialistic and unbelieving generation," another author proclaimed in the magazine that same year, "to show that His arm is not shortened." Gemma was rejected by the people of Lucca, including the nuns in the convents at which she applied for admission, "because she was sick, because she was poor, and, if you please, because she was over-religious." The modern world scorned her, but the great secret truth, according to Paulist Father Richard Walsh, was that the physical pain of this unknown girl in Lucca was fundamental to the church and its endurance against the assaults of modernity. "City lights are not explained by the man who pulls the switch," Father Walsh wrote, introducing the familiar metaphor into Gemma's story, "but only by the hidden dynamos, far from the metropolis[,] which grind night and day to light the skyline." Again pain's dynamo, but this time it was Gemma's pain powering it.[22]

When her oldest son was about fourteen years old, my grandmother took in a boarder, a young woman named Maria Rita, to help pay for the small house into which she and her sons had finally moved down the road from my great-grandfather's farm. The boarder came from Lucca's aristocracy. She suffered from a respiratory ailment, and her family hoped that the clean air of a Tuscan farm would help her. Maria Rita was convinced she was dying. She spun an elaborate gothic—Gemma-like—romantic fantasy that utterly captured my father and grandmother. Maria Rita's family brought her special treats during her stay—apples out of season, peaches, pears—which my grandmother would not permit the young woman to share with her sons. My father was responsible for bringing the sick girl her meals. She was "unbelievably beautiful," my father remembers, "unbelievable."

She lay back on pillows stuffed with straw in a dark, hot room, and over the months Maria Rita stayed with them my father fell in love. He sat at her bedside while she either picked at her food or gave it to him (he was always hungry) and they talked about God and the saints and about pain and suffering in this vale of tears. Every night they said the rosary together. My father came to imagine that Maria Rita radiated a celestial light. "Oh, how beautiful heaven must be," she would sigh to the boy staring at her. One day Maria Rita asked him to vow with her never to get married. He would become a priest, she a nun, and they would be together in heaven someday. "I like you, Mario," she told him often, "but there are more important things to think about" than earthly love. A baby in the house next door died one summer when Maria Rita was visiting. Sixty years later my father remembers that Maria Rita asked him to write on a card, *Il Signore raccolie i fiori piu belli e fa una corona immortale in cielo.* (The Lord gathers the most beautiful flowers to make a crown in heaven). Maria Rita eventually entered a religious order in Torino dedicated to the care of children born with serious birth defects.

Pain bound Gemma and Jesus together. Physical distress and then at the very end of Gemma's life the awful emotional pain of separation and loss were the expressions of their love for each other and the ligature between heaven and earth, nature and supernature. Gemma's yearning for an intimacy with Jesus so total that it obliterated her identity was satisfied only and completely when she was in the gravest pain. "Do you wish to love me really?" Jesus had asked Gemma once in a vision. "Learn first to suffer. Suffering teaches one to love." Jesus appears in Gemma's life as a demanding and insistent lover, a man of intense and unrefusable needs, and the voice and realization of his desire for Gemma was pain. "For a good part of twenty years," the preface to *The White Flower of the Passion* reads, Gemma's "Divine Lover sought for full possession of Gemma's heart; for the remaining five years of her life, He made Himself felt in varying degrees of intensity until at length her heart was so inflamed with the fire of His love that it burned itself out and winged its way to Him in an ecstasy of bliss." Jesus held out a chalice to Gemma in one of her visions (as reported to American readers by Sister Saint Michael of the Sisters of Saint Joseph) and said to her, "On this chalice I have placed my lips, and I want you to drink it." "Upon her heart He wrote His name," James Gallagher says of Jesus in a poem about Gemma, published in 1943, "[t]hen, with a jest that was Divine, / Made her His living valentine, / And in a supernatural whim / Let her exchange heart-vows with Him." So beautiful and desirable was Gemma in this moment, Gallagher says, that she took Jesus' breath away. "Do you know, daughter, for what reason I send crosses to souls dear to me?" Jesus asked Gemma on another occasion. "I desire to possess their souls entirely, and for this I surround them with crosses, and I enclose them in tribulation, that they may not escape from my hands; and for this I scatter thorns, that souls may fasten their affections on no one, but find all content in me alone." When he is done marking her with the signs of his Passion—a sight so awful that when she comes upon it, Gemma's aunt Elena Landi cries out, "Child, what has happened to you?"—Jesus tells Gemma, "Now you are Mine, My little spouse."[23]

Gemma responded with great ardor of heart to Jesus' importuning. She willed what he desired. Every Thursday evening, Cecilia Giannini reported, Gemma, anticipating the next day's pain and bleeding, "prepared herself for suffering as one prepares for a feast." During a vision in 1901, Gemma cried out to the crucifix on the wall, "Jesus, let me come to You. I die of Your love." In February 1900 Gemma wrote her confessor, Monsignor Volpi, "Saturday night I went to make a visit to the Crucified; there came to me a great desire to suffer and with all my heart, I asked it of Jesus. And Jesus that evening made me have a very violent pain in my head." On another occasion, Gemma repeatedly kissed the crown of thorns that Jesus was pressing onto her skull. She often begged Jesus "to help her make an oblation to herself to the point of immolation."[24]

Jesus could also be exquisitely tender to his little lover. In May 1901, Gemma reported dreaming that Jesus had taken her into his arms and invited her to rest awhile with him. As she dozed, "Jesus embraced me ardently." Awakening from this sweet rest, Gemma saw that Jesus was getting ready to leave her. But he turned to ask her, before he departed, "Do you know why I have had you repose on my breast?" And he answered his question for her, "Because I am preparing you to suffer greatly."[25]

My uncle began to take things from his mother's apartment in her last months there when she was too disoriented and depressed to object or even to notice. My grandmother's apartment became my uncle's secret hiding place after he had gotten married. He hid money from his wife high up in his mother's closets, in narrow gray and steel boxes, covering them with old clothes and my grandmother's clean frayed sheets. He brought stale cookies home from the hotel restaurants where he worked and stashed them behind pots and pans in his mother's cupboards. Every week he prepared an enormous package, which he wrapped in old brown paper bags from the A&P and bound with cheap twine, for the Cistercian monastery in my grandmother's village. He took things from his mother to put in these packages: he sent the monks chewing gum and bags of chocolate kisses, old writing paper, promotional materials distributed by corporations that had met at his hotels, jars of instant coffee and peanut butter, gray and tan nylons in thin cellophane packages, striped peppermint candies, pounds of sugar, and cans of Campbell's Alphabet Soup. My uncle went through his mother's drawers and sent off not only her underwear but her nightgowns and dresses ("they give them to the poor *vechiette* that come to beg from them"), opened packages of Dr. Scholl's footpads ("you should see their feet," he said about the monks), emery boards and hairbrushes. He packed up knives and forks from the kitchen, dish towels, and washcloths. He also sent the monks hundreds of white beeswax candles to burn in their chapel for his intentions, rosaries, holy cards, and random pamphlets on various topics he took from churches in Manhattan and the Bronx. "*Pregano per me*," he told me once, "*sai*, these men, they pray all the time, all night too."

For every package the abbot of the monastery sent back a fawning note of thanks, assuring my uncle that he was the community's greatest benefactor. On his trips to Italy my uncle disappeared into the cloister and stayed with the monks for days. He came out loaded down with gifts, among them bottles of the garishly and metallically colored liquors manufactured there. This is where the death bottle had come from. My uncle's attachment to these monks was a family mystery. The only explanation I have ever heard for it came from one of my great-aunts who remembered my uncle's boyhood escapades in the monastery's ditches. "Maybe he goes there to remember his girlfriends."

"You should see how they love this stuff," my uncle told me once, talking about the monks. "They're like little kids."

Now my grandmother's world was disappearing. It was as though her mental deterioration had found an analogue in the space around her. My uncle took the crucifix off the bedroom wall. He made off with pictures of Boston and Tuscany, blurred images of his mother with her husband at the beach, their arms around each other's waists, or strolling through Boston's Public Garden. My grandmother had a small ceramic kitchen blessing, shaped like a peasant cottage, on the wall behind the stove. In one of the little windows of this *casucchia*, as my father called it, darkened by heat and grease, a miniscule piece of cloth was visible. This was a relic of Padre Pio, the southern Italian holy man who bled thickly from large, black-rimmed holes that opened in his hands, feet, and sides, after a vision he had had as a young priest of the Crucifixion—and after he had read Gemma's letters describing her stigmata, in a distinctly Catholic genealogy of blood. At Padre Pio's shrine in San Giovanni Rotondo, on the Adriatic coast the friar's blood-soaked white socks and gloves are preserved and displayed in dusty wooden cases, together with pictures of him leaning over the altar in the middle of saying mass, his grim face blackened by the pain that his followers say was his daily cross. Pilgrims dipped their handkerchiefs in the dark red clots he dripped onto the altar; they tried to steal his bloody socks after his death. Like many Italians, north and south, my grandmother loved this fierce old man, not for his conservative theology (as some contemporary American Catholics do) but for his pain and endurance. She traveled twice to visit and confess to him. The little house disappeared one night, along with my grandmother's ancient Singer sewing machine on which, according to the man who stole it, she had been crucified. It ended up, with everything else he took, piled and packed into a tiny spare room in my uncle's apartment in the northeast Bronx. All that was left at the end were marks and shadows: the little corners that had held the photos in place in my grandmother's albums, the stains of the crucifixes on the walls, and over the kitchen stove the smoky blackened outline of Padre Pio's little house.[26]

Jesus could be a cruel lover for all his tenderness, playing maliciously with Gemma's affections and needs, taunting her by threatening to take away what she most wanted, himself. There are times, Gemma reported to Father Germano, when "Jesus scarcely looks at me . . . it seems to me that He repulses me." Gemma believed herself to be nothing, to have no being or identity apart from Jesus' embrace, and she struggled to steel herself for the moments when Jesus appeared to be toying with her heart. "If

Jesus does not look at me anymore," she consoled herself, an abandoned lover in the night, "what does it matter? I will look at Him always, and if He does not wish me to be with Him anymore, I will nevertheless keep near Him." This is the rejected and deeply hurt lover's ultimate fantasy: separation is an illusion, nothing can truly part us.[27]

It was toward the very end of her life that Jesus especially tormented Gemma by abandoning her. At the moment she was most desperate for him, when she was most sorely beset by doubts and malignant fantasies, Jesus pulled away from her, to Gemma's great sorrow and disorientation. Cecelia overheard the dying Gemma cry out one night to an empty room, "Is it true, you are leaving me, Jesus? Already I notice your withdrawal . . . Why, Jesus, do you not answer me?" Gemma pleaded with her heavenly lover not to torture her with his absence. But after a lifetime of showing his love for Gemma—and demanding hers in return—in the marks of pain, Jesus had found the surest way to inflict the most grievous hurt and therefore, in the lexicon of his relationship with Gemma, the greatest love of all. Or, as Sister Saint Michael says, Jesus had reserved for the end of his lover's life the "last and the greatest" of pains. Gemma's life is bracketed by a love—God's love for her and hers for God—that made itself cruelly and insistently known in loss: God's demand that she love him enough to surrender her mother and then the loss of the one who had come in place of her mother promising never to leave.[28]

After he had stolen everything else from her apartment my uncle stole his mother too and tucked her into a room in his own place, which was now crammed full of my grandmother's old things. For us to see her after this meant enduring the endless rage and bitterness of my uncle's wife, whose husband was forcing her to take care of an incontinent and incoherent old woman who couldn't speak English (as my aunt described my grandmother). The devil came in the shape of a little boy in a white suit and perched on the edge of the bathtub when my grandmother was in the bathroom. My grandmother whispered to me, the last time I saw her alive, that her daughter-in-law had tried to set her on fire, which I assumed was my grandmother's way of expressing her fear and isolation. (But she had been cruelly threatened by her daughter-in-law too.) At last my uncle was the master of his mother's life. She sat in his living room in the high towers of Co-Op City in thin cheap polyester house dresses that her son made his wife buy her at sales in filthy neighborhood discount stores. My uncle walked his mother once a day to the little terrace that opened off the living room in his apartment so she could get some air, but he kept his arm around her as if he were afraid she'd take off and fly away, over the north Bronx marshes, over the boats docked at City Island, back to the smoky fields of Tuscany. His wife's cats ripped at the arms of my grandmother's recliner where she sat in her last long silence. Somehow the holy card of Gemma escaped my uncle's hands and found its way to me.

My uncle's demonstrations of affection for his mother became even more wildly extravagant and insistent in these days of total filial power than they had been when my grandmother was declining but still living in her own home. "*Veni qui, mammina,* come here and sit on my lap." He kissed her and forced her to accept his relentless embraces. "*Carina, carina, sei bella, mammina,*" he crooned. The cats raced away as he forced his heavy body down on his mother in the recliner. A retired couple that lived next door came every night for the show. "Look, look," they said, "look how he loves his mother. What a good boy." "Don't you think she can still turn heads," my uncle asked all of us and brushed his mother's hair, which drooped in thin strands across her face, with an old tortoise-shell brush he had taken from her bedroom off the bureau on which Gemma's picture had rested. Once I saw him grab a tiny plastic spoon out of my grandmother's hand at the kitchen table and try to feed her from the twirled mound of soft ice cream in front of her, but she roused herself from her torpor and pushed his hand away.

Then at the very end of her life my uncle brought his mother to a Jewish home for the elderly in the north Bronx (we learned later). "Why did you put me here?" my grandmother asked him every time he went to see her (he told us afterwards). My uncle didn't tell my father where their mother was until the night before she died, and then he shrewdly (as he must have thought) called too late for my father to get there to see her alive. But every day she was in the home, every day for six months, she asked the man who talked to her in baby talk to explain what he had done to her and why she couldn't see her oldest son anymore. "This was the last thing she said." My uncle was sitting with his brother in my mother's kitchen long after my grandmother's death, when they were speaking to each other again. "The last thing she said to me on this earth was, '*Dov'e mio figlio?*' She meant you." My uncle mopped his face with a damp dish-towel in the hot kitchen. "She wanted to know where you were and why you never came to see her. This was the last thing she said on this earth, and she was sharp right to the end. Incredible, eh? Then she died."

Pain and love were inescapably tied together in Gemma's experience of the world and in the stories told about her in American Catholic popular periodicals and biographies of the saint. The autobiographies of people struggling with illness report that pain is the loneliest experience, disclosing and intensifying the ordinary distances between people and erecting new barriers to intimacy. Again, not so with Gemma: pain obliterated the boundary between her and Jesus, pain was the medium of their connection. "Tonight, Jesus, I alone wish to suffer," Gemma tells her heavenly lover in a vision in 1901, a year of especially intense physical distress and spiritual ecstasy for Gemma. "Or, if Thou willest it, we shall suffer in company. We shall become one victim." Gemma cries to her bridegroom, coquettishly, during one of her ecstasies, "let us suffer together—which one of us will have suffered the more out of love for the other?" Gemma's family and devout describe her dying as a love story. "On Holy Saturday night, April 11, 1903," Sister Saint Michael writes, "Jesus came. Gemma had received the Viaticum, and all had retired for a moment's respite when He stole upon her." Sister Saint Michael ends her story of Gemma's life, "of that meeting none were witness, but of her Easter joy, who could doubt?" James Gallagher imagined a gallant Jesus sending "His chauffeur Death" to bring Gemma to him, as if he were taking her out for an evening on the town. Gemma's cry at the very end of her life—"O, Jesus, I cannot stand it anymore"—is not an expression of defeat but of the fullness of love and pain in her.[29]

I happened to be standing at the back of the funeral chapel on the first night of my grandmother's wake when my uncle walked in and saw his mother's body in the coffin. There was no bottle of vermouth. He moaned and screamed at the threshold of the room, too frightened to enter. The sweat ran in thick ropy streams into his collar and he fell down and rolled back and forth on the funeral home's carpeted floor. The undertaker took me aside and pressed a small pellet covered in thin webbing into my hand. "Break this under his nose if he passes out," he said. So my grandmother never knew that her son failed in the end to keep his promise. She may have doubted at times that he would do what he threatened to do, but she couldn't say with certainty that he would not greet her death with sweet wine. Unless she was looking in on all of us in the funeral parlor, saw us trying to lift my uncle's heavy flesh from the floor, heard his cries for "Mamma!" and smelled the panic on him, she couldn't know that the bottle of vermouth remained corked.

My uncle could not leave the side of his mother's coffin during the three days of her wake. He stroked her face, kissed her forehead, and spoke to her constantly. He lifted my baby daughter into the coffin to touch her great-grandmother's hair. My uncle and his wife sat on one side of the funeral parlor, my parents on the other, and each told their versions of my grandmother's last months to whoever came to the wake. When there was nobody there they took turns speaking to my grandmother in her coffin. "He abandoned you," my uncle said, his forehead on the coffin's edge, close to my grandmother's folded hands. "What son loved you more?" he asked her. "We would have found a good residence for you, a Catholic place," my father whispered to his mother in response, "where you could have had your own room, and other *vechiette* to talk to, but he wouldn't let us. Instead he made you die in a place where no one knew you and couldn't even speak your language." My father spoke to his mother in English, his brother spoke to her in Italian, even though each was actually more comfortable in the other language.

My uncle objected to the shortness of the wake. Three days were not enough, he said. He wanted his mother's body exposed for a week, ten days; he'd pay anything for this. The funeral director refused. Then he insisted that his mother be buried above ground. The cemetery in the North Bronx where Italian Americans bring their dead is called Saint Raymond's. All the dead members of my own family are there. My uncle believed that the dead are under water at Saint Raymond's. The water table is rising in that part of the Bronx, he told me during the wake, and water seeps into even the most expensive coffins, carrying in little fish and worms. The coffin my uncle chose and paid for was a very expensive one with heavy brass handles and a beautiful plush interior and a very tight seal. It was designed to keep out moisture and so in this way to prevent the corruption of the body.

My grandmother was laid to rest in this coffin placed in a wall above the earth. The walls of coffins at Saint Raymond's are arranged in a courtyard off to one side of the cemetery where it is very quiet. The noises of the many highways that surround the grounds and cause them to vibrate, gently rocking the dead in their resting places, do not reach here. People come and sit on stone benches. The cost of such burials depends on where a coffin is situated in the vertical rows. Burial at eye and hand level are the most expensive because here the living can trace the names of their dead with their fingertips and press their palms and lips to the cool stone. My grandmother is buried within reach of our lips and fingers.

The communion of saints exists as stories. The hagiographical tradition associated with Gemma Galgani consists of the stories her contemporaries told about her, the retelling of these stories in various cultural contexts far from Lucca by men and women whose imaginations and moral sensibilities were captured by this ambiguous and passionate holy figure, and (in my family) stories about my grandmother and Gemma. My grandmother and I never talked about her devotion to Saint Gemma Galgani and so there are limits to what I can say about the inner meaning of this bond; but the devotional interior is not the only place to look for understanding. There are things I know for certain about my grandmother and Saint Gemma. I know that it was important to my grandmother that she and Gemma were born in the same place around the same time. I know that the only book family memory records my grandmother reading was Saint Gemma's autobiography. I also know that my grandmother went to sleep every night in her noisy Bronx apartment within sight of Gemma's eyes. Most of all, I have the stories—stories about Gemma and stories about my grandmother—and I have the stories as they wind around and around until they become each other, Gemma and Giulia. It is at the place where the two lives touch in narrative that I can begin thinking about my grandmother's devotion to Saint Gemma and the meaning of the communion of saints. The challenge is to trace the seam made by the narrative conjuncture of these two lives. When she talked about Gemma my grandmother seems to have been telling us, as I understand now after holding these two stories up to each other, that there was something of herself she recognized in Gemma's story and something of Gemma's in hers.

Born in the same time and place, Gemma and Giulia were both early and profoundly shaped by grief and absence that made them both raw and vulnerable to the prospect and the threat of withdrawal and separation. Both were ensnared in bitter domestic entanglements with close relatives who were cruel to them, exploiting their weaknesses, sorrows, and needs, according to the stories. Gemma and Giulia alike understood that pain, sorrow, and loss shadowed all love. Men called both of them to victim lives of sacrificial suffering—Gemma by Jesus in heaven, Father Germano on earth, Giulia by her sons. That there was such resonance between heaven and earth makes sense for the simplest social historical and cultural reasons. Gemma's and Giulia's lives arose on the same imaginative ground of late-nineteenth-century northern Italian Catholicism—passionate, inward looking, mystical, church centered, sacramental, shadowy, and enthralled with the mystery of pain. If any further confirmation of this is needed beyond the details of their respective biographies, there is Maria Rita. It was as if Gemma herself had come to visit, so clearly was this young woman and my family's response to her situated in the idioms of romantic Tuscan Catholic piety. The sufferings of Jesus and Mary, graphically imagined, were central to both Gemma's and Giulia's devotional lives. Both women contended with mischievous devils in moments of terrible fear, sorrow, and loneliness, cultural idiom giving their terror and loneliness a shape. Gemma was robbed by Chiappino, as she called her devil. My grandmother was robbed by her own intimate thief who violated boundaries and intruded into secret places just like Chiappino did. Gemma's and my grandmother's stories constitute a distinctly Catholic diptych.

These social historical and cultural reverberations between nature and supernature are the evidence of still deeper connections below. Sacrifice and suffering were central to both women's understandings of themselves, of how they were meant to spend their lives, and especially of themselves as women. Both took pain as destiny and endurance as a virtue. My grandmother used to say that a person need only three days to get used to anything; Gemma seems to have accepted the onset of supernatural disturbances in her life with similar equanimity. Both understood pain as gift, Gemma as the victim soul, my grandmother as the victim widow and mother. Both yielded to the harsh demands of men who claimed to have loved them and both seem to have taken—with greater or lesser resignation—cruelty as evidence of love. Both were made to think of their pain as a grace they bestowed on others. Every time my uncle declared that his mother "gave her life for us," he was speaking out of and to the spiritual, emotional, and cultural world that Gemma and Giulia shared. He was making Giulia into a victim soul on the model of Gemma.

So there is a social historical and cultural truth to Father Schwitalla's observation with which I began, that the life we live now and the life to come are the same life. But heaven and earth do not merely reflect each other. Heaven and earth are made in relation to each other; the natural and the supernatural are mutually constitutive. Understanding this— understanding in other words that my grandmother and Gemma came from each other, that both were constituted together and in relation to each other by the idioms, motivations, and structures of Tuscan Catholicism in the late nineteenth and early twentieth centuries, and that, in turn, northern Italian Catholicism was made in the intersection of Gemma's life with the lives of men and women such as my grandmother—dissolves some of the mysteriousness of the two stories and something of their otherness. Why didn't my grandmother break the death bottle? How could Jesus love and torment Gemma as he did? How could her sons have failed to protect my grandmother in her last weeks and instead continued to find solace and comfort in her, despite her distress? Why did the Passionist Padre Germano collude in a spirituality that was at once infantile, erotic, and painful? Ways of thinking about these questions (I am trying to avoid the word *answers* here) lie along the hinge of the diptych.

Gemma's bleeding appears, when the two lives are held up to each other, as the outward sign of a family culture in which love and pain were inevitably paired and in which love was demonstrated, expected, and expressed often enough in the language of suffering. In the world made and sustained at the juncture of these stories, the threat of separation served as a vehicle for intensifying intimacy. Gemma's Jesus and Giulia's younger son were alike both masters of the erotics of denial and absence. In the juncture of the natural and supernatural, history and devotion, it becomes possible to see that pain may have served as a guard against the Oedipal fantasies provoked by the intimate overinvolvement of sons and mothers, fathers and daughters, and by the unexamined circulation of desires through families. Indeed, the only language that my family had to think and talk about their needs, desires, and fears was the devotional language that gave shape to Gemma too. Oedipal tensions and struggles come to the surface in the interplay of infantilism and cruelty, desire and baby talk in the stories of Gemma's relationship with Jesus and with her father and of my grandmother with her son. Gemma's certainty that the pain in her body was the mark of Jesus' exclusive love for her parallels my grandmother's long endurance of her son's violence. Where heaven and earth meet, in the tie between Gemma and Giulia, we see that cruelty is often mistaken for love. We are learning something about the Catholic imaginary in the deeper places of people's lives in this time and place.

Death acquires a particular shape in the meeting of these lives. How the border between the living and the dead is constructed, maintained, and transgressed is a matter of history and culture. In Gemma's and Giulia's world, death was not a final separation. Suffering became the bridge between the living and the dead, between those present and those absent. Gemma and Giulia both had absent lovers to whom they were bound by ties of pain and sacrifice and by promises of renunciation. If one suffered enough, the message of this religious world was, distance dissolved. The absent other became present in the pain in the interior of one's body. Pain was the sign of the embodiment of lost love. Finally, in the erotic economy that circulated between heaven and earth, the only way to insert oneself into love that had been sealed by pain against others—such as that between my grandmother and her dead husband and Gemma and Jesus—was by means of more pain. This is what my uncle attempted, to his great grief. But he was inside the story, too, the boy in the sight of the women at the well and in the eyes of heaven.

My family ate well after the funeral in a little Italian restaurant under the grid of the shadows cast by the elevated train on White Plains Avenue. Some childhood friends of mine dropped by, and we found their presence reassuring and comforting. I thought then that I'd seen the last of my uncle but I should have known better. He called one night. "*Non posso dormire*," he said. My uncle had spent most of his adult life on waiter's time and he never seemed to know or care what hour of day or night it was when he had a need to call one of us. "*Non é justo*. Mama's buried in the Bronx and Papa *la nella cimeterie* at Boston." This was a violation of their marriage vows, said my uncle, forgetting that marriage vows promised fidelity to death's parting, not beyond it. A week later he called me again in the middle of the night to tell me that he had begun the necessary paperwork to have his father's body exhumed from the place it had been resting for fifty years. In this culture, not even the absence of the dead can be taken for granted. My uncle revealed now that he had promised my grandmother to do this, a sacred vow, and "*la voleva*," she wanted it. I knew my grandmother had dreamt for fifty years of being reunited with her dead husband and so I knew my uncle was telling the truth.

So Gemma's story, approached in relation to local family and religious history in Lucca at the turn of the century as exemplified by my Tuscan family, takes on a much less bizarre and fantastic cast. Gemma makes emotional sense in the context of family life such as I have described and in relation to gestures, feelings, exchanges—the bottle of vermouth, the Padre Pio house shrine, my father's strange feeling that his aging and distressed mother's home was the safest place on earth, the women at the rocks, and so on—of everyday life in that world. This level of the lived texture of everyday life, through which people move and live, is ordinarily lost to history, which approaches Gemma though her writings, or the discourse of the victim soul, or the history of mysticism, or the politics and ambitions of religious orders in Italy in the late nineteenth and early twentieth centuries. All of these frames are useful and necessary, but there is a still more intimate dynamic at work here between heaven and earth, and to get to it is one of the reasons I turned to the context I know most intimately. I am not proposing a new way of thinking about women mystics or victim souls, simply opening up a bit the world that saints and people make together and live in together.

One of the consequences of the mirroring of the two lives, Gemma/Giulia, is that each normalizes the other. It becomes possible to see what values, dreams, spirituality, and eroticism pressed my grandmother and her sons so deeply into their lives and in turn to understand the troubled social psychological grounds on which the distinctive and dramatic idioms of Gemma's spirituality arose and to which it was addressed. Holding the two lives up in relation to each other opens them both out to history, recovering them from psychopathology. I am personally comforted (one of the private advantages of historiography) by the possibility that the madness (as it seemed to me) in my family, the emotional drama that has always broken my heart, actually makes sense, that we can discern cultural (not purely psychological) and historical meanings in the early morning phone calls, the death bottle, baby talk, the passion for death accompanied by an equally passionate denial of it, the cruelty and the distinctive shape of love. Why else would men and women have loved the saints so intensely, so consistently have brought them into their lives, and so desperately turned to them in moments of the deepest pain and most unsettling hopes if there was not this deep recognition between heaven and earth?

There is no reason to believe, moreover, that my family's story is anomalous. The evidence of the diptych—that the inner dynamics of one family found expression and sanction on the level of culturally shared religious story and that this religious story is so clearly grounded in the most subtle and elusive movements of family culture in a particular time and place—suggests that the interplay of heaven and earth I have teased out in this case study could be used as a lens for a wider study of the social history of love in the northern Italian working and middle classes at the turn of the century, for instance, or for a social psychological history of Tuscan families, or to examine the fate of families caught in the last century's too-rapid succession of immigration, death, and war. It certainly suggests that Gemma and other figures like her belong to the Western history of love.

My personal comfort that my family may be comprehensible is an intimate version of the resolution all scholars of culture, historians among them, and most especially religious historians, seek. Gemma makes sense. We can find the social, historical, social psychological, and cultural tools to explore and account for Gemma's experience, among them family stories. Each side of the diptych accounts for the other.

Therese Elizabeth Alexander was handed a key to Gemma's tomb by the Passionist nuns in whose care the body rested. "Our Lord is there," Alexander described her feelings at the site, "and Gemma is there, united to Him in death as in life."[30]

We have arrived at last at a familiar place. An inquiry that began with blood leaking down a girl's face onto a white tablecloth at Sunday dinner in a bourgeois home in Lucca and a bottle of wine reserved for a mother's death ends with the confident assertion, born of personal need and scholarly training, that there is order, coherence, and meaningfulness in the world in which these things occurred. It is a commonplace in the contemporary study of religion that sacred media are used to make and sustain the meaningfulness of the worlds in which humans find themselves and that it is this work of "meaning making" that makes "reality" livable. The one thing above all else that humans cannot stand is incoherence. So it would appear to be with Gemma/Giulia.

But this is the academic equivalent of Father Schwitalla's belief that Gemma went smoothly from her encounters with the crucified Christ to her kitchen duties. At the very least we can say that if meaning is being made here out of pain and blood, the movement between life and meaning—the social, psychological, domestic processes of meaning making—can be terrible and destructive and that the meanings made, the lives made, with religious media can be dreadful and painful. It is also the case that Gemma and Giulia were born into religious stories that existed before them and that there was a narrative waiting for them that had little to do with their agency or intentionality. What I see when I look at both lives is confusion, cruelty, disorientation, and sorrow; *meaning* is not the first word that comes to mind. For all the meaningfulness we impose on mystical experience, from day to day Gemma seems not to have known what was going on or why Jesus was doing the things he was doing, nor did her family. Gemma was caught up in the narrative flow. My grandmother too and her sons were held in the grip of available meanings—the sacrificial widow who loves by suffering, the woman of sorrow, the saintly son, the evil son. Whether the religious idioms that shaped the stories they created for each other made my grandmother's or my father's or my uncle's lives any more comprehensible or bearable is uncertain. Like the little devil that popped up in my grandmother's last year to torment her, religious idioms were never totally in anyone's grasp. Nor did they add up to a vision of ultimate, overarching meaningfulness.

Another way of thinking about this is to say that the movement between life and meaning or between sacred and profane is not a straightforward one and that the meeting of the two often enough deepens pain, becomes the occasion for cruelty, catches persons and communities in stories that are made against them (or that are supremely oblivious of them in their own particularities), that may alienate them from their own lives, and that bear within them the power to undermine them and make them and the people around them miserable and confused. Religious theories that emphasize meaning focus on the end-product, a story that is said to link heaven and earth, but the solidity and stability of this dissolves if you focus instead on the processes of religious meaning-making. What we see if we do this is the wounding; in this devotional world, as in others, meaning making is wounding. The supernatural bore down hard on the natural in both Gemma's and Giulia's lives. Religious and cultural idioms—among them the devotional piety exemplified in Gemma Galgani's life story, within the broader context of death, wars, immigration, and family conflict—set my grandmother and her sons dancing to impulses, desires, fears, and needs they never fully understood.

Is meaning really necessary to endure? Or is the dreadful resonance between heaven and earth enough? I think the problem lies in the whole notion of "meaning making" (which as anthropologist Talal Asad points out is a distinctly modern, Western preoccupation and a distinctly post-Enlightenment and intellectualist approach to religion). History is the study of the interplay of agency and structure at a particular moment in time. But perhaps we—meaning we scholars of religion and culture living in what has been one of the longest periods of prosperity and comfort in American history (despite war and terror)—put too much emphasis on agency. It is just as true to say that the inner world of my family, each member's intimate experience and the life they made together, was *made by* the meanings embodied, expressed, and available in Gemma. To accept this is to recognize that the convergence of these two stories is a kind of religious tragedy; not to recognize it is to make interpretation itself an act of cruelty.

So meaning making is the wrong register in which to think about my grandmother's devotion to Saint Gemma Galgani. What the saint seems to have offered was companionship on a bitter and confusing journey—bitterness and confusion to which the saint's own stories had contributed. My grandmother asked no grace of Gemma other than that of accompaniment, no miracle beyond the recognition of shared lives. But the sharing was costly. As Gemma's and Giulia's stories teach, in between a life and the meanings that may be made in it, for and against that life is the wound. Meaning making begins in wounding, and the process of meaning making is wounding. Although some have tried—recall here the vita with which I began that failed to mention Saint Gemma's stigmata—neither story can be told without the blood.

"I want to bring them together in death," my uncle told me on the phone, speaking of his mother and father (and echoing Alexander's reflection at the threshold of Gemma's tomb in Lucca), "as they had been in life." A year after my grandmother's death my grandfather's body was exhumed and brought to the Bronx, where it resides now beside his wife. My father retired some years ago after more than four decades as a machinist in a New Jersey factory and very soon afterwards took up his retirement occupation, which is bringing refreshments to dying cancer patients in a hospice in the Bronx that is not far from where my grandparents are buried. My father has seen hundreds of people die over the last several years. He says that some people wait until he comes back after a day off or a weekend so they can die holding his hand. He imagines that these hundreds will be lined up waiting for him someday together with his mother and father when he gets to heaven.

Chapter Five

"HAVE *YOU* EVER PRAYED TO SAINT JUDE?"

REFLECTIONS ON FIELDWORK IN

CATHOLIC CHICAGO

> To decide whether or not you are prepared enough to start
> translating, then, it might help if you have graduated into
> speaking, by choice or preference, of intimate matters in the
> language of the original.
> *Gayatri Chakravorty Spivak*, Outside in the Teaching Machine

I AM SITTING toward the back of the Church of Our Lady of Guadalupe in South Chicago, watching clusters of people arrive for the night's novena service in honor of Saint Jude Thaddeus, patron saint of hopeless causes, whose national shrine is housed here. It is in the late 1980s and I have been working on this devotion for some time, reading through archives at the devotion's headquarters in the Loop, and now I am trying to find my way into the world of Jude's devout. The people coming into the warm glow of the church's electric candles from the darkened, already chilly October streets are wearing windbreakers emblazoned with the names of local unions, fraternal organizations, sports teams, and police and fire auxiliaries over old sweaters. One young woman sports a white quilted sateen bomber jacket with the words "Club Flamingo" arching across her shoulders above the bird itself, silhouetted against a blazing hot pink tropical sun.

The neighborhood around us is dominated by the abandoned piles of old steel foundries along the lake. In good times, I have been told by older residents, when the mills were working, the skies over South Chicago were darkened already at noon by cinders cleaned out of the tall smokestacks all around the church at regular intervals during the day. But it has been a while since times were good in South Chicago, and the skies are clear now. A big sign outside a dry cleaning establishment half a block from the church promises, "Not just cleaned—disinfected."[1]

The people coming to the shrine are of all ages, although the younger ones—couples sitting close together in the pews, family clusters of many generations—are Latino mostly, while the older ones, among whom women significantly outnumber men, are from the old eastern and southern European immigrant enclaves that had surrounded Guadalupe in the days of steel but have been shrinking ever since. The church itself was founded in 1928 as a Mexican national parish by a Spanish congregation of priests, the Missionary Sons of the Immaculate Heart of Mary, also known as the Claretian Fathers after their founder, Saint Anthony Mary Claret. But Saint Jude's shrine, opened in 1929 as a way of supporting the order's various works, has always drawn more on the "Anglo" population (as Mexican Americans in South Chicago refer to everyone else), both locally and across the nation, than on the Mexican community immediately around it.[2]

I think as I watch the pews fill up that all these people have once had (or may be having) an experience so terrible and disorienting that they identified it as hopeless and called on Jude for help (or they have come to call on him tonight), because this is the saint's special province. By now in my research I know well what sorts of crises these could be: long unemployment, bitter family troubles, abandonment or betrayal by loved ones, difficult challenges with changing technologies at work, problems with drug and alcohol addictions, and life-threatening illness. I am struck by all the stories of pain Saint Jude has already heard (and will be hearing this evening). The shrine is a place where awful things may be talked about to friends, family, and clergy, and to Jude, as part of a larger process of healing body and spirit. Often this healing work meant coming to accept tragedy and loss. The stories Jude's devout tell do not always have predictably happy endings. Tonight the place seems charged with all the needs, fears, and hopes brought to it over the years.

Then immediately after this thought come two others, which jar me by the contradiction between them.

First, flushing with pride edged by anger, I think: I am here among these working-class people in this postindustrial landscape because I want to hear their stories. I take their voices seriously. This is what research in religion means, I fume, to attend to the experiences and beliefs of people in the midst of their lives, to encounter religion in its place in actual men and women's lived experience, in the places where they live and work. Where are the theologians from the seminaries on the South Side, I want to know, with all their talk of postmodernism and narrativity? When will the study of religion in the United States take an empirical and so more realistic and humane direction?[3]

But then, still warmed by these satisfying feelings on this cold night, I hear another voice in my head. Do these people really want you here? it asks me. They could care less about your *discovery* of their spirituality, your reclamation project, like the ones periodically proposed and forgotten by the steel industries. Their prayers and their relationships with Saint

Jude existed long before you came to study them and will go on after you leave. What need do they have of you, the voice taunts, and what do you contribute to their experience? You are *studying* them, which means that they have sat down and told you stories about their experiences of hopelessness and about what they asked Saint Jude for in those times. But what have you given them, what stories have you told them, or what will you give them, especially after you translate what you understand of their experience into other, academic idioms so that they will not be able to recognize it any more as their experience?[4]

What could have been responsible for this unsettling convergence of pride and doubt? I spent the service meditating uneasily on my ambivalent place in the congregation that night.

My discomfort was deepened the next morning by an exchange I had with a woman I will call Clara, who first turned to Saint Jude three decades ago when she was nursing her father through his last illness. We had met very early, before Clara went to work, and now the sun was up and we were finishing our talk. The tape recorder had been put away. Suddenly, Clara turned to me with her coat half on, half off, and asked, "Have *you* ever prayed to Saint Jude?"

No, I told her, I had never prayed to Saint Jude. I explained that although I had grown up in a devout Italian Catholic household, none of my relatives had prayed to this saint. Since then my own relation to the tradition had become unsettled and tenuous, and so I could not really bring myself to pray for the intervention of the saints as I once had.

"Then how do you expect to understand what we're doing when we pray to Saint Jude?" she asked.

This was not an unfamiliar question to me, and I considered myself prepared for it. I told Clara that I hoped to learn something about the meaning of devotion to Saint Jude by talking to women like her and attending carefully to the specific ways they described the saint's place in their lives. I would ask them to tell me about their feelings toward Saint Jude and about how they engaged him in their everyday experience. We would talk together about how to think about their relationship with Saint Jude. I was also reading all the historical material I could find about the devotion, such as the letters published in the shrine's periodical, *The Voice of Saint Jude* . . . Clara interrupted me.

"You have to promise me," she said, "that someday you'll ask Saint Jude for something you really want, at a time when you really need him." She insisted that I do this "not just because I asked you to or because you think it'll help your research" but in order to experience the saint the way his devout do. "Then maybe you'll understand what we're doing." The saint might even help me, she added.

I made a noncommittal response, agreeing at least to think about her suggestion, and this is how the conversation ended. But Clara's challenge stayed with me. I had assumed that because I belong more or less to the same culture as the people I study, I had special access to the ways they looked at and acted in the world and could count on an intuitive grasp of the point of their practices. I knew these people in a deep and intimate way, I assured myself, so my work was not comparable to that of the ethnographer who goes far from home to study a culture that is alien to him or her, at least initially. Clara forced me to recognize the error of this belief. However I had grown up, my childhood was long ago, and since then I had been trained in disciplines that generally sought to conceptualize religious experience in categories other than those that practitioners themselves used to think about their lives—academic categories, moreover, that insisted on their own primacy, authority, and universality. I was asking outsider questions now, mostly. Furthermore, my complex autobiographical relationship with the community I was working in was as much barrier as meeting ground. I was less inside the tradition than I had thought, or more precisely, I seemed both thoroughly inside and outside it at the same time, which now, after Clara's question, seemed a uniquely difficult place to be.

Could I really take Clara's suggestion? Even though I was brought up with the saints all around me and still obviously found them (and people's relationships with them) compelling, they were no longer part of my own intellectual or spiritual life. What would it even mean for me to "pray to Saint Jude"?

Other women would later broaden and sharpen Clara's challenge by inquiring into my motivations. Why are you interested in us? they wanted to know. Why do you want to understand practices and beliefs you do not share? I might have protested that I once did share these practices and beliefs or that my grandmothers and my mother did (more interesting and relevant in terms of my motivations, as the last chapter should have made clear, but no more reassuring to the women I was talking to). I also could have told them that I believed that their questions reflected the devaluation of women's experience in Catholic and American cultures (and many others), the belief that women's lives were not as historically significant as men's lives. (Although the irony of my making this statement would have been that I was coming to these women from the world of modern religious and historical scholarship that had played such a large part in marginalizing and trivializing women's experience.)[5]

But I had to acknowledge the fairness of what they were saying. There had been a break between me and the world I studied, and the rupture had occurred on the most intimate levels, involving deep intellectual, emotional, spiritual, and existential questions. I was no longer confident that

I could ever find my way to anything like a second naïveté, the revived
sense of mystery and awe on the other side of critical inquiry. I would
have to be content, I told myself, with the more prosaic satisfactions that
came from disciplined, careful, and precise analysis that was also empa-
thetic and engaged. But I was still humbled by these exchanges with the
women I was speaking with and by the doubts they raised in me. My
confidence in my own intuitions was shaken. Now it seemed to me that
of all the traditions I might study, I was least equipped, emotionally, existentially, and intellectually, to study my own.

Back in the university, meanwhile, a colleague of mine offered another
sort of challenge from within what she understood to be the canons of
the discipline of religious studies. "They're wrong," of course, she said
after hearing me describe women's prayers to Jude and their beliefs about
his response to them. "It seems to me that your interpretation of the material has to begin with the recognition, at least to yourself, that imaginary
beings do not change men's work schedules or military orders or help
women find places to work or to live. This isn't the way the world works."
The women who believed that Jude acted in their lives, my colleague continued, drawing out the implications of her perspective, are deluded, and
the more fervent their faith, the deeper their delusion. One of the responsibilities of scholarship, one of its moral and political imperatives, was to
point out such delusions as a way of helping women liberate themselves.
My colleague was speaking out of the tradition of modern critical inquiry
that assumes, as historian Dipesh Chakrabarty has recently put it, "that
the human is ontologically singular, that gods and spirits are in the end
'social facts,' that the social somehow exists prior to them." Jude's devout
needed to be released from their religious illusions so that they might
become aware of the real conditions of their lives and respond appropriately to them.[6]

   Clara's question had to do with hermeneutics—how would or could I
understand her?—and in this she was an advocate of knowing through
experience, in particular through the experience of pain: I would find the
meanings of the devotion to Saint Jude in the depths of my own distress.
At the time I dismissed this (to myself and sympathetically) as a kind of
romanticism (which shows how much I still had to learn). My colleague,
on the other hand, whose comments also had to do with hermeneutics,
had aligned herself with the modernist traditions of suspicion that fundamentally shaped the history, sociology, and anthropology of religion. It
may have been possible to engage either of them separately, but it was very
difficult to remain in meaningful conversation with both. As a student of
my own tradition's recent history and contemporary experience, I fell in
between these two challenges; I was not *in* enough to contribute to the

ongoing life of the tradition, share its consolations, or experience the power of its account of the world, but not *out* enough to assent to my colleague's sharp dismissal. I could not really defend Jude's devout to my colleague (because it is not the task of religious scholarship to defend religious worlds or to speak for them and because I had been trained in the same suspicious disciplines as she and so I could not shake its orientations at this moment in the evolution of the project) nor could I share the faith of the devout. This is the predicament of many scholars of religion. As Grant Wacker, a distinguished historian of American Pentecostalism who grew up Pentecostal but then left the tradition, writes in the preface to his study of the movement, "I suspect that the posture of being half out and half in, though awkward, defines the fate of many religious historians." At the time this seemed to me an unhappy fate, but I learned otherwise, thanks to Clara, and in any case, what choice did I have?[7]

So my conflicting feelings on the night of the novena reflected the peculiar position of religious studies as a modern academic discipline, caught somewhere between religious practice and imagination, on the one hand, and critical analysis, on the other. Sometimes these divergent orientations are held by different people, but often they exist within a scholar caught as I was. Some practitioners of the discipline want scholars of religion to sanction particular religious beliefs and practices or to endorse religion in general against its modern detractors, and some even maintain that only those who share a particular religion are capable of studying it; others insist on explaining religious belief and practice in terms extrinsic to them, in the languages of psychology, for instance, politics, or sociology. Clara's challenge and my colleague's counterchallenge mark out the dominant poles between which the discipline exists, and these challenges can become most acutely felt when a scholar sets out to study what is or had been his or her own religious culture. I have experienced two levels of difficulty in this regard, one historical and historiographical, having to do with the moment when in the development of American Catholicism, I came to study Saint Jude; the other existential and psychological.

First the problems occasioned by recent history. Around the time I was just beginning my work on devotion to Saint Jude I went to a dinner at a friend's place in New York. My friend had been chaplain of the Catholic Worker House in Lower Manhattan in the last years of Dorothy Day's life, and he was widely connected in the New York Catholic community. On this particular evening he wanted me to meet an old comrade of his, a prominent liturgist who was in town to visit the Worker house around the corner. This liturgist, whom I will not name (he has since died), had been deeply involved in promoting the changes in ritual practice, church aesthetics, and ecclesiology following the Second Vatican Council. It was a beautiful warm spring evening. We drank great amounts of red wine and ate lamb and potatoes; the lively sounds of the East Village at night came through the open windows.

Then the visitor who had been reminiscing about the days after the Council asked me about my work. I started to tell him about Saint Jude, about the founding of the shrine in 1929, and about the feelings that people, especially women, had toward this saint, the way they treated images and statues of him, taking him into their beds, kissing him, punishing him when he did not . . . until slowly I became aware that he was becoming very agitated, turning this way and that in his chair, splashing wine from the glass in his hand onto the tablecloth and onto his pants. Suddenly he pushed himself back from the table and said loudly and furiously as he got to his feet something along the lines of *You are trying to bring back everything we worked so hard to do away with*. Then he walked out.

To recall a discussion I introduced in the second chapter that I want to elaborate here, in the middle years of the twentieth century amid tremendous social and religious change Catholics in the United States struggled to redefine their relationship to the sacred, which entailed a new conceptualization of their bond to the past as well—to their own immediate past, their childhoods in the church—because the past had been filled with sacred presences no longer tolerable or even recognizable in the changed circumstances of lives directed now to new and unfamiliar horizons. Rethinking the sacred for Catholics in the 1960s meant repositioning themselves to what had gone on in relation to the sacred in their past; telling stories about the past became a medium for reimagining the holy. Father Grabowski had located the saints in the time of the "old," "older," and "outdated," which was an argument both about the sacred and about the past. The past to be grown up and moved away from came to be represented by many things—by the dull rhythms (so it was said) of memorized prayer, for example, or by the steady clicking of rosary beads through people's fingers during mass, or by the invisibility of nuns' bodies—but above all it came to be represented by the saints and the Blessed Mother, and denying and forgetting the saints, putting them out of memory and out of history, became the way of closing off the past from the present. In this way the saints performed one last service for modern Catholics in the United States: they became the pivots of the constitution and authorization of a new "past."

Dipesh Chakrabarty says that moderns basically take two attitudes toward the past. One, which he calls "historicism," is "the idea . . . that once one knows the causal structures that operate in history, one may

also gain a certain mastery of them." Historical inquiry frees the present
from the dead hand of the past because it takes as given that the past is
"genuinely dead." The historicist approach to the past may be enacted
confidently, certain of the present's liberation from what had gone before,
or it may be ambivalent and anxious. Chakrabarty associates this latter
mood with Marxism. Marx had written that "the tradition of all the dead
generations weighs like a nightmare on the brain of the living." The danger as Marx saw it was that the new world which was to come into being
out of the rupture with the past necessarily had to be constructed with
tools of the past and so "could end up looking like a return of the dead"
(in Chakrabarty's words). Nevertheless, in both historicist attitudes there
is the assumption that historical knowledge frees the present from the
past. The other stance toward what has gone before Chakrabarty calls
"decisionism," meaning "a disposition that allows the critic to talk about
the future and the past as though there were concrete, value-laden choices
or decisions to be made with regard to both. . . . The critic is guided by
his or her values to choose the most desirable, sane, and wise future for
humanity, and looks to the past as a warehouse of resources on which to
draw as needed."[8]

Some Catholics in the 1960s and 1970s approached the past in such a
decisionist spirit. The process of renewal in many women's religious orders, for example, was guided by a reawakened attentiveness to the visions of their respective founders. Study of the past enriched sisters' reflections about how they might live in faithful witness to the distinctive
vocations of their communities in the changed circumstances of their
times (including new opportunities for women). Liturgists, who were the
most passionate proponents of the new order after the Council, explained
changes in the Mass with reference to ancient practices ("the new yet old
Mass," one liturgical handbook called the reformed service).[9]

But the impulse to hold the present and the past together in relationship
was not the dominant one in the culture and became even weaker as the
decade of the 1960s proceeded. More common was derision and contempt for "yesterday," a sense of its uselessness. What had come before
was spiritually and psychologically "sick," Daniel Berrigan, S.J., declared
in a 1962 article on church art—this language of the past as pathological
was becoming ever more common—and Catholics in this sick past were
"wounded" by being cut off from the altar and from God. "So much for
the past," Berrigan concluded confidently. Not even the Middle Ages,
once the greatest of eras in Catholic imagination and a source of cultural
and religious pride, escaped reevaluation. The past was inauthentic. It
was characterized by secrecy, dishonesty, and alienation. There was a
widespread sense among American Catholics that the past—that *their*
past—had done little to prepare them for their particular present. The

ninant temporal metaphor of the time—one that resonates deeply with language and history of Western modernity—was that Catholics needed to mature and to come of age (although the terrible irony here is that by denying the past, Catholics deprived themselves of anything to grow up from).[10]

"The mood of so many Catholic writers of the past two years," the great historian of American Catholicism Thomas T. McAvoy, C.S.C., wrote in *Ave Maria* in 1965, "has been a kind of fear to look back, as if opening the window of the church to let in fresh air meant closing the door on the past." Catholics were prepared to celebrate those aspects of their common past that authorized their credentials as moderns—the U.S. Catholic endorsement of American democracy, for instance, or the role the church played in making good citizens of immigrants from southern and eastern Europe and Ireland. But the past that would not be engaged was the past that the generation coming of age in the 1960s had most intensely lived, that had formed them and given shape and structure to their everyday lives and to their imaginations, and that had oriented their deepest senses of self, namely the past of devotionalism—that array of practices, objects, liquids, images, ceremonies, and gestures by which Catholics had engaged the presence of God, the Mother of God, and the saints, in the spaces of their everyday lives.[11] Catholics looked back in the 1960s and 1970s, across what they thought of as a tremendous temporal distance, at religious practices that had in fact existed in their own experience, that still characterized the faith of many contemporary Catholics, and that were receiving new spiritual vigor from migrants from Latin America.

The American Catholic devotional past had to be rendered utterly over and done with. But "the past . . . is a position," philosopher of history Michel-Rolph Trouillot writes, meaning that the pastness of any particular past is not given and natural but achieved, secured, authorized, and maintained. The pastness of the past has to be constructed and reconstructed, over and over, often in the face of the dreadful (to those who fear it) and unavoidable evidence of the past's enduring presence. Fundamental to the work of rendering the past past among 1960s Catholics were the saints: toppled from their niches in the churches that had been built with countless small donations to them, the saints and the devotional practices associated with them, the varied practices of sacred presence, were repositioned in the firebreak between the present and the past. Their strangeness guaranteed the otherness of the past.[12]

To Chakrabarty's typology of modern attitudes toward pasts construed as premodern we need to add another, a renunciatory impulse toward one's own and one's community's religious history, a deliberate work of sealing off, in memory and history, by denial, contempt, exclusion, and silence, ways of being in relation to the sacred that are no longer acceptable within the normative construction of the modern. This peculiar impulse of renunciation does not belong to Catholics alone; it is widely shared among moderns and indeed is a constitutive feature of modernity as this is normatively defined. The earliest modern historians would not even consider the history of religion lest writing about churches implicitly endow them with unwarranted prominence or place. Middle-class African Americans, north and south, labored in the late nineteenth and early twentieth centuries to excise from memory and from their own religious worlds any trace of the religious idioms of poor, southern, rural African Americans. Idioms of presence were recast as "survivals" in modern religious theory, their doom foretold in their naming. The historical project of the renouncing of a particular religious past is fundamental to the religious history of modernity and to the practice of modern historiography.[13]

If the point of such renunciation was to build a firewall against the past, it not only failed, it ensured that the past would remain a compelling object of desire among Catholics and ex-Catholics across the religious and political spectrum, who return today obsessively to the world of pre-Conciliar Catholicism in fiction, film, memoirs, plays, therapy modalities (the recovering Catholics movement), in the angry newsletters of Catholic separatists (those so dismayed by the changes in practice and theology in the church that they separate from it in independent congregations), in the bitter or jejune satires of liberal Catholics and ex-Catholics, and in the endless rounds of shared Catholic school memories. The members of no other religious community in the United States return so compulsively to their past. Catholics in the United States today insistently reenact the past so that they can literally enter and move around inside it. The popular theatrical production *Late Nite Catechism*, for instance, offers Catholic audiences (who else would go?) in cities across the United States the opportunity to reexperience their parochial school days. An actress dressed up as an old-fashioned nun bustles around a re-creation of a 1960s classroom demanding penalty money from latecomers, collecting coins for "pagan babies," making the bad boys in the audience (and each time I have seen the production there have been men willing to rise, or regress, to the occasion) kneel on their hands or come to the front of the "classroom" to put their noses in circles Sister draws on the blackboard, and fines the "Bobs," "Joes," and "Kathys" in the theater for not going by their baptismal names. Theatergoers weep at memories of abuse while Sister holds them and begs their forgiveness. *Late Nite Catechism* has become one site of the wider psychodrama of memory in contemporary American Catholicism.[14] Meanwhile, Catholic separatists attempt to "recreate" what they see as the glorious world of Catholic practice before the Council at their parishes, convents, seminaries, and schools, purchasing the statues, vestments, and holy objects discarded by mainstream

Catholics in a peculiarly national and international Catholic exchange economy of remembering and forgetting, and then using them to remake what they "remember" as the lost world. Separatists have generated an extensive iconography of memory: nuns and priests in these environments gather for photographs that directly recall 1950s Catholic imagery. Sister, all but invisible within her habit, smiles beatifically in front of a classroom poster that gaily, in fifties style, instructs students about the "Holy Rosary." A demure seminarian looks tenderly into the distance, his hands folded piously in front of him.[15]

The culture that tried to build so high a barrier against the past wound up creating an obsessive culture of memory. But because contemporary Catholic remembering and forgetting has its origins in the rupture between the present and the past that opened in the 1960s—in the wound between the present and the past—it is marked by this trauma. The not-so-long ago appears utterly sacred and magisterial among those who "remember" with longing and sorrow, but bizarre and ridiculous and cruel among those who "remember" with relief and contempt. In the early 1960s, amid vast social change, liberals told stories about the "past" that heightened its otherness, and conservatives told stories about the "past" that emphasized the beauty and holiness of it, and the two memory discourses first became parodies of each other and then "memories." Memory, in other words, was put at the service of forgetting. Memory became not the practice of engaging the past but another medium for fending it off and keeping it distant. Catholic "remembering" since the 1960s has assumed the task of denying the past for some, and for others of celebrating and canonizing the past, and as a result the lived complexity of the past, especially of the devotional past, was lost. Catholic memory served to ensure that adults did not have to assess what was lost and what was gained—religiously, socially, and culturally—in the era of revolutionary change of the 1960s and 1970s. Lamenting and celebrating, they could forget.

My work on devotion to Saint Jude fell right into the rupture that Catholics were so assiduously enforcing between present and past. To the liturgist at the dinner party I must have seemed a revenant, an unwelcome visitor from a past that should have been dead. But the past was not dead, first of all. As the full pews at the Chicago shrine showed, many contemporary Catholics were still deeply involved in the cult of saints. The liturgist might have responded that these were atavistic holdovers, lingering "survivals" among poorly instructed Catholics of practices and beliefs that should have been uprooted and will be uprooted in due time. But such a claim uncritically accepts and endorses the normative teleology of modernity, which maintains that there is a premodern, which must yield to the modern in all areas of life. This is not what the evidence shows. The undeadness of the supposedly dead past was also evident in the liturgist's rage: if he had believed the devotional past to be securely dead, why would he have been so enraged with me? Perhaps this is the fate of sacred presence in the modern world: excised from objects, moments, and representations, it migrates into memory, where it reestablishes itself behind the masks of denial, forgetting, terror, and desire. Had he been deeply grounded in a historicist sensibility, the liturgist would not have gotten so agitated because he would have known that the past was dead—what risk could its study pose? If he had been decisionist in his approach to the past, we would have gone on to talk about how Jude's devotion might remain relevant, if changed, in the contemporary church (which is how some liberation theologians approach "popular religion"). But in any case, I was not proposing to revive the past, only to study it and its enduring impact on the present. This was enough to drive the liturgist from my presence.

In the emerging post-Conciliar culture of the 1970s and 1980s, the saints and the Virgin Mary were to be reimagined in the languages of friendship, morality, or mythology, deemphasizing what the reformers considered an inappropriate culture of excess and emotionalism and of the miraculous. Above all the reformers insisted that popular devotions, if they were to remain a feature of the post-Conciliar American Catholic Church at all, be surrounded by *words*: one way of understanding the transitions of the early 1960s, which continue to shape the intellectual climate of contemporary studies of American Catholicism, is as a shift from an ethos of presence and sacred intimacy toward a culture bounded by, and even obsessed with, words. Words were not absent from pre-Conciliar culture, of course, with all its prayer cards, novena booklets, and pious ejaculations. The difference is that the words of the old devotionalism were efficacious not simply in themselves but in relation to specific cultic practices and disciplines, such as vows, perpetual novenas, and devotion to particular saints. Devotional words mattered in circumstances of intimacy between heaven and earth. The new words belonged to a professionalized class of ritual specialists whose development and expectations reflected the higher educational levels attained by middle-class Catholics in this era. The new words derived their legitimacy from a strict and precise connection to church authority and not from their association with a beloved saint. Devotions were necessarily now to be accompanied by some sort of discursive practice—explanatory sermons, clerical reflections on the meanings of particular expressions of piety, readings of Scripture or some other devotional text—as if by hedging these practices about with the written and the spoken word their improvisatory and disruptive potential could be controlled or at least diminished.

It is virtually impossible to work on devotional culture without becoming embroiled in modern controversies in Catholic culture. People expect the researcher to condemn or condone, and I found myself when I was working on the devotion to Saint Jude alternately denounced as a liberal and castigated as a conservative. This dilemma is not unique to scholars of Catholic culture, although it is more exigent in this context and more explicitly charged for reasons of recent history. Scholars of lived religion—of religion as people actually do and imagine it in the circumstances of their everyday lives—often find themselves called on to judge, which is to say they are called on to reassure readers of the safety and otherness of religious idioms brought too vividly close through empirical research. It was my brief account of the specificity of the research I had begun—how women prayed to Saint Jude, what sorts of petitions they brought to him, what they thought about his responses—that so dismayed the liturgist. The danger of empirical work in religion on one level is that it appears to endorse, in its initial suspensions of judgments and its refusal of the comforts of otherness—the religious worlds it describes. On a deeper level, however, what may be upsetting about the study of lived religion is that such research appears to align itself with the realness of religious worlds, with presence, thereby threatening to reawaken presence. You're trying to bring back everything we worked so hard to do away with, the liturgist had accused me. Scholars of religion who operate explicitly from a confessional perspective, who do endorse what they study, in other words, do not provoke such anxiety, nor do scholars who openly espouse the modern creeds of suspicion. It is the path in between that causes such dismay and that seems to some impossible. I will return to this issue in the next chapter. Trying to maintain this in-betweeness in relation to my own tradition had proved difficult indeed.

Just as there was obviously a generational impulse to the reformers' contempt for the old ways, so my fascination with those ways had a child's spirit about it. I felt that I knew the people at the shrine so well because not only did they do the same things my father and mother did, they looked like them too, and when I reflect on the question scholars of religion are most often asked by students and friends—"What got you interested in this in the first place?"—I have to admit that when I am working in the field or in archives I often feel like a child again peering into the strange and mysterious world of adults and trying to figure out what is going on in there. This is the existential ground of studies of one's own religious culture—however attenuated one's relationship with this has become—and perhaps more generally of our curiosity about religion. There is both promise and danger here.

That question about the origins of my interest in religion has always provoked annoyance and uneasiness in me, but peevish displeasure hides something else (as I might have suspected). In a commentary on the relationship between anthropologists and their informants, Vincent Crapanzano writes of the prominence in such engagements of a "guilt-inspiring voyeuristic intention that can be rationalized away no more in the anthropological endeavor (by science) than in the psychoanalytic endeavor (by cure)." Or, we might add, in the religious studies endeavor, by either explanation or understanding (the two familiar poles around with the field's methodologies are commonly clustered). What is this intention in the study of religion and especially in the study of one's own religious culture, past or present? By what do we rationalize our voyeurism and to what end?[16]

When I try to remember my childhood curiosity about my mother's and my father's—and everyone else's in the Italian American community in the north Bronx where I grew up—religious worlds, it seems to me that I was fascinated first of all by the depth of their emotion and by the realness of the sacred that this evidenced. Something very important was going on here. My parents and my grandparents withdrew from me in the intensity of their prayers in a way they never did otherwise (and perhaps this is one motivation of religious scholarship, to close this frightening distance) except maybe in grief. They seemed so completely absorbed and at the same time so vulnerable (a projection perhaps of my own unease, which again may account for the anxieties that circulate through scholarship on religion). Who or what was so powerful and so real that they bowed to it, pleaded and argued with it, sometimes were bitterly angry toward it, and at other times made joyous by it?

My family's engagement with sacred presences was not limited to extreme moments, although they prayed with particular intensity then. We have seen how the saints and the Blessed Mother were household companions, as familiar and unpredictable as grandparents and aunts and uncles. The grown-ups around me were forever bringing their pleas, hopes, and furies directly to these holy figures. The first memory I have of a religious practice that intrigued me (and still does) was hearing about a cousin who rushed home from the hospital where his wife had died in childbirth and smashed all their statues and images. What was going on in these fierce engagements between the grown-ups I could see and those I couldn't (or not quite in the same way)? There was something mysterious and frightening about the sacred world to me as a child, frightening because I could sense in the postures and tonalities of adults engaged with the saints secrets and stories I couldn't fully understand, like a child trying to figure out what's going on at an adult dinner party.

Peering into the adult world is hardly an innocent enterprise. This is a dangerous place, with threatening shadows, incomprehensible gestures and signs. Grown-ups do things to each other there that are fraught with implications for children's lives, as children themselves well know, so a child's curiosity is always to some greater or lesser extent defensive, depending on specific family situations. Sneaking peeks into the territory of adults, children are trying to figure out what the adults are up to and what this will mean for them; the stakes are high. They are gathering information not on the way the world *is* but on the way the world is for this group of adults (which is the only world particular children really know). And the key religious question is: what do these invisible beings contribute to the local configuration of reality? To come upon an adult in prayer is to be aware that something of extraordinary power is happening, that the world is being constructed and engaged in a compelling and authoritative way. It is also to experience oneself as excluded, awakening the desire to enter the world for oneself, to explore it, and perhaps also to master it and to make it safe.

This is how I understand the anxiety I feel in the field, the inevitable discomfort that grips me just before I sit down with someone to talk with them about their religious understandings, practices, and experiences. This is not bad faith. It is not that I anticipate debunking them, and the analogy is not of going behind the curtain like Toto in Oz to uncloak the impostor (although this is right for the modernist impulse in the discipline—see, Dorothy, it is social class pulling the levers, or the unconscious, the social or the psychological). Rather, the parallel experience is of a child glancing over his folded hands at his mother at prayer beside him or picking out her voice speaking in tongues above the din of an excited church, or watching her cry on a riverbank above a muddy baptism. Of the many feelings that characterize and shape fieldwork, mine have always included a sense of intrusion, of interrupting and prying, which seems to be built into the enterprise. I am outside the practice. I do not think we need stop here, as I will argue below, but it is useful to remember it—or to be reminded of it, as Clara so compelled me. I do not pray to Saint Jude and I had better respect this difference. And we feel uneasy about this difference because we realize, however dimly, that we are looking for something that frightens as much as it intrigues and excites us. Furthermore, the powerful feelings I had of recognizing the people I was working among—recognizing not only what they were saying but the look on their faces as well, their postures and their gestures, hearing familiar echoes in their voices and their laughter—evoked in me always a range of emotions that included contradictory impulses to protect them and to accuse them, as well as the need to be taken in and accepted by them.

The consequences of all this for our work is that unless we recognize first the elemental fascination and power of religious goings-on and then all the things we want to do with them—share them, control them, mute their power over us and over our memories—our writing about religion will become an exercise of boundary making. This is the emotional ground of the impulse toward functionalism in the field: to tame what is wild and threatening and dangerous specifically to us because of the details of our particular childhoods about different forms of religious experience and practice. This is what makes so much religious scholarship dull and beside the point. It is also the reason why scholars of religion spend so much time in making sterile taxonomies, gridding what we study into safe—and discrete—categories. These various complex anxieties, needs, and discomforts constitute the existential difficulties of fieldwork in one's own religious tradition.

I went back to my old church in the Bronx on a rainy late winter afternoon as I was finishing this chapter. This is absolutely true: wet sparrows clustered in the plaster folds of the statue of Saint Francis in front of the rectory as they had when I was little and first noticed them there, to my delight. I managed to convince the person who opened the door, who didn't know me but remembered my family, to let me wander the church by myself and I made my way behind the altar, down the long narrow corridor crowded with old Italian saints' statues that no one can identify anymore to an almost secret little side chapel to Saint Anthony. I spent a lot of time in this place when I was an altar boy in this church. The chapel then glowed smoky and dark from the scores of candles the old Italians in black clothes lit for their families and for their memories; now there are electric candles. It's a powerful experience to be able to walk around inside a space like this, to be able to touch its walls and holy images and listen to the sounds of people at prayer, to sit beside them, and to hear the noise of the street coming in through the stained glass widows donated by long-gone Italian families once prominent in the neighborhood so that the sun warms the community's memory. When I am asked, "Why do you study what you study?" what I think of is this chapel.

To study a world of meaning and practice other than one's own, as many scholars do, whether this is in another country or in another time, means making one's arduous way from an initial experience of difference that may be deeply disorienting or even alienating toward understanding. Ideally, this transformation comes about by means of a careful, thoughtful, self-reflective engagement with the ways of these other worlds and a deep and disciplined attentiveness to language, practice, history, and geography. Slowly people and practices that had seemed quite alien no longer

do. In the best outcome, difference is acknowledged, but there is also recognition on all sides of a shared human destiny across space and time. Difference is not otherness, in other words. To understand something about another time or place does not necessarily mean claiming to own this other world, to efface it by insisting that one's own representation is definitive, to speak *for* this other world (as opposed to speaking about it), to emphasize sameness, or to accept everything about this other world as good (although historians and anthropologists have done all these things). Scholarship on other worlds, other times, is always chastened by a sense of difference and exhilarated by the experience of recognition. As the exchanges multiply in the field or in our imaginative encounters with historical others, difference becomes a double lens that allows the scholar and the people he or she has gone among to see each other and themselves in new and revealing ways. (If they want to: Clara was happy enough before she met me and happy afterwards, I hope, and it would be morally and intellectually presumptuous of me to suggest that she needed to see her devotion to Saint Jude through the lens I was grinding. If she wanted to, it was there, and, as I will describe in a moment, I certainly saw things differently as a result of our conversations.)

The dilemma of fieldwork in one's own religious culture is that difference is either never clear and sharp enough or else—as my discussion of the overwrought nature of contemporary Catholic memory indicates—difference is constituted by factors outside the researcher's experience and then inherited by him or her. The fieldworker in one's own tradition faces difference that is at once both too little and too much, and this paradox can be paralyzing. The people we are talking to are simultaneously and disconcertingly both other and not, and we cannot respect and use the distance between us because we cannot establish it securely—it is forever shrinking and expanding. On the one hand, difference is undermined by memory, desire, rejection, and anger, so that we are in danger of being swamped by the undertow of the unconscious, or, on the other hand, distance is reinforced, in the case of Catholicism, by the authority of modernity and the rupture of the 1960s. There is a muddle of unacknowledged transferences—the fieldworker in one's own discipline is kind of recognizable to practitioners and kind of not, and vice versa, and so each fills in the space of who they think the other is or wants them to be or fears they are, or all of this at once. In the end either the people among whom we have gone (themselves confused by our ambivalence and ambiguity) reject us, or we come to identify with them so closely that we lose the distance necessary for understanding and wind up defending and celebrating them.

These then were the two concurrent, subterranean, and not completely discrete levels of meaning and experience, historical and psychological, that shaped both my work in the field and the attitudes of the people with whom I was talking toward me. Now I want to show how they played out in my actual experience in Chicago.

The following are some selections from my fieldwork journal, followed by brief commentary:

> *October 30, 1987.* The older woman (maybe seventy years old) sitting in front of me at the 2:00 service—the one who elbowed her husband in the ribs when the priest made the joke about retired men driving their wives crazy—handed her well-worn novena booklet to her husband to put into his pocket after the novena. People come with these booklets in their purses and pockets.
>
> *October 30, 1987.* One woman, V., refers to me as Father Orsi, even after I've told her I'm not a priest.
>
> *October 30, 1987.* After the 5:30 service, a *very* obese woman, who looked to be more than seventy years old, came over to me to tell me about a miracle Saint Jude had accomplished for her. (She smelled very bad, was wearing old, gray, stained slacks and a greasy brown quilted ski jacket.) Her sister and brother had stopped talking to each other, "wouldn't even eat at the same table," and this, she insisted several times, was "real suffering," "real trouble." She prayed to Saint Jude for them, and they started talking again, and—this is how she ended her story—"they sat down together again at the same table." She was very emotional while she was talking to me; her eyes were filled with tears, and several times she had to stop, overcome.
>
> *October 31, 1987.* At the 5:30 service this evening, a woman going down the side aisle toward Jude on her knees. Father D. is careful in his sermons to make sure that people understand that Jude points the way toward Jesus and that the important thing is not to make of this a private cult. D. also spends a great deal of time in his sermons on Central America [this was a period of great American involvement in El Salvador and Nicaragua that many Catholics in the United States found morally objectionable] and points out that this is Jesus crucified again. He says that the church, taking its stand with the "emarginated," is itself being crucified in Central and South America by the "power structure."
>
> *November 1, 1987.* I overheard the following conversation at the shrine: one woman says to another: "Have you filled out the questionnaire? [some very general questions I distributed on these evenings to the congregation, with the clergy's permission, as a way of inviting people to think about their

attachment to Jude and then either talk to me in person or on the telephone or write to me]. "Who has the time to do that?" her friend replies. "Oh, come on," says the first, "you can sit on the toilet and do one question at a time."

December 29, 1987. I am reluctant to discover that Catholics under thirty have a devotion to Saint Jude, perhaps because this would obliterate the neat periodization of Before/After the Council.

January 7, 1988. S.A. called tonight to cancel her [I crossed this out and over it wrote "our"] appointment tomorrow. "If it's not inconvenient, Professor, I'd like to know if I can cancel my appointment." What could I say? I was apprehensive about the power relationship implicit in her question. *Could* she cancel? What would she have done if I'd said, "No, S., tomorrow we must meet"? I had a feeling throughout our conversation that her husband was on the other side of the phone table. She said that her husband was home on vacation and they were wallpapering the house, "and tomorrow night I go running with the kids, and they have basketball and everything." We agreed to meet in June, when I'll be back.

January 8, 1988. 12:40 P.M. From outside, the sounds of the schoolchildren on their lunch break. A neighborhood street person circles the church, perhaps making the stations of the cross, more likely just wandering around; I'd seen him reading the paper in Sonny's this morning when I went in for breakfast.

January 8, 1988. Long and deep reflection on certain religious and existential questions can lead Jude's devout into heterodoxy. C.G. used to believe in reincarnation; less so now, she says. But this emerges out of their serious engagement with Catholic questions, and not necessarily through an encounter with other currents in American religion.

The first thing that even this brief selection of entries illustrates is how minor a part of the total religious experience words are. If American Catholic spirituality, liturgical practice, and religious aesthetics (all those banners proclaiming PAX and AGAPE in the spaces where the saints once stood) have come to be ordered around words and the safety words offer against the embarrassing spontaneity of practice, my time at the shrine pointed me away from words. Fieldwork forces an acknowledgment of and engagement with something messier than the controlled marshalling of letters on a page, something less predictable, and demands a different kind of attentiveness. The world of the text is really not the world.[17]

While the priest was speaking about the political concerns that did indeed occupy American Catholics at the time, a woman was crawling toward him down the aisle of the church. Which represents the contemporary life of this religious culture—either one, or both, or the contradiction between them? What matters—the sermon or the range of interactions and exchanges taking place among the congregation in the interval of the sermon's time? My attention was inevitably drawn away from the official words and postures occurring on the main altar and toward the secret, subtle, but persistent interpersonal connections—nudges, glances, thighs pressed against one another, hands held or withheld—going on all around me during the service. I noticed that women kept their prayer books in their purses, tucked in among their other private things. What relationship did this indicate between the shrine, with all its powers to heal and to comfort, and the intimate spaces of a woman's life? What kind of place is a pocketbook, and how is it connected to the other places—desk drawers at work, kitchen counters, bedside tables and bureaus—where Jude also resides? I became interested in the movement of prayer books from hand to hand during the service. What was a woman doing when she asked the man accompanying her to hold her prayer book? What kind of bond was she establishing, confirming, or enforcing? What places did the invisible persons—saints and absent family members—occupy among the visible ones? These are the questions of an inquisitive child, and from the perspective of the pew they seem like the right ones.

The sounds of the children that filtered into the shrine demonstrate the porousness of such spaces. Among the sounds that matter here are not only those coming from the organ, choir, and priest up front but those that penetrate from the outside, too, posing both challenges of endurance and possibilities of interpretation for believers. So too did the appearance in the sacred space of the confused street person and the drunken (a detail I omitted in my notes for some reason) and troubled woman. Any honest description of very many religious spaces in contemporary America would have to include some reference to the presence there of strange, disturbed, possibly psychotic people loudly sharing their distress with the worshippers (or else to the measures taken to keep them out). I have been saddened by such people when I have come across them and uncertain about what to do with them in my descriptions; worshippers, however familiar they are with these visitors, must learn to deal with the eruptions. What else do we routinely edit out of our representations of sacred environments (dirt, noise, children, the psychotic, animals, the smells of perfume, and so on) and what do our elisions disclose about our anxieties and the limits we want to impose on our religious materials? How are these figures to be included in understandings of sacred space?

The notes illustrate, finally, the density of the interpersonal world in which researchers in religion take their places. When women spoke to me about Jude, they necessarily had to talk about very bleak moments in their lives, and the ones who sought me out to tell me their stories (often over many hours) brought their needs and hopes to me: to be recognized, praised, respected, heeded. Listening to tales of illicit romance or of the consequences of bad choices, I knew I was being called on at least to bear witness to the lives in question, to help by understanding, to share emotions—all of what people ask of each other when they tell stories about painful experiences in their lives. While women talked about mastectomies, abandonment, domestic violence, adultery, and loneliness, I could feel myself being transposed, without any encouragement on my part, into other men in their lives, not only the protagonists of their stories but also doctors, priests, and counselors.

Working beside all field researchers are dreaded doubles, figures like Malinowski's missionaries, who are close enough in education, class, and style and in the specific nature of their concerns and interests to make them particularly vexing figures, since we need to distinguish ourselves from them in order to get work done. Their numbers in my own experience have included journalists (who often spread mistrust and suspicion), church officials, parish workers, overly zealous parishioners, and clergy. Our being confused with these other categories of persons can complicate our conversations with people, and I have always felt these proximities demanded a certain delicate diplomacy from me. As my conversation with the very nervous S.A. indicated, however, this effort to set and respect boundaries was not always successful or possible. The researcher is perceived through multiple frames and becomes the object of displaced resentments and expectations. All his or her conversations with practitioners about important things take place in this charged emotional, religious, psychological, and social setting.[18]

Clearly, a lot more goes on at a shrine (or a Pentecostal meeting, or a Baptist summertime revival, or a neopagan festival) than its sponsors, promoters, and spokespeople intend or hope, and a lot more takes place in fieldwork in religious worlds than a simple gathering of information. What happens at the ritual center represents only the smallest part of the total interaction of the event, and the explicit topics pursued by the researcher and the people with whom he or she speaks are but one dimension of their encounter. A season in the field shatters the givenness of the various borders we seem committed to maintaining in thinking about religion and repositions religious practice and experience amid other domains of human life, just as it calls into question the way we structure our research (with questionnaires and research instruments of various sorts). To paraphrase Geertz, scholars of religion do not study churches, mosques, synagogues, and so on, they study *in* these religious environments, and what we learn is about life itself in these places, not about "religion." There is always an earthier ground for what happens in a sacred space, as my notes indicate. The laughter in the old woman's eyes as she teased her husband with her sharp elbow during the novena reflected the complexities of aging, the strains of retirement, and the pleasures of a long life together. That this gesture took place in a shrine amid many other gestures, official and not, opened this space up to the rest of experience. Religion cannot be understood apart from its place in the everyday lives, preoccupations, and commonsense orientations of men and women.

Historians say that the dilemmas of ethnography are not their concern because after all the past is not a place we can visit (all such metaphors aside). But still I think what I saw at the shrine can speak the work of religious history too. The intimate gesture of the old woman toward her husband, the ravings and wanderings of the street people around the shrine, the pink flamingo glowing in the shrine's dim and holy light, the discrepancy between Father D.'s sermon and the behavior of the woman in the aisle all suggest there are aspects of people's lives and experiences within religious worlds that must be included in our vision and attended to beyond what is officially sanctioned. This is a call, then, for attention to religious messiness, to multiplicities, to seeing religious spaces as always, inevitably, and profoundly intersected by things brought into them from outside, things that bear their own histories, complexities, meanings different from those offered within the religious space. It is also a call to surrender dreams of religious order and singleness or of being able to organize descriptions and interpretations of religious worlds around sets of publicly shared and efficiently summarized meanings and practices. So much else is going on in these spaces. There are those who might want to insist that what matters about the shrine of Saint Jude is changing Catholic teaching about the saints in Europe and the United States in the middle years of the twentieth century, the history and practice of shrines, maybe the changing ethnic composition of neighborhoods—and that once you have gotten through all this, you know what you need to know about those nights in October 1989 in South Chicago. I don't think so. The joy and the revelation of fieldwork is that it opens up to us the fact that running through these realities are other more subtle and elusive possibilities just as important to the making and unmaking of religious worlds. Where is the action at a Pentecostal meeting? In the looks exchanged between siblings as they watch their mother or father fall out or hear their grandmother tongue-speaking, in small gestures of love and fear among people, in the pathways of memory opened by the smell of sweat and perfume, the cadences of the preacher's voice, the sound of the lawnmower in the house next door to the church, and so on.

This means that religious cultures are local and to study religion is to study local worlds. There is no such thing as a "Methodist" or a "Southern Baptist" who can be neatly summarized by an account of the denomination's history or theology. There are Methodists in Tennessee in the

1930s struggling with particular realities of work and home, politics and gender, with children leaving, old people dying, work closing, and so on. There are Southern Baptists in Virginia suburbs in the 1970s, with certain political affiliations, racial attitudes, fear and hopes about work and family. Uncovering the realities that course through a religious world, in other words, demands historical and cultural analysis that goes well beyond the "religious," which is why "religious history" strictly speaking does not exist. What exists are histories of people working on their worlds in specific ways at specific times and places.

The study of religions in this way is the description and examination of the varied media in which men, women, and children who were formed by inherited, found, made, and improvised religious idioms within particular historical, cultural, and political contexts engage shared human dilemmas and situations. These ways of taking hold of the world—prayer, acts of the imagination, visions, petitions to the spirits, theologies of grief and suffering—evolved over time and carry deep within them the marks of this development, the impress of old conflicts, circumstances, and strategies—as we saw with my uncle's participation in devotional life, my grandmother's prayers to Saint Gemma, the diverse encounters of men and women with the Blessed Mother in different times and places. Inherited religious idioms—a theology of pain, for example, or the saying of the rosary—represent diverse ways of being in the world that are, moreover, not always at home in the present. They reach back into the past, although they are always made in the present, and as the world that comes is engaged by people in religious practice, reality itself is in play and the outcomes are not predictable. Crafted and recrafted by many hands, in many different places, and in contradictory circumstances, religious media constitute the way that living people experience and construe events in their social world (war, economic distress, the organization and experience of work, to cite three examples) and perennial human problems (always encountered within specific historical frames, although never completely and securely so).

Such religious patternings of feeling, imagining, and thinking do not remain constant over the long duration. As they are taken up in people's efforts to deal with the challenges of their experience, they are subtly altered, just as the people and their worlds are changed by their use of religious media. People are free to the extent that they may make something of what has been made of them, according to Sartre, and one of the ways that religious men and women have exercised this freedom is by improvising with the inherited idioms of their traditions—with idioms that constrain them as they enable them to live and change at the same time.[19] Religions provide men and women with existential vocabularies with which they may construe fundamental matters, such as the meaning and the boundaries of the self (what may be expected in relation to oneself, for instance), the sources of joy, the borders of acceptable reality, the nature of human destiny, and the meaning of the various stages of their lives. It is through these various religious idioms that the necessary material realities of existence—pain, death, hunger, sexuality—are experienced, transformed, and endured, for better or worse. Religious idioms are neither sufficient nor discrete. They interact with other competing, alternative, or complementary configurations of experience that are available outside the religious world. Growing up in a particular religious context at a particular moment in its history—and it is the work of research in religion to delineate these moments with precision—is to be provided with what Geertz calls a "sentimental education," an orientation in ways of feeling and patterns of thought.[20]

Religious cultures function as one of the primary mediators between historical circumstance and individual experience and response. Religions have provided Americans in the turbulent and distressing circumstances of life in this society over time—its high geographic mobility, periodic economic fluctuations and consequent unemployment and financial vulnerability, fierce competition among groups for work, and attendant domestic and psychological distress—with a repertoire of feelings and orientations with which to take hold of their world as it takes hold of them. Anthropologist Michael Jackson writes that "our concept of culture must . . . be made to include those moments in social life when the customary, given, habitual, and normal is disrupted, flouted, suspended, and negated, when crises transform the world from an apparently fixed and finished set of rules into a repertoire of possibilities, when a person stands out against the world and, to borrow Marx's vivid image, forces the frozen circumstances to dance by singing to them their own melody." In American history and experience, many of the dance tunes have been limned by religions.[21]

It has become axiomatic in the last several decades that understanding human cultures requires a different kind of inquiry than that which characterizes the natural sciences. Psychologist Stanley Leavy's comment about psychological understanding seems broadly applicable to the study of the worlds humans make and inhabit: "Meaning, and the interpretive process through which meaning is disclosed, exists in dialogue." Understanding emerges out of conversation and though the processes of interaction. It was not there at the beginning, waiting to be discovered. Research in this way parallels the work of culture itself: as Peter Berger has written, the world hangs on a thin thread of conversation, on the rounds of intersubjective engagement that make and sustain any social world. To interpret a culture means to join this conversation, alongside and together with the people already engaged in it. As they interpret and reinterpret their worlds, we do too. Leavy says, "When we interpret personal meaning, we must ask one another, for this kind of meaning exists between us." The nature of what is learned through this kind of research will be different too. "A person differs from any other 'object' in that it is a person alone whom I address as 'you,' " to quote Leavy a last time. "As soon as I recognize that, I can see that my explanations with regard to persons must be fundamentally different from any other explanation."[22]

A note of caution is in order before I proceed to the closing intersubjective part of this chapter. Anthropologists Jean and John Comaroff warn against what they call "ontologies that give precedence to individuals over contexts." They point out that embedded in the personalist or intersubjective orientation (of the sort I am about to embark on) is a set of fundamental political, moral, and epistemological assumptions about the world that are distinctly modern and Western, including "that human beings can triumph over their contexts through sheer force of will, that economy, culture, and society are the aggregate product of individual action and intention." The bearer of this ontology has long been (since Geertz's 1973 essay on culture that had a vast impact in religious studies) *the meaning-making subject*. Once this figure has made his or her way to the center of cultural analysis, "culture becomes the stuff of intersubjective fabrication . . . and ethnography becomes 'dialogical,' not in Bakhtin's thoroughly socialized sense, but in the narrower sense of a dyadic, decontextualized exchange between anthropologist and informant."[23]

In the first part of this book, especially in chapters 1 and 4, I suggested replacing the meaning-making subject with a more tragic figure whose engagements with the world, within particular circumstances of power, proceed through media that may embody meanings against him or her. Persons working on the world do so always in the context of the world's working on them. This leads to a more chastened view of culture generally and of religion in particular, one that steers clear of words like *empowerment, agency* (simply), and *transcendence* and instead moves in the register of the tragic, of the limited and constrained, or what I would think of as the real. This is not to endorse hopelessness or political or religious apathy. To be able to construe the gestures of others, the Comaroffs continue, "we have to situate them within the systems of signs and relations, of power and meaning, that animate them." And in this context, "ethnography . . . is an exercise in dialectics rather than dialogics, although the latter is always part of the former. In addition to talk, it entails observation of activity and interaction both formal and diffuse, of modes of control and constraint, of silence as well as assertion and defiance." To approach religion in the way I have proposed in this book is to enter into the dialectic of the possible and the impossible, to acknowledge limits, to recognize the tragedy of meaning.[24]

Religious studies as a discipline in the United States has not done well with the analysis of religious idioms as constraint and discipline, a subject I will address in the next chapter. There has long been a tendency (again to be elaborated) to divide religions up into good ones, in which the self finds the resources to live a purposeful life in an orderly social world to the making of which the good religion has contributed, and bad ones, which deprive the individual of will and autonomy and self-control either by the imposition of authority or by excessive emotional stimulation. But religious imaginings and practices do not grid quite as neatly on the pragmatic axis so beloved to Americans. The very same religious idioms do tremendous violence in society and culture and bring pain to individuals and families all the while that they ground and shape the self, structure kinship bonds, serve as sources for alternate imaginings of the social world, and so on. So before I foreground the notion of intersubjectivity in the study of religion it might be useful to underscore what I have been saying all along in this book: religions arise from and refer back to discrete social and cultural worlds and they are inevitably shaped by the structures and limits of these worlds as they engage them. This is the dialectic of religion, which takes place within and in complex relationship with the dialectics of culture. The intersubjectivity I am about to propose is one that very much operates with a clear and chastening awareness of these dialectics.

Now back to Clara. On what grounds would she and I meet? What does it mean for me to come into her religious life with my concerns and perspectives and questions, and how do I respond to her questions back to me? What kind of dialogue could we have about Saint Jude? Did I really need to pray to him in order to understand Clara's relationship with him—is this what it means to have meaning and understanding develop in between Clara and myself?

About two and a half years after my initial conversation with Clara at Saint Jude's shrine, I found myself in circumstances that were hopeless in the way I think Saint Jude's devout mean this term. One terrible evening as I was agonizing over my situation I recalled Clara's challenge.

"What would it be like," I asked myself, "to pray to Saint Jude now?"

I used to have a big statue of the saint in my study. (Just after I published my book on devotion to Saint Jude my mother asked me if I would give this statue to a young woman she knew in the Bronx who had been raped and badly beaten, as a way of offering her hope and encouragement, and I did; whether I wanted to or not, I kept getting drawn into this devotion that I had set out to "study.") It would have been a simple thing to look into the saint's eyes, as his devout do, and plead with him. But I just could not do it. I had to respect my own intellectual and spiritual culture as much as I did Clara's. So I shifted the ground of the experiment and instead of actually praying to Saint Jude I tried to find some analogue to this act in my own emotional and behavioral repertoire on the basis of what I already knew of the nature of women's prayers.

Women who call on Saint Jude in these circumstances tell him what they want. They make their desires explicit, naming what they see as the best possible outcome of their hopeless dilemma. Strictly speaking, their prayers are petitions. So I did this, although I did not direct my petitionary "prayer" to Saint Jude (I might have called a friend but could not). In this way I learned my first real lesson about the devotion: it is tremendously difficult to put one's desires and hopes into simple words, even to oneself, when realistically one knows, as the devout claim they do, that there is no earthly chance that these will be realized. This is what I most want to happen now! It is easier for the purposes of endurance and survival to hunker down and accept the situation without the unsettling distraction of hope.

But I did it (to the extent that I understood what I really wanted or that what I allowed myself consciously to want was really in fact what I wanted—levels of ambiguity and ambivalence that are shared by Jude's devout). This taught me the second lesson: It is a tremendous relief to admit to oneself clearly and as honestly as one can just what one would like to have happen. Once I had spoken aloud in the empty room what I wanted, I found I had opened up the closed space of my despair a tiny crack. It was as though this other possibility now had a more substantial presence just for having been spoken and acknowledged. I could reimagine the world and my situation in ways I couldn't just moments before. At the very least it made clear to me what I had been denying or repressing.

Now I was at the edge of hope (another lesson: the process of hoping has many stages). Would I take the next step, as Jude's devout do, and actually surrender myself not simply to the hope that I would get this one thing that I acknowledged wanting but to whatever would happen, which they express by adding to their prayers the proviso that they were prepared to accept Jude's decision for them whatever this may be? Could I go through with this difficult movement from despair to acknowledgment to resignation and hope?

By using my own experience as a way of probing Clara's suggestion, I was slowly working my way not into the devotion itself (which was im-

possible for me) but into the experience of vulnerability, risk, and acceptance that serves as the ground of the devotion. "Experience in this sense,"
Jackson writes, "becomes a mode of experimentation, of testing and exploring the ways in which our experiences conjoin or connect us with
others, rather than the ways they set us apart." I had to involve my life
in the process of reflection; I could not withhold myself. I was learning,
as Clara had suggested, by entering into my own distress, by bringing my
own struggles into play.[25]

It was a night of rich (and distracting, to my great relief) discoveries. I
learned the particular courage of Jude's devout by observing in myself the
enormous strength of will it takes simultaneously to risk hoping while
conceding that I had come to the end of my own powers in the situation.
I am not saying that I found this strength, only that I glimpsed the kind
of courage the work of hoping took. (This in contrast with the usual
perspective on religious pleading in desperate times that sees it as weak,
self-interested, and cowardly.) Most of all, as the possibility of hoping
and the realization that I might have to accept whatever happened both
grew stronger, I felt a subtle shift in my experience of the world, a slight
realignment, a change in atmospherics, and this helped me understand
the feeling that women describe after praying to Saint Jude or helped me
think about it better.

I intended to study Catholic ways of understanding and responding to
psychological and physical suffering. In the process, under the prodding
of the people I was working with, I was forced to admit the ways they
and I differed from each other, religiously among other ways. But coming
around in a circle again, what I learned as I tried to take Clara's challenge
seriously is that we were alike nonetheless in our need, vulnerability,
and risk. This was, to paraphrase philosopher Paul Ricoeur, a second
solidarity: the recognition after the necessary discipline of distanciation
of a shared human fate. I had gone from otherness to a new more open
place of otherness/not-otherness, different from the one I started from,
an appreciation of shared experience on a level other than that of specific
religious practice or belief. To reach this, however, I had to respect the
integrity of my own convictions and to be straightforward about the real
difference between Clara's experience and understanding and my own.
Difference remained important, not only for the way I did my work—I
did not want to write a confessional account of prayers to Saint Jude—
and for the quality of my understanding, but for relationships in the field
as well. I wanted these to be genuine, and for this, difference had to be
acknowledged; when it was appropriate, differences between myself and
my conversation partners could be discussed and explored together. I

l not pretend to pray to Saint Jude; I was not identifying with Clara
ırticipating in her religious practice. I respected the disciplinary and
personal necessity of what Gananath Obeyesekere calls a "disengaged
identity" or "distanciation" as necessary to the "capacity to imaginatively and empathically project oneself into an alien life world."[26]
"Participation," Obeyesekere goes on to say, "is participation in dialogue, not identification with the other culture." Clara and I together
had identified the ground of our dialogue or conversation. To understand, one does not have to share it, to believe what practitioners believe
and do what they do, only to acknowledge a common human project,
within the framework of different histories and different ways of being
in the world. Then fieldwork becomes not a matter of taking notes but
of comparing them.[27]

That I ever thought I could engage other people's responses to pain and
suffering without putting my own on the line became a great source of
embarrassment to me, but I believed that this was what was required by
the discipline. I held on to this mistaken sense of disciplinary propriety
even though I already knew that Clara was not as different from me as
my colleague suggested. But I felt I had to occlude myself in order to
properly examine her experience. Now I know that the best moments of
our conversations were precisely these recognitions of shared fears and
hopes and our acknowledgment of the different idioms we relied on to
experience and endure them. Furthermore, what I was doing on that bad
night—testing, exploring, pushing at the edges of my anxiety and sorrow
with whatever came to hand (including Clara's challenge itself, which
offered me another medium for engaging my situation)—is not different
from what Jude's devout have always done when they call on him in
similar situations. They have also been improvising with the materials at
hand, not always certain what the outcome of their experiment would be.
The devout say that they turned to Jude when all else had failed, to see if
this would work instead. So the kind of research I am proposing here—a
tentative, interpersonal examination of particular religious idioms within
a carefully described social field that includes both the researcher and the
persons he or she talks with, in which the conversations they have are
both what is being studied and how it is being studied—resembles the
nature of many kinds of praying and religious acting too. The end of both
prayer and research is not simply there at the start of the process but
comes into being through the process. "Research is a relationship" between human beings, Sartre wrote, "and the relationship itself must be
interpreted as a moment of this history." Things happen in the course of
conversation. Emotions are generated, fantasies provoked; we find in the
other things we need or want as they find such things in us, as both of us

create and recreate each other, and this complex process must be monitored and studied.[28]

Religious fieldworkers face a double challenge, then. The people they talk to ask them to share in some way in their religious worlds—this is one of the facts of ethnographic research in religion in relentlessly and ubiquitously evangelical America: you will be asked if you are born again, if you want to lead a prayer, if you want to be prayed over—and the people they talk to back in the academy will want all this translated into familiar, comfortable, and safe academic language. The space between these challenges is rich terrain; this is the ground of religious studies. Moving around in this space may require that we try some methodological experiments (I tried a couple in the first part of this book). We may want to include the voices of our sources more clearly—and disruptively—in our texts, inviting them to challenge and question our interpretations of them, to propose their own alternative narratives, to question our idioms from the perspective of their own, and in general to break into the authority of our understandings and interpretations and to reveal their tentative character. We might want to examine openly and critically the emotional and intellectual sources of our own implications in the practices and beliefs we study. We could take as one of our subjects the ways in which we, as scholars of religion, and they, as practitioners of religion, respectively make things of the other in our initial encounters, critically examining the fantasized versions of each other that parade across the space between us, and we can be clear about the changing nature of this engagement over time.

This is not an argument for "subjective" research. I have stressed the necessary disciplines of fieldwork, the need for scrupulous and careful attention to the practices encountered in their social field, the necessary historical framing, the resolute difference of our sources and their autonomy, as well as the importance both of respecting one's own culture and of being attentive to the conscious and unconscious motivations for our work and the directions of our inquiries. It is not sufficient to append an autobiographical prologue or epilogue to the old studies. We need to rethink the nature of cultural research itself, and of research in religion. The point of all these experiments and all this critical attention to the unfolding relations in the field is to clarify and to understand particular religious ways of living and thinking and of our scholarship in relation to them.

Of all the dichotomies we use to structure our work in religion, says the great theorist of religion Jonathan Z. Smith—popular/official, heresy/orthodoxy, good/bad—the most fundamental is us/them.[29] At the very least the discipline would benefit from a season of experimenting with ways of rethinking this great boundary that has been so long and so carefully enforced. Fieldwork in religion provides a rich opportunity to conduct this sort of boundary-crossing experiment. The outcome of this experiment would not necessarily be the dismantling of this border, but even rendering it problematic would be something. Our work as scholars of religion could then become as porous as the life of the shrine, a site of many voices talking on top of each other and against each other, a place of unexpected intrusions and uncertain borders, built in the middle of and from the same stuff as what Sartre calls the "equivocal givens of experience."

Chapter Six

SNAKES ALIVE: RELIGIOUS STUDIES BETWEEN
HEAVEN AND EARTH

> He was just a man, just like everybody else, but in my
> opinion, he was a man that loved everybody. And he taught
> his children to love God and their neighbors, no matter what
> color people were, no matter where they come from, if they
> was rich or they were poor. He was a man on a mission from
> Jesus Christ, and sometimes we didn't agree on things,
> spiritual things and Biblical things, but it never put any ill
> feelings between us. He made his mistakes along the way, but
> he never tried to hide his mistakes.
> *Cameron Short describing his friend Punkin' Brown,*
> *in Fred Brown and Jeanne McDonald*, The Serpent Handlers:
> Three Families and Their Faith

> Religion is strange business. You shouldn't expect to
> figure these things out.
> *Jonathan Rosen*, Eve's Apple

AT THE END of an account of his two-year sojourn among snake handling Christians in southern Appalachia, Dennis Covington, who at the time was a Georgia-based reporter for the *New York Times*, describes the night he realized that he could not join the snake handlers whom he had come to love and respect in their faith. I want to borrow this instance of one man's discovery of radical religious otherness—a discovery that led him to turn away in sorrow and disappointment from his friends—as an opening onto the question of how critical scholarship in religion is not only possible but compelling, exciting, and revealing, especially given the challenges—moral, political, and epistemological—that have so profoundly shaken scholarship in the humanities in the last quarter century.

We scholars of religion go among people in other times or in other places who are working on their worlds with (among other things) religious tools they have found, made, or inherited, in relationships with each other and with gods, spirits, ancestors, and other significant beings. Mostly we do not share these ways of living and imagining, or do not

quite share them, or even if we do share them or once did, we train ourselves to approach them now in another spirit and with different questions. Yet we want to understand these persons in their worlds in order
to discover something about human life and culture, about religion and
about ourselves; we would not be doing this work unless we believed that
we would learn something essential about questions and problems that
press themselves upon us with great urgency. How is any of this possible?
How is it possible given legitimate concerns about the political implications of studying other cultures, our disturbing awareness of the limits of
Western rationalities for understanding (let alone assessing) other ways
of construing the world, or simply given the formidable linguistic, historical, and existential difficulties of making one's way into a religious world
that one does not share?

Critical scholarship on something called "religion" (as opposed either
to theological reflection within a religious tradition or polemical commentary on religions, one's own or someone else's) first appeared in the early
modern era in the West amid the ruins of the religious wars between Protestants and Catholics and just when Europeans were encountering the
ancient religious cultures of Asia, Africa, and the Americas. The study of
religion then developed through the ages of European colonialism and
industrialism. Discourse about "religion" and "religions," in which the
dilemmas, judgments, hatreds, and longings of modern Christian history
were inevitably if unconsciously embedded—nineteenth- and early-twentieth-century scholarship on "Hindu" ritual, for instance, echoed with
anti-Catholic contempt for corporal religious idioms and revealed less
about religious practices in south Asia than about internecine European
hatreds—became one medium for construing the peoples dominated by
European nations, at home (in factories, on slave plantations, in urban
working-class enclaves) and abroad. Discourse about "religions" and "religion" was key to controlling and dominating these populations, just
as religious practice and imagination were central to the way that the
dominated themselves submitted to, contested, resisted, and reimagined
their circumstances. So the history of the study of religion is also always
a political history, just as the political and intellectual history of modernity is also always a religious history. The epistemologies, methods, and
nomenclature of scholarship in religion are all implicated in this history.[1]

Within this political and historical frame, the academic study of religion
has been organized around a distinct and identifiable set of moral judgments and values that are most often implicit and commonly evident more
in convention and scholarly ethos than in precept. Theorizing about "religion" has proceeded in accordance with these embedded moral assumptions even as religious studies has increasingly claimed and vehemently
insisted on its "scientific" status in the secular university. The usually

unacknowledged imperative of these values in the working life of the discipline has limited the range of human practices, needs, and responses that count as "religion." It is true that over the past twenty years in response to criticism from various quarters the discipline has intermittently made room for less socially tolerable forms of religious behavior within the scope of its inquiries. But the social and intellectual pressures against this are great and the odd inclusion of a anxiety-provoking ritual or vision has not fundamentally changed the meaning of "religion" in "religious studies." It is understandably preferable to write and think about people and movements that inspire us rather than those that repel us, that make us anxious, that violate cherished social mores, and that we want to see disappear. However understandable this may be, though, the question is how this hidden moral structure limits the study of religion.

Scholars of religion, moreover, are often requested by journalists, lawmakers, and fellow citizens to map the complex and frequently troubling landscape of contemporary religious practice and imagination in a way that makes normative distinctions among religious behaviors and that reassures people that despite the wildly profligate and varied nature of religions on the world stage today, only some are really religions, while other apparently religious expressions—such as the fury unleashed against the World Trade Center in 2001 in the name of Islam—represent perversions or distortions of "true" religion. A lot of public talk about "religion" in the media works to stir up terrible but also thrilling anxiety, which is not surprising in a country enthralled and titillated by movies and stories of gothic horrors, imaginative creations that rose up from the bloody soil of the violence between Protestants and Catholics in the founding age of American culture. These frissons of titillating anxiety in the media call forth the need—and create the occasion—for expressions of reassurance and authority.[2]

People want to be reassured that the men who flew their planes into the World Trade Center on September 11, 2001, were not representatives of "real" or "good" Islam, or that the Christians gunning down abortion doctors do not reveal anything about contemporary American Christianity, or that priests abusing the children in their care cannot have anything to do with Catholicism. Such concerns are understandable, and there are important distinctions to be made in all these cases. Islam is a rich and complicated religious culture now and in the past; in the fall of 2001 and since, many Americans were appropriately concerned that Muslim fellow citizens and visitors not be persecuted by baseless identification with the acts of terrorists. Evangelical Christians span the political spectrum and most of them abhor the vigilantism of the very radical religious Right. Some of the commentary on the clerical abuse scandal in the media and in the courts does draw on deep anti-Catholic roots to malign a faith because of the actions of a few. How can we scholars of religion face the world today or our students, who are so troubled by that world, and not make such moral distinctions?

I am not here to argue for relativism, for scholarship that ignores or denies its perspectives or politics, or least of all for learning that does not address the haunting and urgent questions of our times, nor am I suggesting that "Islam," "evangelical Christianity," or "Catholicism" are each respectively one unified coherent entity. But the tools that scholars of religion use to make moral distinctions among different religious expressions were crafted over time in the charged political and intellectual circumstances within which the modern study of religion came to be, and before introducing or reintroducing moral questions into our approach to other people's religious worlds, before we draw the lines between the pathological and the healthy, the bad and the good, we need to excavate our hidden moral and political history. Otherwise, the distinctions that we make will merely be the reiteration of unacknowledged assumptions, prejudices, and implications in power.

Dennis Covington first entered the culture of snake handlers on assignment from the *Times* to cover the trial of a minister accused of attempting to kill his wife by forcing her hand into a box of poisonous snakes.[3] Drawn by a religious idiom that fused domains that others considered irreconcilable—heaven and earth, spirit and snake, above and below, vulnerability and control—and that generated experiences of tremendous visceral power, Covington stayed on. He came to see snake handling as a way for poor, displaced people in a ravaged land to contend with and to surmount, at least once and a while, with the snakes in their hands, the violence and danger that bore down on them in their everyday lives. Covington vividly describes local life and religious practice, and he does not stay aloof from the people he writes about (although some scholars working in the same area and many of the people with whom Covington spoke about their practices later challenged his descriptions and interpretations). He smells the "sweet savor" of the Holy Spirit moving in the room when the snakes are taken out of their boxes—a smell like "warm bread and apples" discernible just beneath the reptile fug—and finally he takes up serpents too. Until the last night of the time he spent with the snake handlers, Covington offers a worthy model for an engaged, interpersonal, participatory religious study.

But on this last evening, at the Church of the Lord Jesus Christ in Kingston, Georgia, Covington is appalled when his photographer, a young woman well known by then to the handlers, is verbally assaulted—by a minister Covington had considered his spiritual father—for what this minister and others in the congregation saw as her usurpation of the place assigned to men in church by Holy Scripture. Covington rises to witness against this denial of spiritual equality to women, but his mentor silences him. Then another preacher, the legendary figure Punkin' Brown, who was known among other things for wiping his sweat away with rattlesnakes bunched in his hand like a handkerchief, reached into the serpent box, pulled out a "big yellow-phase timber rattler, which he slung across his shoulders like a rope." As he does so, Punkin' Brown makes a sound that Covington records as "haaagh," an explosive, angry grunt, and as he bears down into his nasty, woman-hating sermon, the preacher uses this sound to set the cadence of his attack and to underscore his rage. Covington makes sure we hear this. "Haaagh" appears ten times on a single page—and it is thus—"haaagh!"—that he reestablishes the border between himself and the handlers that he had up until then so courageously been tearing down.

Covington signals and solidifies his new position vis-à-vis the handlers with a change in rhetoric. Before this evening in Kingston he had seen an eerie, otherworldly beauty in the moans and movements of the handlers. His descriptions of women taking up serpents, sobbing and trembling as they drew bundles of snakes close to themselves in religious "ecstasy," in particular are charged with a fierce (and unacknowledged) erotic intensity. But now he gives us Punkin' Brown, a vile, primitive force, "strutting" about the sanctuary with the big snake across his shoulders, his body contorted, his face flushed with blood and hate. The evangelist brushes his lips with the serpent and wipes his face with it and always there is the brutal "haaagh!" like "steam escaping from an *underground vent*" (I have added this emphasis). Punkin' Brown has become a nightmare figure, a subterranean creature, a snake himself.[4]

Covington believes that he was saved at the last minute from descending into such strangeness himself. He tells us he was all set to give up his work at the newspaper, stock his car trunk with snakes, and head out across the land as an itinerant, snake-handling evangelist. But the "haaagh!" brought him to his senses and restored his world to him. This appears to be the existential impulse behind the abrupt change in voice—to shield himself from otherness and to impose closure on a two-year experience that threatened in the end to penetrate the boundaries of his own subjectivity. The description of Punkin' Brown—or rather, the construction of "Punkin' Brown" not the man but the character in this drama of Covington's imagination—is a barrier enacted in the language of the text against the compulsive attraction of otherness. "Punkin' Brown" makes the world safe again for Covington and his readers. Protected now against this alien—who would ever confuse the author or oneself with this wild creature, one's own fantasies, needs, and hopes with his?—Covington can find Punkin' Brown ridiculous, "grotesque and funny looking, with his shirttail out and a big rattlesnake draped over his shoulder." His description of "Punkin' Brown" is humiliating. The work of rendering Punkin' Brown into "Punkin' Brown" first secures the identity of the observer as safely separate from the other and then establishes the observer's superiority.[5]

Before moving on I want to say something about what I just called the compulsive attraction of otherness—not of difference that can be bridged but otherness that cannot and that offers only the alternatives of surrender or repulsion. Punkin' Brown died some years ago in church with a snake in his hands (his friends maintain it was not the bite that killed him but a heart weakened by the venom of many prior snakebites). Brown appears to have been a compelling man. But the wider reality here is that Americans have long been deeply fascinated by such powerfully complex religious figures, who blur gender or racial categories, for example, or do forbidden and dangerous things with their bodies or with others' bodies. Brown and his fellow snake-handling Christians were the subject of several television show and documentaries, of many research projects, and tourists came from around the county to watch them in action. Brown believed that it was God present before him that caused him to pick up snakes at meetings; he embodied, in other words, the enduring power of sacred presence in the modern world and in modern persons' imaginations and memories, from which presence is disallowed. Americans want to be protected from these religious actors, but at the same time they want access to some of their power, an unstable mix of desire and prohibition.

Having turned Punkin' Brown into a snake, Covington makes another move. At stake that night in Georgia, he maintains on the closing page of the book (so that the handlers will not have the opportunity to say anything further for themselves), was not simply the role of women in the church. Nor was it the rightness of taking up serpents, even though this is how Punkin' Brown understood the conflict. If the Bible is wrong about women, the preacher believed, then it is wrong about the Christian's invulnerability from poisonous snakes too, so that we who take up such serpents will die, and so will our beloved family members. ("This wasn't a *test* of faith," a Tennessee minister commented on Punkin' Brown's death, "this *is* our faith.") Rather, according to Covington, at issue that night in Georgia was "the nature of God." Punkin' Brown's God, Covington reassures himself and his readers, is not, cannot be, my, our God. This is the final, and most damning, step in the rendering of Punkin' Brown as radical other: he has been cast out of the shared domain of the sacred.[6]

What has happened here? How could a writer who managed to bring the alien world of snake handlers so close end by repositioning them at the margins of culture? Covington has inscribed an existential circle, taking a long detour to reestablish the prejudices against snake handlers many readers started out with, alongside whatever fascination drew them to the work as well. I want to explore how this happens, how the religious figure that confounds and challenges us with his or her difference is silenced and securely relegated to otherness, and then I want to propose another way of approaching religions.

It seems to be virtually impossible to study religion without attempting to distinguish between its good and bad expressions, without working to establish both a normative hierarchy of religious idioms (ascending from negative to positive, "primitive" to high, local to universal, infantile to mature, among other value-laden dichotomies familiar to the field) and a methodological justification for it. These resilient impulses take on special significance in light of the well-known inability of the field to agree on what religion is: we may not know what religion is but at least we can say with certainty what bad religion is or what religion surely is not. The mother of all religious dichotomies—us/them—has regularly been constituted as a moral distinction—good/bad religion.[7]
   One of the main sources or contexts for the development of this moralizing imperative in the study of religion had to do with the way that the nascent discipline of religious studies was situated in American higher education as this was taking modern shape in the late nineteenth and twentieth centuries. The academic study of religion in the United States developed within a university culture struggling with the conflicting claims of Christian authority (widely accepted in the culture) and secular learning. Christians did not speak with a single voice in the United States and so whatever compromises were sought in response to this intellectual and cultural tension had to be acceptable within the broader social context of American denominational and theological diversity, to Calvinists, Arminianists, Quakers, Spiritualists, Christian Scientists, and so on. The solution to the dilemma from the early Republic until the years after the Second World War, according to a distinguished historian of religion in American higher education, was "morally uplifting undergraduate teaching," on the one hand, and voluntary, extracurricular religious activities on the margins of academic life, on the other, in order to satisfy the concerns of Christians inside and outside the academy. Morally uplifting undergraduate teaching: *ethics* came to stand for Christianity in American university culture but ethics defined in a broad, universal, nondogmatic, nonsectarian, and nondenominational way designed to appeal to a broad clientele. A modern and liberal creed, what the historian just cited acidly

but justly calls "pious nonsectarianism," became the official religious culture of the American academy.[8]

This was a pragmatic position too: the challenge of the educational marketplace in which colleges and universities competed was to attract students from many different denominations because not even church-affiliated schools could survive on enrollments from a single church. But the emphasis on moral learning of a sort that all Protestant Americans could have access to as the crown of their education was also congruent with the understanding among American educators of the role of the academy in the turbulent and pluralist democracy the United States was proving itself to be. The rationale for building colleges in the early Republic was explicitly understood as civilizing the population, taming it and creating out of its diversity a common culture of shared values and behaviors. This aspiration persisted down to the Progressives and John Dewey at the start of the twentieth century and it remains alive among educational theorists today and among defenders of religious studies departments in secular settings. "Civilized" has always included in American nomenclature particular forms of acceptable religious belief, practice, and emotion. What counted as civilized religion has varied somewhat over time, in different regions of the country, and according to changing economic fates associated with practitioners of particular religious ways, but not that much. The nation with the soul of a counting house would make its universities into Sunday schools of moral and social values and of appropriate and tolerable Christianity.[9]

This ethos further coincided with broader trends in the reorientation of academic culture in the nineteenth century, in particular the insistence on critical research as the mainstay of learning, the professionalization of the professoriate, and the secularization of methodology. Already in the early Republic, academic leaders influenced by Scottish Common Sense philosophy asserted that science, morality, and "true religion" were all allied. American evangelicals, whose own religion did not resemble this, went along with the notion of a broad intellectual alliance between tradition and modern learning secure in their own cultural authority. This would change later, particularly as the social and natural sciences came to pose an increasingly serious threat to Christians, subjecting the Bible and Christian history to the requirements and procedures of critical scholarship.

Many of the progressive social scientists at the turn of the twentieth century who played important roles in shaping the contemporary university world in the United States were children of orthodox Christian households. They rejected the faith of their families in favor of a scientific approach to social and psychological knowledge that was nevertheless deeply and passionately informed by Protestant values. These intellectuals and scholars replicated in their careers the development of the American academy from Protestantism to secular science. But while liberal religious concerns informed the scholarship and pedagogy of this group of explicitly post-Christian Christian academics, those concerns had no effect on the commitment among these men and women to the university as a place of secular, critical, scientific learning. "After a century of resistance from more traditional Christians," writes historian George Marsden, "the dominant educational ideals were defined by a synthesis of Enlightenment ideals and an enlightened Christianity, or religion of humanity." Outside the gates of the academy, meanwhile, increasingly alienated fundamentalist Christians waged a campaign to restore what they understood to be the primary purpose of education at all levels—"to learn the wisdom of the elders" in Marsden's formulation of their position—in direct opposition to modernists who "gave their ultimate intellectual allegiance to the scientific method as the essence of true education." A liberal and enlightened civic Protestantism became the essential buffer within the academy against the ever more intransient fundamentalists outside it.[10]

It was in this intellectual environment that the academic study of religion first appeared in the United States. Certain key issues had already been settled in the wider academic culture, such as the authority of the scientific method and the primacy of critical research. The new discipline would have to meet these standards and comport itself by these rules if it wanted to be a player in the modern academy. Moreover, the distinction between a "Christianity" amenable to the aims of modern learning and "sectarianism" hostile to them had by now been embedded in academic culture in its confrontation with fundamentalism. The entire curriculum was understood by liberal Christian educational leaders to be morally uplifting, oriented to the shaping of human spiritual and moral development. Students would emerge from the American university knowledgeable in the sciences and morally formed as virtuous persons and good citizens.

The impact of these converging forces on critical scholarship in religion can be seen in University of Chicago founder William Rainey Harper's rationale for including the study of religion in the curriculum of a major research university. According to Marsden,

> Harper shared with many of his contemporaries enthusiasm about the powers of "scientific study" to settle longstanding human debates in all areas. He accordingly justified the inclusion of the Bible and other distinctly religious subjects in the broadening university curriculum on the grounds that they could now be studied scientifically. There were "laws of religious life" just as there were laws of health and physical life. Yet "men and women of the highest intelligence in matters of life and thought are discovered to be cultivating a religious life far below the plane of their intellectual life." Advances in the

scientific study of religion, not only in biblical studies, but notably also in the
psychology of religion, now made possible a scientific approach to this part
of life as much as any other.

The true religion long established within American academic culture—
what another historian calls a domesticated Christianity tailored "for use
in public life"—now became the "religion" studied in the academy.[11]

It was inconceivable that "religion" would be anything but good religion in this social and intellectual setting, "good" meaning acceptable
in belief and practice to this domesticated modern civic Protestantism.
Proponents of the academic study of religion claimed a place in university
culture by asserting that the study of "religion"—meaning the denomina-
tionally neutral version of Christianity recast as an ethical system—was
good and even necessary for American democracy. Outside the walls of
the academy, the winds of religious "madness" howled (in the view of
those inside)—fire-baptized people, ghost dancers, frenzied preachers and
gullible masses, Mormons and Roman Catholics. "Religion" as it took
shape in the academy was explicitly imagined in relation to these others
and as a prophylactic against them.

Fear was central to the academic installation of religious studies. Religious difference overlapped with ethnic and racial otherness, and this
combination produced and fed upon the pervasive and characteristically
American idea that dangers to the Republic were germinating in the religious practices of dark-skinned or alien peoples congregated in areas beyond the oversight of the Christian middle class. Religious paranoia has
been as deep in the American grain as political paranoia, deeper even
because it came first; religious paranoia always shadows times of political
fear. Early American scholars of religion, searching diligently for scientific
laws of religious behavior, explicitly committed themselves to the project
of social order. "I have undertaken not simply to discriminate spurious
and genuine revivals," sociologist of religion Frederick Davenport told
readers of his highly influential survey of the contemporary religious landscape in the United States in 1905, "but to show that in genuine revivals
themselves there are primitive traits which need elimination or modifica-
tion in the interest of religious and social progress."[12]

"Primitive" is an important word here. One way that Davenport and
other scholars of religion contributed to social order was by constructing
and authorizing scales of religious practice and imagination that went
from "primitive" to modern—where modern or mature meant the domesticated Protestantism tolerable within the academy—and mandating
movement up the developmental ladder as prerequisite for modern life.
(Such culturally obtuse schemas attained substantial psychological authority later in the century in models of religious "faith development.")

American psychologists of religion created categories and terms to pathologize unacceptable forms of religious behavior and emotion—a scientific nomenclature of containment—and countered bad religious expressions with a normative account that designated as "religion" that component of human personality that moved it toward emotional, spiritual, and existential maturity, unity, success, and happiness. Sociologists of religion correlated unacceptable religious behaviors with certain environments and "types" of people—immigrants, migrants, African Americans, women, children, poor rural folk. "Religion," on the other hand, was socially integrative. These sociologists emphasized "religion's" role as the pivot of social stability and solidarity and relegated to categories other than "religion" any phenomenon that did not serve this consensual function. Normative terms were presented as analytical categories, and their implicit moral and cultural assumptions went unchallenged. Such was the authority of "real" or "good" or "true" religion in the academy.

All this had dreadful social consequences when it converged with broader racist discourse in the world outside the academy. It contributed to destructive federal policies toward Native Americans. Northerners who wanted to temporize about (or even to justify) the grim realities of lynching used sociological accounts of African American popular religious culture, defined in racist terms, as mitigating explanation. Teaching domesticated Protestantism as "religion" would protect American democracy and inoculate the young against the contagion of American religious imaginings, which scholarship would contain and enclose by nomenclature and analysis. No wonder religious practitioners often do not recognize what passes for "religion" in religious studies.

The point here is not simply that the normative account of real religion that took shape within the academy or at the anxious intersection of the academy with the extravagance of American religious life excluded from the study of religion ugly, violent, or troublesome matters (although it certainly does this). Rather the entire notion of "religion" had been carefully demarcated to preserve it from ambivalence and ambiguity, from anything not in accordance with certain sanctioned notions of self and society. Religion came to be gridded along a graph of diametric opposites, and the possibility that religion can transgress these various dualities, that it does its cultural, psychological, and political work precisely by disregarding boundaries between one self and another, or between past, present, and future, or between the natural and the supernatural, is disallowed.

So what is real religion?

There is a nomenclature problem here. As I have noted, the distinction between "religion" and "spirituality" is an important one in contemporary American popular culture. *Religion* in this context—"I'm spiritual but not religious," as even the most religious Americans characterize themselves today—is a bad word. On the other hand, I cannot really call the kind of religious practice and posture that has normative status in this culture "spirituality," a relatively recent term, because it carries too many connotations of its own. So I will retain the word *religion* but qualify it as "good religion" or "true religion." Readers can transpose "true religion" to "spirituality" if they wish, on the understanding that "spirituality" is a term crafted in this culture to designate the opposite of "bad religion." It is a disciplinary word, built out of and for exclusion.

True religion, then, is epistemologically and ethically singular. It is rational, respectful of persons, noncoercive, mature, nonanthropomorphic in its higher forms, mystical (as opposed to ritualistic), unmediated and agreeable to democracy (no hierarchy in gilded robes and fancy hats), monotheistic (no angels, saints, demons, ancestors), emotionally controlled, a reality of mind and spirit not body and matter. It is concerned with ideal essences not actual things, and especially not about presences in things. Students of mine over the past twenty years in classrooms in New York City, Indiana, and Massachusetts have unfailingly refused to acknowledge as "religious" the practice of putting holy water into an automobile's transmission (as pilgrims to a Bronx Lourdes shrine commonly do). Whatever this is, it is not "good religion." All the complex dynamism of religion is thus stripped away, its boundary-blurring and border-crossing propensities eliminated. Not surprisingly, there is only one methodology and one epistemology for studying this "religion," critical, analytical, and "objective" (as opposed to "subjective," existentially engaged, or participatory).

In this way the discipline reflects the religious politics of the United States as well as the particular history of American higher education. The embedded, hidden others against whom the "religion" in religious studies is constituted are the religions on the American landscape that appeared so terrifying and un-American to the guardians of the culture—Mormonism, Catholicism, certain forms of radical Christian evangelicalism, Pentecostalism, among others. The discipline was literally constructed by means of the exclusion—in fact and in theory—of these other ways of living between heaven and earth, which were relegated to the world of sects, cults, fundamentalisms, popular piety, ritualism, magic, primitive religion, millennialism, anything but "religion."

The academic study of religion is not an American phenomenon, of course. American academics who study religion participate in an international network of scholars institutionalized in various sorts of academic arrangements, scholarly exchanges, and symposia. But in this broader context, too, liberal notions of religion allied to particular political agendas came to be authoritative. Scholars shaped in liberal Christian traditions played important roles in the formative period of the modern development of the discipline in Europe and in Asia; a vision of "religion" that developed out of liberal and modernist Christianity acquired a normative status in the work of nineteenth- and twentieth-century scholars of comparative religion. Nineteenth-century scholars of south Asian religions, for example, "invented what might be called a Euro-Buddhist canon," according to anthropologist H. L. Seneviratne, "by portraying a rationalized and sanitized Buddhism in keeping with the imperatives of the sociology of their own intellectual life."[13]

Indeed, this Christianity was seen as the telos of the evolution of world religions. At the World Parliament of Religions in Chicago in 1893 an authoritative and hypostasized "Christianity"—identified by its superior moral teachings—was compared with other essentialized religious entities—("Islam," "Buddhism," and so on)—to create a class of "world religions" identified by enlightened liberal and rational characteristics and to set Christianity up as the highest realization of global religious culture. The Columbian exposition performed this distinction spatially, by putting the world religions into massive buildings and everyone else on the Midway. While representatives of the former traded pieties, a carnival atmosphere took hold of the latter space, where religions marked as other were depicted in mock demonstrations of cannibalism and human sacrifice. As the colonial period came to a close, scholars proposed a broadly inclusive, universal religion of man as the goal of both the study and the practice of religions, aspiring to gather the world's many different traditions into a single, global narrative of the progressive revelation of the Christian God.[14]

Given the commitment within modern scholarship on religion to the evolutionary model—from primitive to modern, infantile to mature, religions—many practitioners insisted that the academic study of religion itself make a positive contribution to human culture and to the betterment of life on earth, to facilitate relations across cultures and to deepen human tolerance. This seemed particularly imperative after the Second World War, when many figures in the discipline held that academic study of religions had a role to play in the reconstruction of Western culture devastated by war and totalitarianism. A hard-core group, comprised mainly of European scholars, held to an "empiricist" vision of the field and insisted that the renewed emphasis on the moral responsibility of professors of religious studies represented the intrusion of theology and normative ethics into the discipline, but their voices were overwhelmed by the ameliorative imperative. Both in content and method the academic study of religion has been preoccupied with the study and defense of "good" religion for a long time.[15]

By the time I arrived as an undergraduate at a small New England college with an excellent religion department this combination of a liberal Protestant understanding of what religion is and a sense of the moral responsibility of the field had become institutionalized in the curriculum and heightened by the increasingly urgent debate over the war in Southeast Asia. Religion departments around the country, with some exceptions, taught Christian and Jewish scriptures, theology or the philosophy of religion, Christian and philosophical ethics, and some religious history; the dominant ethos was Protestant; other religions when they were taught at all were taught precisely as such—as *other* religions (this usually included Catholicism and Judaism). What was meant and valued by "religion," in other words, was exactly the domesticated liberal Protestantism that had been pressed deep into religious scholarship at the turn of the century. ("Christianity" remains the default religion in the discipline of religious studies today despite the enormous development of scholarship on Asian religions in the last three decades. *Scriptures*, for instance, unless otherwise specified refers to the texts important to Christians.) My professors were all educated at Union Theological Seminary in New York, where they learned theology from Paul Tillich and ethics from Reinhold Niebuhr, the two figures whom I thus came to see as the alpha and the omega of the study of religion (an unusual conclusion for an Italian American Catholic from the Bronx but not one that seemed odd at the time).

Eric J. Sharpe, a historian of the study of religion, points out that "scholars trained in one or other liberal religious tradition [came] to occupy a prominent position in the newer religious studies enterprise since the early 1970s," a reflection of broader cultural trends in the 1960s. The discipline is far more varied and complex today, but it is still oriented, as Sam Gill, a prominent scholar of Native American religions has lamented, toward "the broadly held essentialist view of religion—that is, that religion is 'the sacred' or 'ultimate concern' and that attributes of the 'sacred' and 'ultimate concern' are goodness, purity, and unity." To study religion from this approach, Gill writes, "means to discern and appreciate these desireable qualities in any culture." Departments of religious studies are really thus departments of the study of desirable religions. The enduring confusion today between the fact of the "plurality" of different religions in the United States and in the world (an empirical observation) and the notion of "pluralism" (a theological position that encourages the search for common ground that different religions may share or on which they might meet) is an example of how the normative vision of a certain kind of modern liberal Protestantism was embedded in the analytical tools of religious studies and represents itself as theory.[16]

The work of the discipline in constituting itself this way has had grave social consequences beyond the academy. By inscribing a boundary between good and bad religions at the very foundation of the field, religious studies enacts an important cultural discipline. There is no end to human religious creativity (a comment that has nothing to do with whether this is a positive thing or not). One would have to look to the staggering varieties and complexities of what humans have made of sexuality to find another site of such explosive and inventive activity. Yet is has been the impulse of religious studies since its inception to impose closure and discipline on religion, to control and contain this complexity. When the Branch Davidian compound was incinerated at Waco, Texas, in April 1993, much was made of the failure of the government and of federal law enforcement officials to recognize the religious character of leader David Koresh's movement. It was not as widely noted that the government's failure paralleled the limitations of religious studies, which has long offered an authoritative map of religious experience that excluded such a "marginal" group.

Any approach to religion that foregrounds ethical issues as these are now embedded in the discipline obstructs our understanding of religious idioms because religion at its root has nothing to do with morality. Religion does not make the world better to live in (although some forms of religious practice might); religion does not necessarily conform to the creedal formulations and doctrinal limits developed by cultured and circumspect theologians, church leaders, or ethicists; religion does not unambiguously orient people toward social justice. Particular religious idioms can do all of these things. The religiously motivated civil rights movement is a good example of a social impulse rooted in an evangelical faith and dedicated to a more decent life for men and women. But however much we may love this movement and however much we may prefer to teach it (as opposed to the "cultic" faith of Jonestown or the "magical" beliefs of "popular" religion) this is not the paradigm for religion, nor is it the expression of religion at some idealized best. There is a quality to the religious imagination that blurs distinctions, obliterates boundaries—especially the boundaries we have so long and so carefully erected within the discipline—and this can, and often does, contribute to social and domestic violence, not peace. Religion is often enough cruel and dangerous, and the same impulses that result in a special kind of compassion also lead to destruction, often among the same people at the same time. Theories of religion have largely served as a protection against such truths about religion.

It is the challenge of the discipline of religious studies not to stop at the border of human practices done in the name of the gods that we scholars find disturbing, dangerous, or even morally repugnant, but rather to enter into the otherness of religious practices in search of an understanding of their human ground. Practitioners must find a way of honoring their own moral and political values while not masking the common humanity that both researcher and religious adept share—share with a man Punkin' Brown, for instance, who was, after all, as his friend pointed out, "just a man." The point of engaging other religious worlds should not be to reassure ourselves and our readers that we are not them, that Punkin' Brown and I belong to different species.

But in attempting such a morally and existentially demanding engagement with the men and women they study, practitioners of religious studies will run into a problem. Although the discipline authorizes an implicit account, freighted with moral value, of what religion is, religious studies in its quest for academic legitimacy has also explicitly insisted that scholars adhere to canons of critical and analytical scholarship as defined by the secular academy. Scholars of religion must maintain a remove that is understood to be the necessary precondition for analysis and interpretation. (This is why there is such trepidation in the discipline about studying one's own tradition.) Scholars of religion are trained to keep their lives out of their research; not to do so exposes them to charges of subjectivism, of writing autobiographically (which is a critical comment!), journalistically, or theologically.

Religious studies acquired its contemporary shape in the American academy after the Second World War in explicit distinction from—and rejection of—seminaries and schools of theology. The severity of the injunction against theology, and more broadly against the moral and religious presence of the scholar in the conduct or presentation of his or her research (other than to articulate the discipline's domesticated Protestant moral assumptions), reflects this origin. Theology is the reflection upon the thought and practice of a religious tradition by its adherents; religious studies is an outsider's discipline by definition, aspiring to critical knowledge through a strategy of distance. But of course this paradigm is under attack now, from several different quarters.

Among the most severe contemporary critics of religious studies are evangelical Christian academics of various denominational affiliations who have felt that the hegemony of the liberal definition of religion and the dominance of liberal approaches to research have precluded their own full participation in the discipline or in the wider university culture. Evangelical perspectives have survived in the liberal university, according to these critics, only to the extent that evangelicalism denies its own distinctiveness, severs its connections to the believing community, and becomes a branch of cultural studies. Could a Christian biologist, grounded in a particular faith community and certain of the truth of Scripture, conduct her research according to her faith? Would such an alternative be allowed in the academy, which is otherwise so open by its own account of itself to the perspectives of the marginalized, oppressed, and voiceless? The liberal secular university, in the view of these evangelical critics, is the site of manifold prohibitions masquerading as permissions. Liberal piety opens the space for anything to be studied critically as long as the critical perspective brought into play is not religiously particular, and thus theology, which is always particularist, has been exiled by academic liberalism.

Religious studies is an egregious expression of this prohibitive environment since it sets out to study matters of greatest concern to others from a nonconfessional point of view—ostensibly demanding, indeed, the suppression of the researcher's own values in the process. Could a Christian scholar of religion frame her classes by what she understood to be the authoritative witness of her church? But how does one assess one's understandings of Christian history or doctrine apart from the guidance of tradition as articulated in a believing community? Some have even seen religious studies as corrosive of religious practice generally on college campuses: writing as an evangelical and neoconservative critic of the discipline, D.G. Hart notes that "religious studies reflects the very same intolerance of religious points of view or normative religious judgments that characterizes the university's culture of disbelief," with the result that "the academic study of religion is a failure when it comes to making the university a more hospitable place for religion."[17]

Christian theologian Stanley Hauerwas has also written harshly of departments of religious studies as being "comprised of people who are willing to study a religion on the condition that it is either dead or that they can teach it in such a way as to kill it. The last thing they would want to acknowledge is that they might actually practice what they teach, because such an acknowledgement might suggest that they are less than objective." Religious studies departments might introduce students to Thomas Aquinas or Karl Barth, but these programs would never hire such intellectually rigorous but religiously committed thinkers for their own faculties. The discipline is literally founded on the distortion of its very subject, by this account, or worse yet on an act of academic—and personal—bad faith. It demands the intellectual and religious deformation of scholars who believe as the condition for admission to the guild. For God's sake, Hart concludes his critique of religious studies, do away with it: "by excluding religion as a field of academic study, the university may be paying religion great respect."[18]

These Christian critics now sense that the moment is right for a challenge: insurgent groups of younger conservative Christian scholars, many of them trained and credentialed in departments of religious studies at secular universities, have set out to undermine the authority of older, modernist, liberal scholars and perspectives in biblical studies, philosophy of religion, theology, and even religious history. The notion of a critical and unaffiliated study of religion has come to seem almost fusty to some, a vestige of modernist confidence long ago chastened by postmodernism, and indeed, ironically, or perversely (depending on one's politics), the Christian critique of the liberal, secular university echoes themes of radical critics of modernity. Scholar of education Warren A. Nord, for instance, has suggested that what multiculturalism means is that education "should give voice to various subcultures—religious subcultures included—which currently have little say in the world of intellectual and educational elites." George Marsden argues in a polemical "Concluding Unscientific Postscript" to his history of the secularization of learning in American higher education that "the widespread current critiques of scientific objectivity provide a context for reconsidering the near exclusion of religious perspectives from the academic life of American universities of Protestant heritage." Once one admits that "everyone's intellectual inquiry takes place in a framework of communities that shape prior commitments," there is little reason for excluding explicitly religious claims from the teaching and research that take place in the academy. Confessional pedagogy slips its nose into the academic tent through the opening created by postmodernism.[19]

An alternative account of contemporary university culture maintains that it is Christianity in any form, modern or postmodern, that stands as an obstacle for intellectual work, generally and particularly in the study of religion. Marsden claims that contemporary university culture is anti-Christian, and surely anyone who has spent any time in this world must agree that there is a measure of truth in this charge. Some of this is simply prejudice; some of it is a reaction against the long Christian domination of thinking about other religions in the world; some of it is a way for university intellectuals to draw an unmistakable boundary for themselves—and for their students—between the culture of learning they value and a surrounding society that can be anti-intellectual on explicitly Christian grounds. (I certainly came to understand that providing my students with an environment in which they were free to think critically about religion came as a necessary antidote to their teenage religious environments in which such open inquiry was not welcome. It would have been dreadful for these students to have come into a religious studies classroom only to discover the same constraints on their thinking they were encountering in their churches.)

But for some the critique of Christianity is linked with a broader political and epistemological agenda and is meant to challenge the hegemony of Western ways of knowing and living. Articulated by scholars who have worked in cultures that endured the burden of Christian authority under colonial regimes, this perspective on Christianity is politically charged. Christianity is understood to have been indispensable to Western imperialism, providing its cultural legitimacy, moral confidence, and epistemological grounding while spiritually underwriting the military and economic campaigns of the Western powers. Intellectuals, including scholars of religion, crafted the philosophical framework that constituted native populations as empty of culture and therefore not only open to but actually requiring Western conquest and domination for their own good. Representations of native cultures as either primitive, proto-Christian, or crypto-Christian were the intellectuals' contribution to imperialism.

The postcolonial world since the 1950s has exposed the cruelty of Western intellectual authority, unmasking practices of domination and exploitation enclosed within the culture of enlightened reason and liberal tolerance. Intellectuals in Asia, Africa, and South America have challenged the canons of Western culture. The task for American university intellectuals now, some say, is to rethink American culture from the perspective of the once-dominated other and from alternative and once-oppressed vantage points, a process of defamiliarizing and decentering as the first step to reinterpretation. Globalism as an economic, demographic, and political reality demands an intellectual reorientation, a reimagining of the place of the United States in world culture. Western styles of knowledge, which typically give priority to detachment over engagement, textuality over vocality, mind over body, are to be exposed to radically different ways of understanding and inhabiting reality.

In the context of this broader criticism of Western knowing and given the history of religious studies' implication in Western power at home and abroad, the challenge now, say scholars of religion working from this political vantage point, is to become radically aware of the discipline's implicit Western and Christian biases, of the hidden, normative Christianity within the basic methodologies and philosophical orientations of religious studies, and to expunge them. Just as postcolonial intellectual culture calls into question central tenets of Western thought, so a new kind of moral inquiry must be open to construals of the "ethical" that are profoundly at variance with Christian ideals and formulations.

One example of what this sort of ethical inquiry would look like is Karen McCarthy Brown's now-classic discussion of Haitian vodou morality in *Mama Lola: A Vodou Priestess in Brooklyn*. Unlike the radical distinction made within Christianity between absolute good and absolute evil, a boundary authorized and presided over by a singular deity and an authoritative clergy equipped with the varied tools of moral discipline, Brown maintains that vodou asserts multiplicity, diversity, and contradiction. Vodou notions of subjectivity understand the self to be multifarious, the site of conflicting energies, capacities, and possibilities without the Christian insistence on consistency in self-presentation. "A moral person, in Vodou," writes Brown, is one who lives "in tune with his or her character, a character defined by the spirits said to love that person." Such moral "flexibility," she adds, "is provided in the midst of moral dilemmas by the support these favorite spirits offer to different and sometimes contradictory values."[20]

Vodou locates fault not inside persons (which by rendering them evil exposes them to harsh moral proselytism if not persecution or destruction for their own good) but in relationships between persons in the social field. As a healing medium, vodou seeks to dissolve whatever is holding people in hostile and antagonistic relations. It may be quite extreme in this work of unblocking, heating up the contradictions, conflicts, and inconsistencies within a person or in the social setting—disorientingly, shockingly at times—in order to create a liberating and revealing excitement. In Brown's account, vodou is the paradigmatic idiom by which a poor, politically oppressed, economically marginalized people live their lives with grace, dignity, and compassion in the spaces between the absolutes composed by intellectuals of more politically powerful and materially comfortable regimes.

Brown and other scholars who have spent personally and intellectually formative years in other cultures call us to juxtapose the language of American reality with the reality of those other worlds. They propose to bring the religious, and moral vision of the colonized into creative tension with the moral sensibility and religious idioms of the colonizer. The goal is a creole scholarship that draws from the epistemological, aesthetic, religious and moral idioms of different cultures to decenter and rethink the idioms of the West. Christianity itself—as well as the normative, dualistic, crypto-Christian categories of religious studies—looks very different when viewed from Mama Lola's living room in Brooklyn or her ancestral home in Haiti.

It may appear that there is little common ground between the evangelical and the postcolonial critiques of the liberal paradigm for studying religion, but surprisingly and perhaps ironically there are significant convergences. Proponents of both perspectives propose that the universalistic ambitions of Western enlightened rationality give way to local orientations: there is no essential, singular truth, only situated truths. Both understand the scholar herself to be situated at a particular cultural location that fundamentally shapes her vision, and both place passion and commitment at the center of research methodology and pedagogy. Stanley Hauerwas has said that the confessional teacher "witnesses" in the classroom, makes his or her faith present and invites students into a dialogue about it, holds it up as a lens for examining and challenging the dominant arrangements of culture. Critical anthropologists also propose a radical critique of Western culture as an appropriate classroom stance. They draw on the experiences of people in distant places, and especially their often-disastrous encounters with Christianity, to frame students' examinations of Western religions and their assessments of the claims of Western reason. Conversion—to Christianity or to other religions—is not necessarily the explicit goal of either evangelical or postcolonial pedagogies, but there is a heightened existential edge to this kind of teaching as compared with the older critical liberal model, so that students may find themselves attracted to the religious worlds represented in both of these classrooms. The evangelical and the political critiques challenge the authority of liberal Protestantism in the discipline of religious studies and demand that scholars in the field transgress, in method and in the subjects they choose, the authoritative boundaries of religious studies.

I find both critiques compelling and welcome the challenge each represents to the way we have gone about the study of religion in the United States. But I am not sure that either one ultimately avoids the pitfall to which Covington succumbed in reestablishing his barrier against Punkin' Brown. Evangelical and postcolonial scholars themselves rely on the constitution of others in doing their work—the Christian other, in the case of postcolonial critics (for whom non-Western religions are valued in part as expressions of not-Christianity, a perspective that often informs how these religions are described and interpreted), and for evangelicals, either the liberal, secular other or, just as likely, ways of being Christian other than those espoused by evangelicals. The postmodern Christian scholar in the postliberal university would presumably assess Punkin' Brown's Christianity from the perspective of a distinct set of Christian beliefs and perspectives, much as Covington himself did in his own criticism of the snake handler. (Covington's argument at the end is a liberal Christian theological one about God and human equality.) Encountering such a figure would be a ripe moment for normative theological engagement and criticism, the explication of the scholar's own faith through a dialectical interplay between his or her religious world and the religious world of the other. Covington secured the boundary between himself and Punkin' Brown by evoking God as his witness, explicitly placing himself in a debate within the Christian community over the "nature of God," in his words, and the role of women in the church and society. The confessional professor too might witness to her own faith by affirming that in her reading of Scripture, God sanctions the participation of women in religious life. She might say that the God of the handlers is not the God of the New Testament, as indeed Covington did say. How much closer does this get us to understanding the world of the snake handlers, which is the goal of scholarship in religion?

I find it even harder to imagine what postcolonial professors might make of Punkin' Brown given the resolutely anti-Christian animus of so many of them. His rage against women and his apparent determination to dominate them (religiously and probably otherwise too—although this is not the picture that emerges in other studies of the man) disclose what many consider to be the inherent social aggressiveness of Christianity. A cultural critic might help us understand Punkin' Brown's impulse to dominate in global and domestic perspectives. He or she might shift the focus of analysis away from the nature of God to the sorts of social conditions that shaped Punkin' Brown. But the internal power of the man's religious imagination, his relationship with Jesus crucified, and his deep desire to experience the real power and presence of the Spirit with the life-threatening snake in his hands—Brown's passionate love of God in the snakes—might be missed by observers tone-deaf to matters of faith and religious practice, especially to Christian faith and practice.

Punkin' Brown and others like him are just too valuable precisely *as others*, as the unassimilable and intolerable, to be easily surrendered. So long as the point of religious scholarship, even implicitly or unconsciously, is to seal the borders of our own worlds of meaning and morals, whatever these might be—liberal or conservative, Christian or not—against such others, it will be impossible to relinquish the "Punkin' Browns" constituted in the field or in the archives. The challenge facing the discipline today, however, is not to find new others, as both the evangelical and postcolonial approaches do, but to get beyond "otherizing" as its basic move.

There is another alternative to the liberal paradigm that guards more assiduously against the moralistic impulse to construct figures of otherness. This alternative—which I think of as a third way, between confessional or theological scholarship, on the one hand, and radically secular scholarship on the other—is characterized by a disciplined suspension of the impulse to locate the other (with all her or his discrepant moralities, ways of knowing, and religious impulses) securely in relation to one's own cosmos. It has no need to fortify the self in relation to the other; indeed, it is willing to make one's own self-conceptions vulnerable to the radically destabilizing possibilities of a genuine encounter with an unfamiliar way of life. This is an in-between orientation, located at the intersection of self and other, at the boundary between one's own moral universe and the moral world of the other. And it entails disciplining one's mind and heart to stay in this in-between place, in a posture of disciplined attentiveness, especially to difference.

This in-between ground upon which a researcher in this third way stands belongs neither to herself nor to the other but has come into being between them, precisely because of the meeting of the two. This is ground that would not have existed apart from the relationship between researcher and her subject. (Covington forgets that Punkin' Brown was responding to *him* that night; the preacher would not have given that sermon had Covington and his friends not entered his world in the way they did. Covington represents his own presence as a provocation that revealed the real nature of the snake handlers, the depths of their faith, but what it revealed was the snake handlers in relation to Covington.) On this ground, not owned by either party, each person experiences the taken-for-granted world as vulnerable, decontextualized, realigned. Ideally, after such an exchange, neither party is the same as when the exchange opened (which is exactly the problem with the evangelical and postcolonial approaches and with Covington: they wind up just where they started). Scholarship in the third way is transformative. Such a movement onto the ground in-between universes of meaning would not permit the kind of closure Covington imposes on Punkin' Brown and his world. It requires that the scholar of religion abandon the security offered by the discipline, by its implicit and explicit moral certainty as this is embedded in its theoretical apparatuses, and to proceed instead by risk, suspension, and engagement.

To illustrate what I have in mind here, I want to take an example, David Haberman's study of the Ban-Yatra pilgrimage in ancient and contemporary northern India, *Journey through the Twelve Forests: An Encounter with Krishna*.[21] Like Covington's, this is an intensely personal narrative. It recounts Haberman's deep existential involvement with the Hindu pilgrims he journeys with through Braj, as the pilgrimage area is called. Haberman never forgets who he is, and he is always mindful of the history of Western relations with India and of the implications of Western religious and philosophical preoccupations in mapping the landscape of "Hinduism." A sophisticated theorist of postcolonial culture, he is aware that as a contemporary student of Hinduism he steps into and attempts to challenge a tradition of interpretation with its roots in the period of empire. A scholar of the third way remains resolutely aware of the history of religious scholarship in his or her area, conscious that the analytical terminology he or she works with (whatever it is) is formed and marked by this history.

Braj is dotted with sites central to narratives about Krishna—the grove he frolicked in with his consort, Radha, for example, and the prison cell where he was born. Believers claim that Braj *is* in some sense the body of the god: the landscape is so intimately connected to Krishna that it is he.

The god's body is thus uniquely present to the pilgrims during their arduous journey through Braj. This trope of physical presence becomes a central device of Haberman's work. Early in the journey Haberman begins to develop awful blisters on his tender feet, and for the rest of the pilgrimage he must contend with terrible pain and rely on the assistance of fellow pilgrims. Just as the god's body is overpresent in Braj, so is the ethnographer's in his experience and account of the pilgrimage, which as a result becomes a journey through the possibilities and limitations of corporality. On the levels of religious understanding and existential experience, pain is the pathway for Haberman into the intersection between worlds, the suspensive space where a new kind of understanding of other religions is possible.

Haberman could see that many of his fellow pilgrims were also in pain. But this did not prevent them from taking a deep sensual pleasure at sites commemorating Krishna's own pleasures, an incongruity that Haberman found confusing at first. How could these weary bodies stumbling into the groves of Krishna's delight experience joy and pleasure, and how could the anthropologist with his inflamed foot? But as he entered into this apparent disjuncture of pain and pleasure, deprivation and sensuality, distress and celebration, Haberman comes to see it as the dynamic of the pilgrimage. His confusion, disorientation, and pain become means of comprehension (as Clara could have told him). Haberman shows us what Covington might have done differently, at greater personal risk to himself and cultural disorientation to his readers, that night in Georgia. Covington might have used the distress and even revulsion occasioned in him by Punkin' Brown's performance as such a pivot of reflection. By suspending the need to guard himself against whatever fears and revelations Brown's performance evoked, Covington could have been led to discover the common source of both the violence and the beauty of this startling religious idiom. He might have reflected on the roots of Brown's anger; he might have explored the intersection between desire and rage as these swirled around each other in the snake handlers' world, or looked at the convergence of love and pain in the handlers' experience or on the intersection of the sacred and the obscene, and come to grips with his own attraction to snake handling. Instead, he turns away, and asserts a principled commitment to the spiritual equality of women. This commitment may be laudable in itself, but Covington does not see how invoking it where and when he does amounts to a refusal to engage his subject.

The key moment in Haberman's account for my purposes—his version of the Punkin' Brown encounter—comes when he finds himself standing on bleeding feet in a place called Charan Pahari, the "Mountain of the Foot," where Krishna is said to have left a footprint in a white stone that had been softened by his music. The stone is lovingly, regularly bathed by the god's devout with water and smeared with red powder. Haberman's account of his visit to this spot begins with an acknowledgment of otherness. There is a quality to the site that causes him to step out of his role as pilgrim and to admit his place—and confusion—as observer: "Such claims [as that Krishna had stepped on this stone] are naturally met with some doubt on the part of the outsider." He moves still further out in the second half of this sentence: "especially considering the economic benefits gained by the attendants busily collecting money from the pilgrims." A moral distance has opened between him and the caretakers of the shrine. This is the "haaagh" experience: suspicion, detachment, and doubt overwhelm compassion, attention, and understanding.[22]

Haberman might have turned away at this moment in disgust at the venality of the shrine keepers and the gullibility of the devout, as other visitors to India have done. There are indeed good reasons to be suspicious of what goes on at a shrine, in India and elsewhere. Shrine priests do not scruple to take advantage of people in considerable emotional need and religious excitement. Moreover, as countless Western critics have pointed out whenever they have encountered such human practices, the money spent on feeding, dressing, and adoring the gods in this way might better be spent on people's health, clothing, or education. Religious discomfort in this way is transmuted into moral criticism through a posture of pragmatic superiority. Liberal scholars of religion have been as bemused by immigrant Catholics' devotion to the saints as by Hindus in this regard. So this could have been the boundary of Haberman's journey, the point at which he stopped at otherness and confirmed it, and many readers would have understood and even shared his moral concerns.

But he turns back to the experience of the people he is observing and forces himself—and his readers—to recognize that there are many worlds, many different ways of making and inhabiting reality. He writes, "upon observing several women bow down and touch their heads to this stone, come up with tears streaming down their faces, and hug each other crying, 'O Sister, O, Sister!' I began to think that questions [about the venality of the shrine keepers or the ontological reality of the stone's imprint] . . . were inappropriate." Since "reality is not set for human beings [and] multiple realities or worlds of meaning are available to us," moral judgment is rendered problematic. "Judgments of realities are difficult," Haberman continues, although not impossible or unnecessary, "because there is nowhere to stand that is not situated in a particular reality, which by its very nature regards other realities with suspicion."[23] The challenge then becomes to set one's own world, one's own particular reality, now understood as one world among many possible other worlds, in relation to this other reality and to learn how to view the two in relation to each other, moving back and forth between two alternative ways of organizing and experiencing reality. The point is not to make the other world radically and irrevocably other, but to render one's own world other to oneself as prelude to a new understanding of the two worlds in relationship to one another.

Ironically, it is Haberman's constant awareness of his difference that permits him to enter so deeply into the intersection of the two worlds; indeed, there would be no intersection without awareness of difference, no in-betweenness. Covington portrayed himself initially as having passed over entirely to the culture of snake handling, but that apparent immersion ends up telling us less about either his own or Punkin' Brown's world than Haberman's intersectional strategy tells us about Braj. This is where the pleasure, excitement, and risk of religious studies are, its delights as well as its dangers. The space is dangerous because one cannot, after all, simply abandon one's deepest values or tolerate the intolerable, even though something awful and intolerable might make sense in someone else's world. It is delightful because, by staying in the place in between—indeed, prolonging one's stay there by refusing initial opportunities for closure—one comes to know something about the other and about oneself through relationship with the other. Haberman identifies this as an erotic methodology, borrowing from French psychoanalytic theorist Jacques Lacan an understanding of desire as that which arises from lack and rejects closure. The erotic orientation to another's religion resists ending the tension provoked by the unexpected proximity of two diverse worlds. It is this delight in difference that sets religious studies apart from the more conventional orientations of liberal academics, evangelical theologians, and postcolonial critics alike.

Besides imagining himself as a snake-handling minister, there is one other way that Covington attempts to bring the world of the other closer, to himself and to his readers: through an appreciation of the physical beauty of Christian women with snakes in their hands. He invites us to gaze on these women holding snakes and find their spiritual passion beautiful. (This is good spiritual passion, Punkin' Brown's is bad spiritual passion, and Covington knows his readers will know the difference.) His account of Aline McGlockin in particular, the wife of one of Covington's closest friends in the community, emphasizes her haunting, lovely appearance in spiritual ecstasy; and, again, there is a sound. Covington records that Aline cries "akiii, akiii, akiii," as she experiences the spirit's presence, and he finds this unnerving and sexually interesting.

Covington offers us two sounds—"haaagh" and "akiii"—and two choices, the ethical and the aesthetic, one approach through judgment, the other through beauty. Haberman offers a third way, neither ethical nor aesthetic. He calls it erotic. Because I live so far from the delights of Krishna's groves, I will call it instead suspensive. Religious studies is not a moralizing discipline; it exists in the suspension of the ethical, and it steadfastly refuses either to deny or to redeem the other. It is a moral discipline in its commitment to examining the variety of human experience and to making contact across boundaries—cultural, psychological, spiritual, existential. It is a moral discipline in its cultivation of a disciplined attentiveness to the many different ways men, women, and children have lived with the gods and to the things, terrible and good, violent and peaceful, they have done with the gods to themselves and to others.

The classroom is where many of us perform a significant portion of our daily intellectual work; it is where we invite others to join us in our questions. Our students come to us from many different worlds, bearing many different histories. This was true even in the Bible Belt, where I taught for more than a decade: the world's cultures are well represented in midwestern classrooms. Furthermore, "Christian" students bring complex Christianities into the classroom. Many of them—and here I can say *especially* in the Bible Belt—have had truly ruinous experiences in their churches and Christian homes. They are already quite familiar with the power of Christian faith to scar them and, if they have been fortunate, with its powers of liberation and salvation. These students from Bible-reading homes are often sick of witnesses and revivals, of experiencing the "truth" as a prescription about the doable, thinkable, or possible. In response, some have put together intricate Christian understandings that draw on neo-paganism, snippets of Asian religions, popular psychology, and contemporary science fiction. Others simply will have nothing more to do with religion, finding their way instead to religious studies classrooms in hopes of securing the tools to help them reflect critically on their experiences. "Christianity," when it is used in the authoritative singular, as if it had secure, discernible boundaries, makes sense only as a symbol for political or cultural mobilization and the domination of others. The social reality of our classrooms, as of American culture, is that there are many, many Christianities.

Students in this polytheistic world are not well served by a professor's witnessing to a singular truth, nor will they be inevitably awakened by denunciations of their Christianities by postcolonial critics. Nor will students be helped by normative accounts of religion that neglect or exclude all the humiliating, destructive, beautiful, mysterious, and terrifying dimensions of it that they know from their own experience. It is difficult to see these "Christian" students as agents of Western hegemony, since like Punkin' Brown their families have so often been on the receiving end of cultural domination; postcolonial cultural criticism becomes another form of imperial witnessing when it is conducted without a vivid sense of the worlds Americans come from and the varieties of Christianity they have known. Religious witnessing in any case will always fail in the university, where the expectation is appropriately for discussion, critical analysis, and open exchanges (an ideal often enough abandoned but no less desirable or admirable for that). Moral inquiry without communication and conversation is nothing but a covert compulsion.

There is no distinct moment of moral inquiry that comes before and exists separately from the communication of one's moral reflections to others. Discernment does not precede discussion; talking does not represent the outcome of moral analysis but serves as its necessary vehicle. Moral inquiry proceeds, like everything else in culture, through conversation—which is to say, more broadly, that moral inquirers exist in relationship with each other on a social field comprising cultural traditions, economic and political circumstances, and family histories. Such inquiry never exists apart from conversations among real, historically situated people, and moral inquiry is always simultaneous with efforts to make its doubts and decisions public. Understandings of morality represent an engagement in communication; we narrate what we know and we know by what we narrate.

Since moral reflection is in fact the conversations that constitute it, then the presence of many different histories, memories, and experiences converging in our classrooms is a unique opportunity for religious studies. Moral inquiry and religious study proceed in this context not by constituting the other—"Punkin' Brown," "Hinduism," "cult members," "popular" religion, and so on; rather, they work through the recognition of difference and a revisioning of one's own story through the lens of the other openly engaged. It means experiencing one's own world from the disorienting perspective of the other—from Uncle Sal's, for example, or from Gemma's—and this necessarily entails risk, vulnerability, vertigo; it invites anger and creates distress. Like the discipline itself, the religious studies classroom exists in suspension too. The understanding of other religious worlds and of the moral impulses of these worlds comes only through the multiplicity of stories told and stories attended to and to the new possibilities that emerge in the places between heaven and earth, between lives and stories, and between people and their gods.

NOTES

INTRODUCTION
JESUS HELD HIM SO CLOSE IN HIS LOVE FOR HIM THAT HE LEFT THE MARKS OF HIS PASSION ON HIS BODY

1. Richard Wightman Fox, *Trials of Intimacy: Love and Loss in the Beecher-Tilton Scandal* (Chicago: University of Chicago Press, 2000), 5 and 7.

2. Danièle Hervieu-Léger, *Religion as a Chain of Memory*, trans. Simon Lee (New Brunswick, N.J.: Rutgers University Press, 2000), especially chapter 1, "Sociology in Opposition to Religion? Preliminary Considerations."

3. For an especially elegant treatment of this notion of braiding as an alternative way of conceptualizing not simply religion's fate in modernity but modernity itself, see Leigh Eric Schmidt, *Hearing Things: Religion, Illusion, and the American Enlightenment* (Cambridge: Harvard University Press, 2000). My thinking about the tension between presence and absence in modern religious history has benefited from years of conversation and friendship with Leigh Schmidt.

4. Schmidt, *Hearing Things*, 32.

5. Don Kulick and Margaret Wilson, eds., *Taboo: Sex, Identity, and Erotic Subjectivity in Anthropological Fieldwork* (New York: Routledge, 1995).

CHAPTER ONE
"MILDRED, IS IT FUN TO BE A CRIPPLE?" THE CULTURE OF SUFFERING IN MID-TWENTIETH-CENTURY AMERICAN CATHOLICISM

The epigraphs to this chapter are taken from two autobiographical reflections written by Sal in the 1960s and circulated among his friends in mimeograph form.

What I say in this chapter about American Catholic popular theology is based on my readings of the many devotional periodicals that made up the everyday literary culture of this community for most of the last century. Some of these, such as the *Voice of St. Jude*, were published by the shrines that proliferated on the American Catholic landscape in these "heyday" years of devotionalism (as historian Jay Dolan has called them). Others (*Catholic World, Ave Maria,* and *America*) were the work of specific religious orders. Still others were more or less trade journals for clergy (*Homiletic and Pastoral Review* and *American Ecclesiastical Review*). *Hospital Progress* was published for Catholic hospital professionals.

While it is impossible to give a history of American Catholic popular journalism here, I want to note, first, that this kind of popular journalism has existed among American Catholics since the early nineteenth century. These periodicals have always appealed mainly to a middle-class, not a working-class, readership, for obvious reasons, and they have always promoted the devotional piety that has been seen since the early modern period as the foundation of Catholic life and a bulwark against modernity. In the decades considered here, especially in the late 1950s and into the 1960s, Catholic magazines slowly became attractive, accessible, upbeat family periodicals in a self-consciously American voice, offering articles and fiction on subjects of interest to the middle-class children of immigrants. (A popular feature was nostalgic presentations of "authentic" Old World customs.) By the middle of the last century, Catholic popular magazines and newspapers together sustained Catholics' sense of their distinctiveness in American culture as they described the aesthetics of assimilation, articulated the moral ideals of an emerging middle class, served as the training ground for Catholic intellectuals like John Cogley and Donald Thorman, supported a host of Catholic entrepreneurs, gave a Catholic gloss to every dimension of American culture from highways and kitchen designs to foreign policy, and thus became visible expressions of the coherence, integration, and unity of American Catholic culture—a coherence, integration, and unity that did not really exist outside of these magazines and newspapers.

Catholics had other sources for their theology: the pastors and prelates of the airwaves, Catholic fiction, catechisms, sermons, religion classes, book clubs, moral handbooks, and so on. All of these other idioms converged in the devotional magazines, however, which regularly printed excerpts from popular theological books, condensations of Catholic novels, articles by or about Catholic television and film personalities, and the sermons of famous Catholic preachers, along with the usual fare of American family magazines.

Devotional periodicals could be found everywhere. Salesmen sold subscriptions door-to-door in cities, suburbs, and rural areas, often traveling in big cars with the name of their magazines painted on the doors. Magazines were offered as promotions in local parish fund-raising drives, stocked in the libraries of Catholic hospitals, schools, convents, and rectories, and given as gifts, prizes, and incentives. By 1959, at the end of the most intense period of devotional improvisation in American Catholic history, the Catholic Press Association reported that there were 24,273,972 subscribers to 580 Catholic publications. See Jay P. Dolan, *The American Catholic Experience: A History from the Colonial Times to the Present* (Garden City, N.Y.: Doubleday, 1985), 394. I have also been helped in preparing these brief comments on the history of American Catholic journalism by Arnold J. Sparr, "The Catholic Literary Revival in America, 1920–1960," Ph.D. diss., University of Madison–Wisconsin, 1985; and Apollinaris W. Baumgartner, *Catholic Journalism: A Study of Its Development in the United States, 1789–1930* (New York: AMS Press, 1967). See also Marianna McLoughlin, "Catholic Magazines and Periodicals," in *The Encyclopedia of American Catholic History*, ed. Michael Glazier and Thomas J. Shelly (Collegeville, Minn.: Liturgical Press 1997), 274–77; and McLoughlin, "The Catholic Press (Newspapers)," in Glazier and Shelly, 289–92. Many of the most popular periodicals disappeared in the era of revolutionary change in Catholic life in the 1960s, even though they had endorsed the changes in liturgical life and Catholic practice for the most part. Catholics no longer needed their own separate publishing world.

Popular theologizing was practiced with considerable fervor and verve in devotional journals—which until recently have been overlooked as sources for the study of American Catholic culture—literally in response to current events as they unfolded. This was where Catholics commented on what they were becoming as they were becoming it. Clergy read the magazines and talked about them in their sermons, and issues of particular magazines were discussed in Catholic schools. Ample space was allotted for readers' comments, and their letters were generally lively, provocative, and sometimes at odds with editorial positions. This was a thriving and important idiom, in which modern American Catholics not only discovered who they were, but constituted themselves as well.

1. *Cripple* and *handicap* are ugly words and strike contemporary ears (rightly) as harsh and demeaning. But these were the words everyone used in the years under consideration to talk about my uncle and his friends. This is what my family called Sal, priests used them to refer to the disabled in the sermons delivered on devotional outings, and these were the terms applied to men and women like my uncle in the devotional press. It should become clear that my uncle was anything but "crippled" or "handicapped," in spirit or mind. His body was strong too; he hugged his nephews and nieces with powerful arms. But *cripple* and *handicap* were the standard nomenclature of the times, and I use them as such throughout.

Cripple has, not surprisingly, undergone a revolutionary repositioning in the past several years. Persons with disabilities have adopted it in self-conscious political anger and personal defiance, just as gay men and women have done with *queer*. As Joseph P. Shapiro notes in his excellent study of the struggles of persons with disabilities for civil rights, "In reclaiming 'cripple,' disabled people are taking the thing in their identity that scares the outside world the most and making it a cause to revel in with militant self-pride." See his *No Pity: People with Disabilities Forging a New Civil Rights Movement* (New York: Three Rivers Press, 1994), 34. Also useful on this subject are James I. Charlton, *Nothing about Us without Us: Disability Oppression and Empowerment* (Berkeley and Los Angeles: University of California Press, 1998); Lennard J. Davis, ed., *The Disability Studies Reader* (New York: Routledge, 1997); and Kenny Fries, ed., *Staring Back: The Disability Experience from the Inside Out* (New York: Plume, 1997). See also the helpful cultural studies by Rosemarie Garland-Thomson, *Extraordinary Bodies: Figuring Physical Disability in American Culture and Literature* (New York: Columbia University Press, 1997), and Garland-Thomson, ed., *Freakery: Cultural Spectacles of the Extraordinary Body* (New York: New York University Press, 1996). Recent work on the study of religion and the experience and understanding of disability includes Nancy L. Eiesland and Rebecca S. Chopp, *The Disabled God: Toward a Liberatory Theology of Disability* (Nashville: Abingdon Press, 1994); Nancy L. Eiesland and Don E. Saliers, eds., *Human Disability and the Service of God: Reassessing Religious Practice* (Nashville: Abingdon Press, 1998); Sharon V. Betcher, "Rehabilitating Religious Discourse: Bringing Disability Studies to the Theological Venue," *Religious Studies Review*, 27, no. 4 (2001): 341–48; and Helen R. Betenbaugh, "Disability: A Lived Theology," *Theology Today* 57, no. 2 (2000): 203–10.

2. On the devotion to Our Lady of Fatima in contemporary Catholicism, see Sandra Zimdars-Swartz, *Encountering Mary: From LaSallette to Medjugorje* (Princeton: Princeton University Press, 1991), 67–91, 190–219. For a useful tour of the contemporary Marian landscape in the United States, see Mark Garvey, *Searching for Mary: An Exploration of Marian Apparitions across the U.S.* (New York: Plume, 1998). The National Shrine of the Blue Army of Mary is located in Washington, New Jersey, where a periodical, *Soul Magazine*, is published.

3. For this theology of sanctification through suffering, as it was elaborated in American Catholic devotional journals in the twentieth century, see, for example, Marcella Murray, O.S.B., "Magazines in the Catholic Hospital Library," *Hospital*

Progress 21 (February 1940): 50–51; M. Teresita, C.M.H., "Opportunities for the Promotion of Catholic Action in the Teaching of Professional Adjustments in the Catholic Schools of Nursing," *Hospital Progress* 21 (June 1940): 206–12; Thomas A. Fox, "Drama with a Happy Ending," *Homiletic and Pastoral Review* 49 (April 1949): 565–67; Joachim DePrada, C.M.F., "To Whom Shall We Turn?" *Voice of Saint Jude* 24 (December 1958): 34; E. J. Garesché, S.J., "Catholic Hospital Apostolate," *Ave Maria* 73 (5 May 1951): 551–55; and Jerome F. Wilkerson, "Patient-Care Spiritual Needs," *Hospital Progress* 46 (December 1965): 76–80. The ethos was pervasive, and virtually any issue of any devotional periodical contained some expression of it. The ambivalent ethos of suffering and pain in modern Catholicism is evident in the following examples, among many others: "Our Foolish Discontent," *Ave Maria* 11 (10 April 1920): 469; "Sympathy for the Sick," *Ave Maria* 11 (12 June 1920): 757–58; "A Virtue More Admired Than Cultivated," *Ave Maria* 15 (21 January 1922): 84–85; "The Best of All Devotions," *Ave Maria* 26 (16 July 1927): 84–85; "Relief of the Holy Souls," *Ave Maria* 36 (5 November 1932): 595–96; see also Jane Sprenger, "Do It for Mom, Patty," *Sign* 32 (July 1953): 51–52; Ed Willock, "Suffering and Spiritual Growth," *Ave Maria* 88 (12 July 1958): 23–26; and Jerome Dukette, O.F.M., Conv., "Salvation in Suffering," *Homiletic and Pastoral Review* 58 (October 1957): 77–79. An excellent study of the "victim soul" idiom in Catholic popular spirituality is Paula M. Kane, " 'She Offered Herself Up': The Victim Soul and Victim Spirituality in Catholicism," *Church History* 71, no. 1 (March 2002): 80–119.

4. Joseph L. Healy, S.J., "Opportunities for Religious Education in the Hospital," *Hospital Progress* 18 (August 1937): 259–61.

5. For examples of such advice to nurses, see Bakewell Morrison, S.J., "Religion in the Curriculum of the Catholic School of Nursing," *Hospital Progress* 20 (December 1939): 419–27, and "The Nurses' Apostolate," *Catholic Women's World* 2 (February 1940): 30.

6. On Dooley's cancer in American Catholic popular culture, see James T. Fisher, *The Catholic Counterculture in America, 1933–1962* (Chapel Hill: University of North Carolina Press, 1989), 187. On the fascination of Dooley for American Catholic Cold War culture, see Fisher, *Dr. America: The Lives of Thomas A. Dooley, 1927–1961* (Amherst: University of Massachusetts Press, 1997).

7. Katherine Neuhaus Haffner, "One Day at a Time," *Ave Maria* 72 (9 September 1950): 343.

8. Healy, "Opportunities for Religious Education," 261.

9. Rev. Lincoln F. Whelan, "The Sick and Aged at Your Home," *Homiletic and Pastoral Review* 58 (July 1958): 983–84.

10. Vera Marie Tracy, "After Dark: A Hospital Sketch," *Catholic World* 130 (November 1929): 134–39.

11. In "Sick Room Study," *Ave Maria* 54 (6 September 1941): 294, the author imagines the sick person ministering to the priest who comes to call on him or her.

12. Florence White Rogers, "Letters to the Needy," *America* 50 (31 March 1934): 616–17; the quotation about Lourdes is from James Louis Small, "Vignettes of Lourdes," *Ave Maria* 11 (19 June 1920): 771. An excellent recent study

of the cult of Lourdes is Ruth Harris, *Lourdes: Body and Spirit in the Secular Age* (New York: Viking, 1999).

13. Two excellent books have explored this romanticism with great subtlety and insight: William M. Halsey, *The Survival of American Innocence: American Catholicism in an Era of Disillusionment, 1920–1940* (Notre Dame, Ind.: University of Notre Dame Press, 1980), and Fisher, *Catholic Counterculture.* Fisher's book, in particular, superbly limns the darkness. See also Ellis Hanson, *Decadence and Catholicism* (Cambridge: Harvard University Press, 1997), for its European expressions.

14. Ferdinand J. Ward, C.M., "How and Why of Suffering," *Homiletic and Pastoral Review* 58 (February 1958): 498–99.

15. Sister Celestine, "A Sister's Role in Spiritual Care," *Hospital Progress* 33 (October 1952): 75–77.

16. American Catholics were articulating an ancient ambivalence. For a useful overview of the complex understandings of sickness, pain, health, and healing in Catholic cultures, see Darrel W. Amundsen, "The Medieval Catholic Tradition," in *Caring and Curing: Health and Medicine in Western Religious Traditions*, ed. Ronald L. Numbers and Darrel W. Amundsen (Baltimore: Johns Hopkins University Press, 1998), 65–107; and Marvin R. O'Connell, "The Roman Catholic Tradition since 1945," also in Numbers and Amundsen, *Caring and Curing*, 108–43. About the Tridentine tradition, to which American Catholics were immediate heirs, O'Connell notes, "Priests and people were likely moreover to ascribe a specific suffering to a specific moral lapse, their own or others', a habit they maintained in the face of official ecclesiastical and theological disapproval" (112).

17. Boniface Buckley, C.P., "In Bitter Praise of Pain," *Sign* 24 (May 1945): 528. See also, for example, Rev. James J. Murphy, "Human Suffering," *Homiletic and Pastoral Review* 49 (March 1949): 485–86, and C. C. Martindale, S.J., "Making Use of Pain," *Priest* 13 (January 1957): 51–54.

18. Hubert N. Hart, "Notes on the Meaning of Pain," *Ave Maria* 177 (April 1953): 50–53.

19. P.J.C., "Error and Disease," *Ave Maria* 35 (9 January 1932): 53. Patrick Joseph Carroll, C.S.C., was editor of *Ave Maria* from 1934 to 1952. The classic discussion of this politicized use of stories and language about sickness is Susan Sontag, *Illness as Metaphor and AIDS and Its Metaphors* (New York: Doubleday, 1990); see also Paul Farmer, *AIDS and Accusation: Haiti and the Geography of Blame* (Berkeley and Los Angeles: University of California Press, 1992).

20. Dean H. O'Donnell, C.S.C., "Apostolate of the Sick Room," *Ave Maria* 63 (2 March 1946): 263–66.

21. See, for example, Paul Schaeuble, O.S.B., "Lepers and Leprosy," *Homiletic and Pastoral Review* 45 (February 1945): 381–82.

22. On the association between Hansen's disease and immorality, see Gavan Daws, *Holy Man: Father Damien of Molokai* (New York: Harper and Row, 1973), 132–34; on Father Damien, see also Richard D. Stewart, *Leper Priest of Molokai: The Father Damien Story* (Honolulu: University of Hawaii Press, 2000).

23. Alice Blair, "Share Your Fun," *Catholic Women's World* 1 (October 1939): 37.

24. On CUSA, see Mary S. Hessel, "Catholic Action for the Sick by the Sick," *Catholic World* 167 (May 1948): 163–66; Paul Brindel, O.S.B., Oblate, "I Am a Cusan," *Hospital Progress* (September 1957): 32, 34, 173; Anne Tansey, "Catholic Union of Sick Associates," *Ave Maria* 72 (11 November 1950): 622–25; Thomas Shelley, "Find Happiness in CUSA," *Catholic Digest* 22 (March 1958): 24–26; and Joseph LaMontagne, S.S.S., "I Am a Cusan," *Priest* 11 (September 1956): 776–80.

25. Frank J. Mallett, "Overcoming Handicaps," *Ave Maria* 46 (24 July 1937): 105–7.

26. John P. Doran, "One Way Ticket: A Visit to Molokai," *Catholic World* 171 (April 1950): 30–35. Doran's ticket, for the record, was round trip.

27. Thomas Heath, O.P., "From Evil to Good," *Ave Maria* 101 (1965): 16–19.

28. "They Also Serve: A Series of Letters from an Invalid," *Voice of St. Jude* (September 1950): 16–17.

29. See, for example, "One Lesson Taught by the War," *Ave Maria* 15 (4 March 1922): 275–76; Charlotte Wilma Fox, "The Voice of God," *Ave Maria* 35 (30 April 1932): 557–61; Alphonse M. Schwitalla, S.J., "The Influence of the Catholic Hospital in Our Modern Society," *Hospital Progress* 20 (September 1939): 315; Msgr. Patrick O'Boyle, "I Saw the Eyes of Suffering Children," *Voice of St. Jude* (June 1947): 7, 13; Clement H. Crock, "The Mystery of Suffering," *Homiletic and Pastoral Review* 50 (March 1950): 549–51; Jennie Marie Mucker, "Hidden Apostles," *Voice of St. Jude* (February 1954): 10–13; and Owenita Sanderlin, "My Operation," *Voice of St. Jude* (August 1955): 29–31.

30. Mary E. Hoffman, "The Candle Beams," *Ave Maria* 81 (16 April 1955): 16–17.

31. Haffner, "One Day at a Time," 344.

32. For example, Mary Catherine Schuler, "Silver Lining of Convalescence," *Ave Maria* 59 (8 April 1944): 494–96; O'Donnell, "Apostolate of the Sick Room"; Thomas A. Lahey, C.S.C., "A Letter to Shut-Ins," *Ave Maria* 71 (25 February 1950): 245–49; Florence A. Waters, "Religious Communities for the Sick," *Ave Maria* 77 (21 February 1953): 241–43; and Martindale, "Making Use of Pain."

33. Mary O'Connor, "Are You Pain's Puppet?" *Ave Maria* 73 (17 February 1951): 216.

34. "A headache compared with His crown of thorns! Possibly this may make us a little less timorous in asking for 'more'!" (Martindale, "Making Use of Pain," 53).

35. Bruno M. Hagspiel, S.V.D., "A New Hospital Patroness, St. Gemma Galgani," *Hospital Progress* 21 (March 1940): 97–98.

36. "Heroes," *Ave Maria* 46 (11 September 1937): 341.

37. "Pain can bring greatness to us. It can make people great. It need not. We have seen it in some of our sick, making them only discontented till they find life terribly wearisome. But this failure to grow great by suffering is not due to suffering, but to the soul," wrote Bede Jarrett, O.P., in "The Problem of Suffering," *Homiletic and Pastoral Review* 34 (December 1933): 260–65; see also Buckley, "Bitter Praise of Pain," 527.

38. See, for example, the peaceful, productive, and well-organized life of leper colonies portrayed in George J. Renneker, S. M., "Gateway to Heaven," *Catholic Digest* 5 (March 1941): 11–13; Marius Risley, "Damien's Spirit in America," *Catholic Digest* 6 (January 1942): 40–45; and James A. Brussel, "Two-Way Door at Carville," *Catholic Digest* 13 (June 1949): 52–54.

39. "Suffering and Imagination," *Ave Maria* 15 (13 May 1922): 596.

40. Doran, "One Way Ticket," 35.

41. Waters, "Religious Communities for the Sick."

42. See, for example, B. J. Cunningham, C.M., "Is One of You Sick?" *Ave Maria* 81 (21 May 1955): 8–11. Docetic Christologies "denied [Jesus'] real humanity and His actual death," according to Williston Walker, as a way of resolving the terrible contradiction between Jesus' earthly existence and belief in his glory. "The simplest solution of the Christological problem may well have seemed to some the denial of His earthly life all together." See Walker, *A History of the Christian Church* (New York: Scribner, 1970), 51.

43. William P. McCahill, "Christ in the Wounded and the Maimed," *Catholic Mind* 49 (September 1951): 563–69.

44. From an undated prayer card printed by CUSA, 176 W. Eighth St., Bayonne, N.J. 07002.

45. Waters, "Religious Communities for the Sick," 241.

46. For some other examples of this theme, see Rev. G. Hardesty, "The Maintenance of the Individuality of the Catholic Hospital," *Hospital Progress* 20 (October 1939): 338–39; Murphy, "Human Suffering," 484; Bertin Farrell, C.P., "Why the Suffering?" *Sign* 45 (May 1966): 55. An especially poignant meditation on this theme, written by a woman paralyzed from the waist down since the age of seventeen, is Vivian T. Murphy, "Sickbed Voyage of Discovery," *Catholic Digest* 14 (May 1950): 74–76. The writer tells herself, "You are one of the crosses that have made [your family] good."

47. Mary Agnes Boyle, for example, contrasts her own resignation to and acceptance of her incurable cancer with the way her non-Catholic relatives rebel against and get angry with their diseases, in "The Long Journey," *Ave Maria* 78 (19 September 1953): 10–13. That non-Catholics do not know how to take life on the chin as Catholics do was a commonplace in the devotional press and may have been the echo among their children of the pride of working-class Catholics of the ethnic enclaves.

48. Morrison, "Religion in the Curriculum," 423.

49. See, for example, Hart, "Meaning of Pain," 53; and Heath, "From Evil to Good," 18.

50. Jerry Filan's story is told in Shelley, "Find Happiness in CUSA"; and in Tansey, "Catholic Union of Sick Associates," 623.

51. Murphy, "Sickbed Voyage," 76.

52. Dukette, "Salvation in Suffering," 78.

53. Sprenger, "Do It for Mom, Patty," 51.

54. On the subject of pain's historicity, see David B. Morris, *The Culture of Pain* (Berkeley and Los Angeles: University of California Press, 1991); Roselyne Rey, *The History of Pain*, trans. Louise Elliott Wallace, J.A. Cadden, and S.W. Cadden (Cambridge: Harvard University Press, 1995); Edward Shorter, *From Pa-*

ralysis to Fatigue: A History of Psychosomatic Illness in the Modern Era (New York: Free Press, 1992); Caroline Walker Bynum, *Holy Feast and Holy Fast: The Religious Significance of Food to Medieval Women* (Berkeley and Los Angeles: University of California Press, 1987); and Bynum, *Fragmentation and Redemption: Essays on Gender and the Human Body in Medieval Religion* (New York: Zone Books, 1991).

55. Fisher, *Catholic Counterculture*, 187.

56. See, for example, Robert O'Hara, C.P., "The Good Life," *Sign* 29 (August 1949): 52–53.

57. See Fisher, *Catholic Counterculture*, 94–99. Here he is talking specifically about the appeal of Dorothy Day's dark anarchism for college-educated children of the Catholic ghettos, but I think the point can be generalized, as I argue in the text.

58. I have discussed this at greater length, with bibliographical citations on changes in the experience of ethnicity among the many different groups making up American Catholicism, in *Thank You, St. Jude: Women's Devotion to the Patron Saint of Hopeless Causes* (New Haven: Yale University Press, 1996), 9–14. For useful deconstructions of the givenness of white ethnic identity, see Richard D. Alba, *Ethnic Identity: The Transformation of White America* (New Haven: Yale University Press, 1990); Mary C. Waters, *Ethnic Options: Choosing Identities in America* (Berkeley and Los Angeles: University of California Press, 1990); Matthew Frye Jacobson, *Whiteness of a Different Color: European Immigrants and the Alchemy of Race* (Cambridge: Harvard University Press, 1998); David Roediger, *The Wages of Whiteness: Race and the Making of the American Working Class* (London: Verso, 1999); and Werner Sollors, ed., *The Invention of Ethnicity* (New York: Oxford University Press, 1989).

59. The best English-language biography of this unusual holy figure is William R. Bonniwell, O.P., *The Life of Blessed Margaret of Castello* (Madison, Wis.: IDEA, 1979). Bonniwell's book is based on archival sources that date to the fourteenth century. I have discussed this devotion in "The Cult of Saints and the Reimagination of the Space and Time of Sickness in Twentieth-Century American Catholicism," *Literature and Medicine* 8 (1989): 63–77. Margaret's cause is promoted in the United States at two shrines both in the care of the Dominican order and located in Dominican parishes. One is in Saint Patrick's Church in Columbus, Ohio, the other in Saint Louis Bertrand's in Louisville, Kentucky. The Columbus shrine is the oldest: devotion to Blessed Margaret there dates to the 1930s, the actual shrine to her was constructed in the 1950s, and it was renovated in the 1970s. The shrine in Louisville was founded in 1980. (This shrine was moved for the period 1981–86 to Philadelphia when its director was reassigned to a parish there but returned to Louisville when the Dominicans handed the church over to the Philadelphia archdiocese.)

60. See, for example, *Blessed Margaret: The Cross Transfigured, a Saint for Our Time*, pamphlet published by the Dominican nuns, Monastery of Our Lady of the Rosary (Summit, N.J., 1977); Madeline Pecora Nugent, S.F.O., "Blessed Margaret of Castello," on the website of Priests for Life, Staten Island, New York, undated, http://priestsforlife.org/testimony/castello.htm; "Patroness of the Unwanted," *Naples (Florida) ProLife Council Newsletter*, February, 2001, http://naplesprolife.org/0page4.htm; Nora M. Madden, "The Little Pearl of God," in

"Celebrate Life," online newsletter published by the American Life League, Stafford, Virginia, November–December 1992, http://www.all.org/celebrate_life/cl9211.htm; Father Frank A. Pavone, "The Christian's Voice for Life," on the website of Our Lady of Loretto Online, http://ourladyofloreto.org/ourorganizations/pavone4.htm.

61. I spent 1985–86 in Italy, studying modern Catholic popular religion and exploring both the history of the devotion to Blessed Margaret in Umbria and her cult among contemporary Italian handicapped men and women. The Dominican order in the United States and Italy was extraordinarily generous to me in this research, allowing me access to all the documents relating to Margaret's cult and inviting me to observe their work in promoting her canonization at the Vatican. I especially want to thank A. I. Cataudo, O.P., in Philadelphia, and Innocenzo Venchi, O.P., the order's Postulator General in Rome, at the time and still.

62. Indeed, were Margaret to be canonized, she would be the first saint whose body was not in perfect physical condition at birth, thus effectively severing the ancient Western link between physical and moral soundness—as her devout well know.

63. Devotional writers literally drew a curtain across the sickroom. Addressing himself or herself to an imaginary person in severe pain, an anonymous author in *Ave Maria* intoned: "you enact your monotonous drama of pain in such a divine technique of self-suppression, you make us think that, after all, there is joy in suffering, with sunshine, summer and rose bloom behind the half-curtained window of a sick room" ("Sick Room Study," 294).

64. See, for example, "Visitation of the Sick," *Homiletic and Pastoral Review* 48 (August 1948): 854; and, in the same issue, Donald L. Barry, "Sacraments for the Sick," 824–27; see also "On Visiting Hospitals," *Homiletic and Pastoral Review* 65 (December 1964): 193–94. A study of the history and practice of Catholic hospital chaplains in the United States remains to be written.

65. George A. Mahony, "Our Friend, the Hospital Chaplain," *Homiletic and Pastoral Review* 37 (September 1937): 1260–64.

66. See, for example, Anthony Kraff, C.P.P.S., "The Difference in the Ministry between Hospital and Parish," *Hospital Progress* 38 (November 1957): 83–84. The training and the reputation of hospital chaplains were improving by this time, but Kraff is still conscious of the parish clergy's scorn. "A Hospital Chaplain" of 1930 laments his being compelled to carry a "double burden"—caring for the sick and enduring the contempt of his fellows. He concedes that "until now" it has been "customary to appoint to this position priests who are often semi-patients themselves." (This chaplain was optimistic—the situation persisted for at least another three decades.) See "God's Way with Souls," *Hospital Progress* 11 (April 1930): 172–74.

67. Wilkerson, "Patient-Care Spiritual Needs." For a brief history of the National Association of Catholic Chaplains, see Marilyn N. Gustin with Rev. Msgr. Harrold A. Murray, *The National Association of Catholic Chaplains: A Twenty-Year History (1965–1985)* (Milwaukee: The Association, 1985).

68. On the nineteenth century, see Ann Taves, *The Household of Faith: Roman Catholic Devotions in Mid–Nineteenth Century America* (Notre Dame, Ind.: University of Notre Dame Press, 1986), 57ff. One of the better-known healers in American Catholic history is Capuchin friar Solanus Casey (1870–1957), whose

powers first came to the attention of people outside his order when he was living in a Harlem monastery in the 1920s. On Father Casey see Catherine M. Odell, *Father Solanus: The Story of Solanus Casey, O.F.M., Cap.* (Huntingdon, Ind.: Our Sunday Visitor Pub. Division, 1988) and James Patrick Derum, *The Porter at Saint Bonaventure's* (Detroit: Fidelity Press, 1968). Sister Celestine ("A Sister's Role," 76) reports the case of an older hospital sister in her order who was believed by patients to be a healer. The story of such healers within American men's and women's religious orders remains to be told. A number of shrines on the American Catholic landscape, such as El Santuario de Chimayo in New Mexico and St. Roch Chapel and the Campo Santo in New Orleans, are important healing sites that draw pilgrims from all over the country. A helpful catalogue of such places is James P. Kelcher, ed., *Catholic Shrines and Places of Pilgrimage in the United States* (Washington, D.C.: Office for the Pastoral Care of Migrants and Refugees, the United States Catholic Conference, 1994). The first positive evaluations of religious healing appeared in the devotional press in the early 1960s, not surprisingly just when the ethos of suffering and pain was being called into question. For an example of both reconsiderations, see Heath, "From Evil to Good," 18–19. Some writers in the 1960s sought to transform that ethos into a motivation for political action and social responsibility; see, for example, Father Ronald Luka, "The Way of the Cross Today—through the Streets of Selma and the Trails of Vietnam," *Ave Maria* 101 (10 April 1965): 6–9. For a discussion of the revival of faith healing among Catholic charismatics in the 1970s by a participant in the movement, see Edward D. O'Connor, C.S.C., *The Pentecostal Movement in the Catholic Church* (Notre Dame, Ind.: Ave Maria Press, 1971). O'Connor's discussion of healing is not completely free of ambivalence; he seems uneasy at times with this manisfestation of the Spirit's presence (see, for example, pp. 162–64). Another contemporary evaluation of the Pentecostal movement is Kevin and Dorothy Ranaghan, *Catholic Pentecostals* (Paramus, N.J.: Paulist Press, 1969). An excellent study of the movement is Meredith B. McGuire, *Pentecostal Catholics: Power, Charisma, and Order in a Religious Movement* (Philadelphia: Temple University Press, 1982). For a rich and learned overview of Catholic health ministries in the United States, with some attention to devotional healing idioms, see Christopher J. Kauffman, *Ministry and Meaning: A Religious History of Catholic Health Care* (New York: Crossroad, 1995). The life and writings of Rose Hawthorne Lathrop must be included in any history of American Catholic spiritualities of suffering and pain. See Patricia Dunlavy Valenti, *To Myself a Stranger: A Biography of Rose Hawthorne Lathrop* (Baton Rouge: Louisiana State University Press, 1991).

69. My sense of this is impressionistic. The subject of vernacular healing in European American immigrant communities awaits study. Religiously inflected vernacular healing practice endures to the present day among Mexican American migrants and their children and grandchildren, so there is not a single history of popular healing in American Catholicism, nor do such practices have a common destiny. The latter has also been more carefully studied.

70. I have been helped on this subject by Meredith B. McGuire, *Ritual Healing in Suburban America*, with the assistance of Debra Kantor (New Brunswick, N.J.: Rutgers University Press, 1988); Thomas J. Csordas, *The Sacred Self: A Cultural*

Phenomenology of Charismatic Healing (Berkeley and Los Angeles: University of California Press, 1994); and David Edwin Harrell, *All Things Are Possible: The Healing and Charismatic Revivals in Modern America* (Bloomington, Ind.: Indiana University Press, 1975).

71. Tracy, "After Dark," 138.

72. Dukette, "Salvation in Suffering," 78.

73. Jarrett, "Problem of Suffering," 264. Ferdinand Ward criticizes the idea, which he says is shared by many Catholics, that sedation is spiritually wrong ("How and Why of Suffering," 499). Gerald Vann, O.P., approved what he considered the heroic Catholic refusal of "anesthetic drugs, twilight sleep, psychotherapy, and so forth," a resistance that he proudly claimed had its "roots in a feeling that the naked will should be left to conquer the rebellions and repulsions of the instincts, so that the reward due to fighting the good fight may not be forfeit." See his "True Balance," *Catholic World* 151 (July 1940): 485–86. Vann went on to caution his readers against the "glorification of suffering" that he had just urged upon them.

74. The simile of turning off Niagara Falls is from Timothy Chiappetta, O.F.M., Cap., "Prayers of the Sick," *Priest* 11 (June 1956): 526–27. The Catholic Union of the Sick in America was specifically conceived as a means of preventing the "terrific wastage of suffering that takes place when the sick are unaware or indifferent to the truly marvelous opportunities they providentially have at hand," according to Bishop John C. Cody of London, Ontario, as quoted in Brindel, "I Am a Cusan," 173.

75. Margaret Lehr, "The Advantages of a Handicap," *Ave Maria* 69 (4 June 1949): 728.

76. Lahey was a professor of English, advertising, and journalism at Notre Dame and St. Mary's College; from 1929 until 1959 he was associate editor of *Ave Maria*, to which he contributed a popular column, "Bits Out of Life." From 1959 to 1961, he was chaplain of the university infirmary at Notre Dame. According to his obituary, he was known for his "modesty, his quiet kindness and good humor, his zeal and dedication." Father Lahey makes only a brief and, I realize, not particularly flattering appearance in this chapter. Since it is not the business of historians to dishonor men and women of the past, I want to emphasize that Lahey's article, in tone and theology, is characteristic of the way that "handicapped" people were imagined and addressed in the devotional press rather than being unique to him. The information on his life comes from *Province Review* 18 (December 1970): 3, which is published by the Holy Cross Fathers of the Indiana province; a copy of his obituary was graciously sent to me by David Schlaver, C.S.C.

77. For an example of the way that persons with disabilities now view the language used by others to describe (and possess) them, see Evan Kemp Jr.'s criticism of Jerry Lewis's talk about "Jerry's Kids," in Shapiro, *No Pity*, 20–24.

78. Lahey, "Letter to Shut-Ins," 245–46.

79. Lahey, "Letter to Shut-Ins," 247.

80. Vincent Crapanzano, *Tuhami: Portrait of a Moroccan* (Chicago: University of Chicago Press, 1980), 140.

CHAPTER TWO
THE MANY NAMES OF THE MOTHER OF GOD

1. Hindu goddesses also ride dashboards. See, for example, the sad description of the unnamed narrator's taxi ride to retrieve his recently deceased sister's infant from a hospital in Calcutta, in Raj Kamal Jha, *The Blue Bedspread* (New York: Random House, 1999), 12–13. Jha writes, "There's a black earthen idol of a goddess above his dashboard, two incense sticks burn, their heap of ash trembles when he changes gears" (13).

2. David Freedberg, *The Power of Images: Studies in the History and Theory of Response* (Chicago: University of Chicago Press, 1989), 17–18, 30.

3. David Morgan, *Visual Piety: A History and Theory of Popular Religious Images* (Berkeley and Los Angeles: University of California Press, 1998), 25. David Morgan points out that negative assessments of popular art forms—indeed, the denial of the very possibility of a popular aesthetic—is the outcome of "the history of aesthetics since the eighteenth century," which imposed "disinterestedness as the basis for judgments of taste and artistic quality" (26).

4. On vodou practitioners in relation to the Madonna of Mount Carmel, see Elizabeth McAlister, "The Madonna of 115th Street Revisited: Vodou and Haitian Catholicism in the Age of Transnationalism," in *Gatherings in Diaspora: Religious Communities and the New Immigration*, ed. R. Stephen Warner and Judith G. Wittner (Philadelphia: Temple University Press, 1998), 123–60; and Robert A. Orsi, "The Religious Boundaries of an In-Between People: Street *Feste* and the Problem of the Dark-Skinned Other in Italian Harlem, 1920–1990," in Orsi, ed., *Gods of the City: Religion and the American Urban Landscape* (Bloomington: Indiana University Press, 1999), 257–88. For examples of how media of presence mark neighborhood boundaries and become implicated in the complex work of ethnic self-identification and the maintenance of national identities, see, in the same volume, Thomas A. Tweed, "Diasporic Nationalism and Urban Landscape: Cuban Immigrants at a Catholic Shrine in Miami," 131–54; David H. Brown, "Altared Spaces: Afro-Cuban Religions and the Urban Landscape in Cuba and the United States," 155–230; and Joseph Sciorra, " 'We Go Where the Italians Live': Religious Processions as Ethnic and Territorial Markers in a Multi-ethnic Brooklyn Neighborhood," 310–40. A superb introduction to the relationships between vodou practitioners and the spirits is Karen McCarthy Brown, *Mama Lola: A Vodou Priestess in Brooklyn* (Berkeley and Los Angeles: University of California Press, 1991).

5. On the conflict over the contemporary appropriation of Native American artifacts by whites, see Michael F. Brown, *Who Owns Native Culture?* (Cambridge: Harvard University Press, 2003).

6. This is quoted in Xavier Rynne, *Vatican Council II* (New York: Farrar, Straus and Giroux, 1968), 160.

7. For general discussion of this transitional period in American Catholic history, see Dolan, *The American Catholic Experience*; Philip J. Gleason, ed., *Contemporary Catholicism in the United States* (Notre Dame, Ind.: University of Notre Dame Press, 1969); Andrew M. Greeley, *The Church and the Suburbs* (New York: Sheed and Ward, 1959); Gleason, *The American Catholic: A Social Portrait*

(New York: Basic Books, 1977); Gleason, *Crisis in the Church: A Study of Religion in America* (Chicago: Thomas More Press, 1979); Gleason, *American Catholics since the Council: An Unauthorized Report* (Chicago: Thomas More Press, 1985); Mark S. Massa, *Catholics and American Culture: Fulton Sheen, Dorothy Day, and the Notre Dame Football Team* (New York: Crossroad, 1999); Charles R. Morris, *American Catholic: The Saints and Sinners Who Built America's Most Powerful Church* (New York: Random House/Times Books, 1997); and David J. O'Brien, *The Renewal of American Catholicism* (New York: Oxford University Press, 1972). The quote in the text about Catholics becoming middle class is from Michael E. Schlitz, "The Parish of the Future," *Today* 17 (April 1962): 12–14.

8. For a sense of Catholics' struggles with new liturgical expectations in this period, see Clifford J. Howell, S.J., "Liturgy in Practice: No Parrots in Church," *Worship* 36 (April 1962): 327–35; Bede Scholz, "Participation: How Do We Begin?" *Altar and Home Pocket Missal* 1 (February 1961): 49–55; Scholz, "Our Changing Parishes," *Altar and Home Pocket Missal* 1 (June 1961): 51–53; Joseph H. O'Neill, "A Matter of Choice: The 'Quiet' Mass," *Priest* 17 (April 1961): 342–46; Rev. Robert J. Sherry, "Active Participation—'God's Gift to Our Age,' " *Catholic Choirmaster* 47 (Fall 1961): 106–10; Joseph M. Champlin, "Altars Facing the People," *Homiletic and Pastoral Review* 65 (March 1965): 492–95; Walter J. Schmitz, S.S., "The Liturgy and the Rubrics," *Priest* 21 (June 1965): 519–20; A. M. Carr, "Who May Handle the Ciborium?" *Homiletic and Pastoral Review* 63 (October 1962): 71; G.G., "Benediction after Mass," *Clergy Review* 50, no. 2 (February 1965): 155–56; James J. Higgins, "Why Have Your Home Blessed?" *Liguorian* 53 (April 1965): 37–39; A. M. Carr, "Those Girl Servers at Mass," *Homiletic and Pastoral Review* 66 (February 1966): 427–28. On Catholic experience of changing roles in the church, see, for example, Sister M. Martin, O.P., "What Is a Nun?" *Ave Maria* 93 (11 March 1961): 28–29; Daniel J. Potterton, "Must Our Sisters Be Stylish?" *Priest* 17 (May 1961): 437–39; Donald F. Miller, "How to Be a Good Layman," *Liguorian* 50 (February 1962): 1–7; Beverly Belock and Joanne Ganley, "A Debate: Changing the Nuns' Habits," *Extension* 60 (November 1965): 48; Daniel Callahan, *The Mind of the Catholic Layman* (New York: Scribner, 1963). For discussions of changes in U.S. Catholic spirituality in the 1960s and 1970s, see, for example, the special section of *The Critic*, "Spirituality for the Seventies," Andrew M. Greeley, ed., 29, no. 1 (1970); special edition of *Chicago Studies*, "A Spiritual Life Handbook," 15, no. 1 (1976); and the special edition of *New Catholic World*, "The Rebirth of Spirituality," 219, no. 1310 (1976).

9. The comment about Mary as a "senile grandmother" is from Leo J. Trese, "Hold On to Your Beads," *Sign* 44, no. 10 (May 1965): 36; the description of Holy Rosary Month is from C. J. McNaspy, S.J., "The Fracas about the Saints," *Sign* 44, no. 21 (24 May 1965): 608. Other examples of what I am describing here are Ethel Marbach, "Liturgical Customs from Many Lands for the Family through the Year We Have Tried at Our House," *Ave Maria* 102 (24 July 1965): 14–15; Rev. Robert F. Griffin, C.S.C., "De Senectute," *Ave Maria* 96 (20 October 1962): 20–22, 28; the notion that popular devotions are to linked to old world Europe and not the new world of the United States is suggested by (among many others) Edward Wakin and Rev. Joseph F. Scheuer, *The De-Romanization of the American Catholic Church* (New York: Macmillan, 1966), 278. The matter of the rosary's fate after the Council was the subject of a meeting at Notre Dame in

1966, reported on by Gary MacEoin, "Has the Rosary Survived the Council?" *Ave Maria* 104 (9 July 1966), 12–14, 28; that only old people say the rosary is claimed by "A Matter of Taste," *Sign* 45 (October 1965): 43.

10. The examples offered here about the broader American impulse toward sacrilege in this period are from David Burner, *Making Peace with the 60s* (Princeton: Princeton University Press, 1996), 60, and David Farber, *Age of Great Dreams: America in the 1960s* (New York: Hill and Wang, 1994), 221. A typical account of the discovery of nuns' bodies in the period is Johnnie Fay Duncan, "Nuns Can Be People, Too," *Information* 76 (April 1962): 8–15; see also the treatment of nuns in Mary Gilligan Wong, *Nun: A Memoir* (New York: Harcourt Brace Jovanovich, 1983), 15. On the fate of nuns in modernizing contexts see JoAnn Kay McNamara, *Sisters in Arms: Catholic Nuns through Two Millennia* (Cambridge: Harvard University Press, 1966), 565–99. For examples of what I am calling pornographic sacrilege see Robert Byrne, *Memories of a Non-Jewish Childhood* (New York: Lyle Stuart, 1970); Justin Green, *Binky Brown Sampler* (San Francisco: Last Gasp, 1995) (this includes the classic 1972 graphic novel *Binky Brown Meets the Virgin Mary*); and the zine *Catholic Guilt*, published in Wisconsin in the early 1980s (available at the Wisconsin State Historical Society, Madison, Wisconsin).

11. See Stanley M. Grabowski, "Iconoclasts Anonymous," *Priest* 21 (July 1965): 572–74; for another expression of these sentiments, see John Julian Ryan, "Pity the Poor Pastor," *Worship* 35 (Spring 1961): 560–67.

12. The sentence about the space between the faces here is influenced by my reading of object relations theory, the tradition of psychological reflection and practice concerned specifically with the nature of the bonds between developing humans and their caregivers. My entry into this domain of theoretical work was Jay R. Greenberg and Stephen A. Mitchell, *Object Relations in Psychoanalytic Theory* (Cambridge: Harvard University Press, 1983).

13. The exhibition is chronicled in Melissa R. Katz, ed., *Divine Mirrors: The Virgin Mary in the Visual Arts* (New York: Oxford University Press, 2001).

14. Walter Benjamin, *Illuminations: Essays and Reflections*, ed. Hannah Arendt, trans. Harry Zohn (New York: Schocken Books, 1968), 217–51. Benjamin introduces devotional idioms as an art form distinct from art in the more modern sense; he calls these two "polar types" (224). The cult value of devotional art, he suggests, demands that such objects be hidden, whereas "with the emancipation of the various art practices from ritual go increasing opportunities for the exhibition of their products. It is easier to exhibit a portrait bust that can be sent here and there than to exhibit the statue of a divinity that has its fixed place in the interior of a temple" (225). Clearly, images of the Virgin Mary do not fit this typology. Benjamin sees the shift from one art form to the other as a process of historical development, indeed as liberation. Following Freedberg, I am suggesting that there is always a historically and culturally situated interplay between the two ways of experiencing objects. Sacred representations were, in any case, far more motile in practice than Benjamin's comment about fixed statues in temples allows. See, for example, Patrick J. Geary, *Furta Sacra: Thefts of Relics in the Central Middle Ages*, rev. ed. (Princeton: Princeton University Press, 1990). Marx's theory of the fetish taught us that there is a presence in consumer objects (indeed, Marx is one of the last Western theorists of presence). On this subject, I have been helped

by Michael T. Taussig, *The Devil and Commodity Fetishism in South America* (Chapel Hill: University of North Carolina Press, 1980). For a discussion of American Protestant approaches to religious imagery, see David Morgan, *Protestants and Pictures: Religion, Visual Culture, and the Age of American Mass Production* (New York: Oxford University Press, 1999). On the reproduction of Lourdes grottoes in the United States, see Colleen McDannell, *Material Christianity: Religion and Popular Culture in America* (New Haven: Yale University Press, 1995), 132–62. McDannell writes, "The production of religious replicas was, curiously enough, the production of authenticity" (161). She points out that the Vatican has often granted the same tally of indulgences (units of supernatural merit earned by good deeds of various sort) to reproductions that it makes available to the faithful at the originals, thus further erasing the distinction between them.

15. Susan Stewart, *On Longing: Narratives of the Miniature, the Gigantic, the Souvenir, the Collection* (Durham, N.C.: Duke University Press, 1993), 132–69; the phrases quoted in the text come from p. 135.

16. This emphasis on the intersubjective nature of devotional experience was influenced by Gananath Obeyesekere, *Medusa's Hair: An Essay on Personal Symbols and Religious Experience* (Chicago: Chicago University Press, 1981); and Ana-Maria Rizzuto, *The Birth of the Living God: A Psychoanalytic Study* (Chicago: Chicago University Press, 1979).

17. For a discussion of the methodological debates over Marian apparitions, see Paolo Apolito, *Apparitions of the Madonna at Oliveto Citra: Local Visions and Cosmic Drama*, trans. William A. Christian Jr., (University Park: Pennsylvania State University Press, 1998), 19–26; see also Zimdars-Swartz, *Encountering Mary.* The exemplary practitioner of the psychoanalytical approach to Marian devotions is Michael P. Carroll. See, for example, *The Cult of the Virgin Mary: Psychological Origins* (Princeton: Princeton University Press, 1986).

18. The apparitions referred to in this paragraph are Lourdes (see, most recently, the superb study by Harris, *Lourdes*; Marpingen (see David Blackbourn, *Marpingen: Apparitions of the Virgin Mary in Nineteenth-Century Germany* [New York: Alfred A. Knopf, 1994]); Fatima (see Zimdars-Swartz, *Encountering Mary*, 67–91); and Ezkioga (see William A. Christian Jr., *Visionaries: The Spanish Republic and the Reign of Christ* [Berkeley and Los Angeles: University of California Press, 1996]).

19. Michael P. Carroll, *Madonnas That Maim: Popular Catholicism in Italy since the Fifteenth Century* (Baltimore: Johns Hopkins University Press, 1992); Apolito, *Apparitions of the Madonna at Oliveto Citra*, 109–10, 170.

20. On the history of Marian clubs in the early twentieth century, see Sister Mary Florence, S.L. (Bernice Wolff), *The Sodality Movement in the United States, 1926–1936* (St. Louis, Mo.: Queen's Work, 1939). Marina Warner emphasizes the disciplinary nature of Mary's identity in *Alone of All Her Sex: The Myth and the Cult of the Virgin Mary* (New York: Knopf, 1976).

21. Apolito, *Apparitions of the Madonna at Oliveto Citra*, 171, also 165–79, 178, 191, 205, 210–11. Of the Queen of the Castle Committee, Apolito writes, "The installation of the Queen of the Castle Committee is perhaps the most decisive of the acts that constituted the apparitions. . . . Without the Committee, and in particular without the parish priest Don Giovanni, it is possible that the apparitions would not have existed, and it is certain that they would quickly have faded

away" (44–45). For an example of the reinterpretation of Mary by liberation theologians, see Leonardo Boff, *The Maternal Face of God: The Feminine and Its Religious Expressions* (San Francisco: Harper and Row, 1987).

22. "The Roman Sermon of the American Cardinal on Church and State in the United States," in *Documents of American Catholic History*, ed. John Tracy Ellis (Milwaukee: Bruce Publishing, 1956), 476–79. On Gibbons, see John Tracy Ellis, *The Life of James Cardinal Gibbons, Archbishop of Baltimore, 1834–1921*, vols. 1–2 (Milwaukee: Bruce Publishing, 1952); and James Hennesey, S.J., *American Catholics: A History of the Roman Catholic Community in the United States* (New York: Oxford University Press, 1981), 172–233. On the Washington basilica, see Thomas A. Tweed, "Proclaiming Catholic Inclusiveness: Ethnic Diversity and Ecclesiastical Unity at the National Shrine of the Immaculate Conception," *U.S. Catholic Historian* 18, no. 1 (Winter 2000): 1–18.

23. The best study of this literature is Jenny Franchot, *Roads to Rome: The Antebellum Encounter with Catholicism* (Berkeley and Los Angeles: University of California Press, 1994). For a provocative introduction to the Virgin's place in the imagination of cultural critics of the United States, see T. Jackson Lears, *No Place of Grace: Antimodernism and the Transformation of American Culture, 1880–1920* (Chicago: University of Chicago Press, 1981), 248–49, 279–86, 294.

24. The great American Catholic sociologist Paul Hanley Furfey opened one of his last works, *Love and the Urban Ghetto*, with this autobiographical reflection: "I grew up an Irish lad in Boston. To be such at the turn of the century was to be a member of a minority group. The WASPs were in control. They were the doctors, the judges, the mayors, the bank presidents, the intellectuals. The Irish were struggling upward from the level of pick-and-shovel men or housemaids. But we Irish had one big compensation. We were Catholics. On Judgment Day, the WASPs would be humiliated and we would be triumphant" ([Maryknoll, N.Y.: Orbis, 1978], vii).

25. For a recent study of Black Madonnas, see Monique Scheer, "From Majesty to Mystery: Change in the Meanings of Black Madonnas from the Sixteenth to Nineteenth Centuries," *American Historical Review* 107, no. 5 (December 2002): 1412–40.

26. On the Virgin's place in the context of contemporary transnationalism is Thomas A. Tweed, *Our Lady of the Exile: Diasporic Religion at a Cuban Shrine in Miami* (New York: Oxford University Press, 1997).

27. This is taken from *Catholic Book of Family Novenas* (New York: John C. Crawley, 1956), 329–30.

28. From *The Catholic Book of Family Novenas*, 336.

29. The list of mysteries is taken from *The Catholic Book of Family Novenas*, 336. On the medieval origins of this practice, see Anne Winston-Allen, *Stories of the Rose: The Making of the Rosary in the Middle Ages* (University Park: Pennsylvania State University Press, 1997), esp. 111–52, and Eugene Honee, "Image and Imagination in the Medieval Culture of Prayer: A Historical Perspective," in *The Art of Devotion in the Late Middle Ages in Europe, 1300–1500* (Princeton: Princeton University Press, 1994). For an example of a meditation on the mysteries in light of present-day concerns, see Rosemary Haughton, *Feminine Spirituality: Reflections on the Mysteries of the Rosary* (New York: Paulist Press, 1976).

30. David Morgan identifies this dimension of the viewing of sacred images as the "psychology of recognition" and finds it to be especially present in popular attitudes toward the widely distributed image of Jesus by the American artist Warner Sallman. See Morgan, *Visual Piety*, 34–50, for a discussion of devotional recognition. Morgan considers as well how believers manage to see many different images of a holy figure as all corroborative of this figure's "real likeness." As he writes, "Believers purport to see through the local features and apprehend the transcendent Jesus who stands behind every instantiation of his image" (39).

31. I did not have the opportunity to see Ofili's work, so I cannot comment on it (a scruple that any number of Catholic protesters and the former mayor of New York City, Rudolph Giuliani, did not share with me). Paula Kane's discussion of this incident, in "American Madonnas: Perspectives on Mary since the 1940s" (unpublished paper, Cushwa Center for the Study of American Catholicism, University of Notre Dame, March 2000, 2–4), was helpful in preparing these few sentences of this chapter.

32. *Il Miracolo* (*The Miracle*), second vignette of the 1948 film *L'Amore*, starred Anna Magnani as the shepherdess, Frederico Fellini as the vagabond, and the inhabitants of Amalfi and Maiori as the villagers. Roberto Rossellini directed and Fellini wrote the screenplay (after a short story by Ramon del Valle-Inclan). This was the "half" film Fellini referred to in his famous movie *8 1/2*. (I thank Melissa R. Katz for the information in this note.)

33. In a theological reflection on the *Ave Maria*, Nicholas Ayo, C.S.C., writes, "Sinners know they cannot attract love in their wounded condition, unless that love be unconditional. They must be loved in their sinfulness as a mother loves a child in his or her woundedness. Something of that gratuitous quality of love that goes beyond one's deserts and gives life where there is no claim to life captures the tone of this petition in the *Ave Maria*." *The Hail Mary: A Verbal Icon of Mary* (Notre Dame, Ind.: University of Notre Dame Press, 1994), 110–11. For a study of the mood and self-perception of Catholics in the United States in the early days of the Cold War, see Fisher, *Dr. America*.

34. For a discussion of this controversy, see Frank Walsh, *Sin and Censorship: The Catholic Church and the Motion Picture Industry* (New Haven: Yale University Press, 1996), 241–61.

35. Rubén Martínez reports this in "The Undocumented Virgin," in *Goddess of the Americas/La Diosa de las Americas: Writings on the Virgin of Guadalupe*, ed. Ana Castillo (New York: Riverhead Books, 1996), 100.

36. This litany of the names of Our Lady of Guadalupe is taken from Castillo, *Goddess of the Americas*.

CHAPTER THREE
MATERIAL CHILDREN: MAKING GOD'S PRESENCE REAL FOR CATHOLIC BOYS
AND GIRLS AND FOR THE ADULTS IN RELATION TO THEM

1. Clifford Geertz, "Religion as a Cultural System," in *The Interpretation of Cultures* (New York: Basic Books, 1973), 87–125; quote in the text is from p. 90.

2. A classic locus of this argument is Emile Durkheim, *The Elementary Forms of the Religious Life*, trans. Joseph Ward Swain (New York: Free Press, 1965),

esp. book 3, "The Principal Ritual Attitudes," 337–496; Geertz also emphasizes the world-making powers of ritual. For a recent important discussion of religious ritual see Catherine Bell, *Ritual Theory, Ritual Practice* (New York: Oxford University Press, 1992). The example of the woman associated with devotion to the Sacred Heart is taken from a conversation I had in Phoenix, Arizona, as part of the research for ongoing work on growing up Catholic in the United States in the twentieth century: LL-F-56-Superior, Az./Phoenix, Az.-2/13/01. The format of citations from this research is a variation of the one I have used in other studies: identifying initials for the person with whom I spoke (I have made these up to protect my sources but they are consistent throughout so readers can keep track of what particular people say), age birthplace/location of our conversation, and its date. Most of the conversations took place in small groups of people (usually four to five) who gathered together, at my request, in a group member's home, for several discussions, over a three- or four-week period, about growing up Catholic. I taped the conversations and prepared transcripts afterwards. Participants in this work were chosen by a contact in a particular area I had made through friends, always an older woman with long connections to the community who drew on her friends and neighbors—and their friends and neighbors—in assembling the groups for me. The groups were made up of equal numbers of men and women and ranged in age from mid-thirties to mid-seventies. So far in this research I have worked in Louisiana, Arizona, Indiana, Ohio, and Nebraska. The people I speak to know that I am working on a book on growing up Catholic; I do not make composites and I quote individuals exactly. My sources are assured that I will protect their identities; they also know that they can ask me not to quote something they had said, even long after our conversations (although in all the years I have been working this way, no one has ever made this request).

3. Sister Mary I.H.M., "Preparing the Little Child for Christmas," *Journal of Religious Instruction* 8 (December 1937): 303–6; quotations in this paragraph are from p. 305; quotations in the next are from p. 306.

4. "Preparing the Little Child for Christmas," 306.

5. "Preparing the Little Child for Christmas," 306–7.

6. For a recent, useful discussion of the meanings of relics, see Gregory Schopen, "Relic," in *Critical Terms for Religious Studies*, ed. Mark C. Taylor (Chicago: University of Chicago Press, 1998), 256–68.

7. Elaine Scarry's discussion of torture is in *The Body in Pain: The Making and Unmaking of the World* (New York: Oxford University Press, 1985), 27–59.

8. My thinking on childhood has been influenced by a number of recent works on the history, sociology, and politics of childhood, among them Karin Calvert, *Children in the House: The Material Culture of Early Childhood, 1600–1900* (Boston: Northeastern University Press, 1992); Anne Higonnet, *Pictures of Innocence: The History and Crisis of Ideal Childhood* (London: Thames and Hudson, 1998); Chris Jenks, *Childhood* (New York: Routledge, 1996); James R. Kincaid, *Child-Loving: The Erotic Child and Victorian Culture* (Routledge, 1992); Kincaid, *Erotic Innocence: The Culture of Child Molesting* (Durham, N.C.: Duke University Press, 1998); Ashis Nandy, *The Intimate Enemy: Loss and Recovery of Self under Colonialism* (New York: Oxford University Press, 1983); and Neil Postman, *The Disappearance of Childhood* (New York: Delacorte Press, 1982),

Jackie Wullschläger, *Inventing Wonderland: The Lives and Fantasies of Lewis Carroll, Edward Lear, J.M. Barrie, Kenneth Grahame, and A.A. Milne* (New York: Free Press, 1995).

See also the important collections, Paula S. Fass and Mary Ann Mason, eds., *Childhood in America* (New York: New York University Press, 2000); Henry Jenkins, ed., *The Children's Culture Reader* (New York: New York University Press, 1998); and Elliott West and Paula Petrik, eds., *Small Worlds: Children and Adolescents in America, 1850–1950* (Lawrence: University Press of Kansas, 1992).

9. Scarry, *The Body in Pain*, 204–5. The anticipation of seeing the interior of Isaac's body "makes the dimly apprehended incontestably present; for the object of conviction acquires a compelling and vibrant presence from the compelling and vibrant sequence of actions which the human willingness to believe, to be convinced, is enacted" (205).

10. For a striking meditation on the enduring implications of the religious trope of child sacrifice for Western cultures see Carol Delaney, *Abraham on Trial: The Social Legacy of Biblical Myth* (Princeton: Princeton University Press, 1998).

11. Jenks, *Childhood*, 3.

12. For citations on these various modern apparitions, see notes 8 and 9 of chapter 2. The shift in the late twentieth century from child visionaries to adults (of all social classes) is a problem for historical, cultural, and social psychological analysis.

13. Igino Giordani, *Pius X: A Country Priest*, trans. Rt. Rev. Thomas J. Tobin (Milwaukee: Bruce Publishing, 1952), 93–95. Giordani sees the popular scrupulousness about bringing very young children to the Communion rail as evidence of Jansenist influence. As a result of Pius's initiatives, Giordani writes, "immediately, there was a great enrichment of the Eucharistic life of the Church, as throngs of children crowded about the altar" (95). The story of the English visitor is told in Katherine Burton, *The Great Mantle. The Life of Giuseppe Melchiore Sarto, Pope Pius X* (London: Longmans Green, 1950), 203. Other popes in the modern era also aspired to be the children's pope, which was a sentimental fascination among American Catholics. See, for example, Frater Barry B. Brunsman, O.F.M., " 'We Wish to Be the Pope of Youth,' " *Priestly Studies* 25 (Winter 1957): 13–21, on Pius XII.

14. Benedict XV is quoted on St. Thérèse in John Clarke, O.C.D., introduction to *Story of a Soul: The Autobiography of St. Thérèse of Lisieux*, trans. Clarke (Washington, D.C.: ICS Publications, 1976), vii; see also the discussion in Monica Furlong, *Thérèse of Lisieux* (London: Virago, 1987), 127–28. La Soledad de la Torre Recaurte is discussed by William A. Christian Jr., *Visionaries: The Spanish Republic and the Reign of Christ* (Berkeley and Los Angeles: University of California Press, 1996), 225–29. Raymond J. O'Brien's pamphlet on the boy saint is *A Boy Who Loved Jesus: Guy De Fontgalland, 1913–1925* (St. Louis: Queen's Work, 1933). O'Brien tells his readers that as the boy was dying, Jesus whispered, "My little Guy, I shall take you. You will die young. You will not be my priest. I desire to make you my angel" (14). O'Brien closes his work with accounts of priests praying to little Guy (28). Sentimental Victorian Roman Catholic piety insisted that Mary remained Jesus' mother in heaven; as historian Carol Englehardt remarks, Frederick Faber addressed Mary as "dearest Mamma." She notes

that non-Roman Catholic Victorian writers "vociferously rejected any meditations on Jesus 'as a little child in the arms of Mary' " because this was seen as a diminishment of Jesus' power and masculinity. (She is quoting here from Michael Hobart Seymour, *A Pilgrimage to Rome*, 1848.) Englehardt explains that Anglican visitors to the continent complained about depictions of Jesus as a child; indeed, so terrifying was this that "some Protestants even objected to any suggestion that Mary had guided or directed Jesus when he was a baby." Charles Kingsley explicitly mocked Catholics in *Yeast: A Problem* (1851) for seeing themselves as children of Mary. As Englehardt concludes, the contrast between "masculine, rational Englishmen who worshipped Christ and childlike, effeminate Roman Catholics who worshipped the Virgin Mary" was central to Victorian anti-Catholicism. "Victorians and the Virgin Mary: Religion, National Identity, and the Woman Question in England, 1830–1880," Ph.D. diss., Indiana University, 1997. Quotations here are from pp. 172, 175, 185.

15. The Third Plenary Council is discussed in Timothy Walch, *Parish School: American Catholic Parochial Education from the Colonial Times to the Present* (New York: Crossroad, 1996), 61–62.

16. For example, "Mass Server in Sisters' Chapel," *Ecclesiastical Review* 99 (December 1938): 558–59, typically states, "The office of server of Mass cannot be discharged by a woman. According to all theologians it would be a mortal sin for a woman (even though a religious) *to serve at the altar*" (558; emphasis in the original). See also "Mass without a Server," *Ecclesiastical Review* 91 (September 1934): 298–301.

17. The teacher quoted in the paragraph is Sister Marita, O.S.F., "Marshaling Troops for Christ," *Catholic School Journal* 53 (September 1953): 204–5 (quotation from 204). For other expressions of this pervasive martial spirit, see, for example, Paul E. Campbell, "Enlisting the Little Ones for Christ," *Homiletic and Pastoral Review* 40 (December 1939): 291–98; Kaye B. Green, "Youth—'An Army of the Altar,' " *Catholic Action* 35 (November 1953): 6–8.

18. The comment about children bridging the gulf between their parents and the priests is from Rev. Daniel F. Cunningham, "Teaching Children the Mass," *Report of the Proceedings . . . NCEA* (National Catholic Education Association) vol. 27 (November 1930): 352–59; this quotation is on p. 352. The lament about "those armies of children" is from M.V. Kelly, C.S.B., "The First Friday and Children's Confessions," *Homiletic and Pastoral Review* 37 (October 1936): 65–67, quotation on p. 66. For an example of the critical rethinking of the Catholic school enterprise in the 1960s, see Wakin and Scheuer, *The De-Romanization of the American Catholic Church*, 61–83. Walch discusses this moment in *Parish School*, 169–240. Influential contemporary discussions about the relevance, or not, of Catholic schools were Mary Perkins Ryan, *Are Parochial Schools the Answer? Catholic Education in the Light of the Council* (New York: Holt, Rinehart, and Winston, 1964); and William E. Brown and Andrew M. Greeley, *Can Catholic Schools Survive?* (New York: Sheed and Ward, 1970). On Protestant childhoods in the United States see Margaret Lamberts Bendroth, *Growing Up Protestant: Parents, Children, and Mainline Churches* (New Brunswick, N.J.: Rutgers University Press, 2002).

19. Sanctifying grace is defined for little readers in "Is Your Name in Heaven?" *Junior Catholic Messenger* 6 (15 October 1943): 41–42. As abstract as this may have been, readers were assured that "you ought to be willing to give up everything to get it" (42). My understanding of children's role in rituals associated with Saint Joseph's altars in New Orleans is based on conversations held in Louisiana in fall 2000, as part of the research for a cultural study of modern American Catholic childhoods with adult men and women now in their late sixties and seventies. For an example of how very, very young children were introduced to the possibility of a vocation, see Sister Marie Imelda, O.P., "God and His Partners: For the Kindergarten Teacher," *Journal of Religious Instruction* 13 (March 1943) 508–11. Sister Imelda recommends playing with children in class with a "Sister Doll." "Having been dressed by a Sister, the habit was perfect in every detail, even to a tiny rosary dangling from a black leather belt. Sister displayed the doll to the children who admired it longingly" (509). For an example of vocational literature for young people see Daniel A. Lord, S.J., *Shall I Be a Nun?* (St. Louis: Queen's Work, 1927).

20. The mother who wonders if people saw her boys on the altar is Catherine K. Ingalls, "Altar Boy Problems," *Ave Maria* 57 (20 February 1943): 247–48; her question is on p. 248. The definition of the true altar boy as one who likes to be seen is from J.P.R., "Church Management: Altar Servers, 1," *Clergy Review* (London), vol. 18 (May 1940): 459–61, quote on p. 459. The priest who stressed the visibility of altar boys in a manual detailing their proper conduct is Rev. David E. Rosage, *Letters to an Altar Boy* (Milwaukee: Bruce Publishing, 1952); quotes on pp. 61 and 62. The comment about Mary's gaze is from Charles G. Houston, "The Acolyte," *Catholic Educator* 18 (April 1948): 406.

21. EL-76-Tyrone, Az./Phoenix, Az.-2/8/01.

22. CL-46-Phoenix, Az./Phoenix, Az.-2/11/01.

23. Janet L. Nelson's comments on the supernatural power of children's actions are found in "Parents, Children, and the Church in the Earlier Middle Ages (Presidential Address)," in *The Church and Childhood: Papers Read at the 1993 Summer Meeting and the 1994 Winter Meeting of the Ecclesiastical History Society*, ed. Diana Wood (Oxford: Ecclesiastical History Society by Blackwell Publishers, 1994), 81–114; quote appears on p. 89. Pius's remark to the French children is reported in Giordani, *Pius X*, 96. By receiving Holy Communion, the pope told these children, "you have become higher than the angels," because angels cannot take Communion. Burton also discusses this visit in *The Great Mantle*, 209, adding the detail that as the children parted, the pope said to them with great feeling, "Catholiques et Françaises toujours! Dieu protège la France!" A rich and helpful collection of studies of Western theological accounts of children is Marcia J. Bunge, ed., *The Child in Christian Thought* (Grand Rapids: W. B. Eerdmans, 2001).

24. The loving evocation of altar boys is from Houston, "The Acolyte," 406; the poem cited is "Little Altar Boy," by Annamae Kelly, *Ave Maria* 62 (1 December 1945): 348. For examples of adult men warmly recalling their altar boy days, see for example, W.A.W., "Remembering," *Ave Maria* 38 (8 July 1933): 50–52; John C. Hanley, "The Bell and the Book," *Catholic Digest* 5 (December 1940):

7–9; and S.C.M., "Remember Your Altar-Boy Days?" *Catholic Digest* 12 (June 1948): 89–91.

25. The remark about "hooligans" is from Ernest Graf, O.S.B., "Choice and Training of Altar Boys," *Homiletic and Pastoral Review* 38 (March 1938): 623–24, on p. 623. Benediction competition is described in "Sketches Illustrating the Way . . ." *Orate Fratres* 17 (21 February 1943): 182. Father Graf notes that boys will not always serve unless there is "pecuniary inducement." (623). Father Graf also claims "a priestly vocation is easily fostered in an altar boy."

26. George P. Johnson, "The Priest and His Sanctuary Boys," *Ecclesiastical Review* 86 (January 1932): 7–29. Quotations in the text are on pp. 10, 11, and 27.

27. Edward J. McTague, "To the Unknown Altar Boy," *Ecclesiastical Review* 104 (June 1941): 506–13. In the paragraph that follows, the description of the funeral is on p. 506, the boy's dutifulness as an acolyte on p. 507, the murder on p. 508, and the little admonitory poem on p. 509.

28. The volume of commentary in the Catholic popular media on the teenage problem in the middle years of the twentieth century is huge. Rarely was an issue of a Catholic family periodical or journals for nuns or priests published without some reference to troublesome teenagers, male and female, and the danger they posed to the culture. Here are some examples of this literature from the 1930s to the 1960s: Mary D. Chambers, "What a Girl Should Know," *The Magnificat* 48 (May–October, 1931): 18–20; Anna E. King, "The Adolescent Girl," *Catholic Action* 15 (August 1933): 23–24 (King writes about girls' "bored air of condescension, the occasional direct defiance of parental edicts, the exaggerated emotional reactions to the most minor frustrations, the display of lack of consideration for others, spells of moodiness and apathy" [p. 23]); "Solving the Youth Problem in the Chicago Archdiocese," *Catholic Action* 16, no. 2 (February 1934): 3–4; Most Rev. Bernard J. Sheil, "Problems of Youth," *Catholic Mind* 34, no. 18 (22 September 1936): 365–68; Daniel A. Lord, S.J., "The Training of Girls for Catholic Action," *Homiletic and Pastoral Review* 35 (January 1935): 332–36; Felix M. Kirsch, O.F.M. Cap., "Adolescence: A Challenge and an Opportunity," *Homiletic and Pastoral Review* 35 (August 1935): 1195–1201 ("We are all familiar with the faults of our young people," 1195); "Young Women," *America* 57 (15 May 1937); "How the Adolescent Loses Faith in Adults," *Journal of Religious Instruction* 8 (September 1937): 59–63; Joseph A. Coyne, O.S.A., "The Boy, His Home, and His School: Disciplinary Problems in High Schools," *Catholic School Journal* 41 (January 1941): 1–4; Daniel A. Lord, S.J., *Love, Sex, and the Teen-Agers* (St. Louis: Queen's Work, 1947); Dr. Clement S. Mihanovich, *Understanding the Juvenile Delinquent* (St. Louis: Queen's Work, 1956); John Thomas, S.J., "Parents and the Youth Problem," *Apostolate* 3 (Autumn 1956): 47–54; Sister Ancille, O.S.B., "Teenagers, Emotions, and Music," *Musart* 9 (March 1957): 6–7, 37; John B. Sheerin, C.S.P., "What Troubles Teen-Agers?" *Catholic World* 186 (March 1958): 401–4 ("The teen-agers of today are killers," 401); Pacificus Kennedy, O.F.M., "Sister Makes the Gang," *Columbia* 39 (April 1959): 29, 48; Robert Meredith, "Our Rebellious Teen-Agers," *Priest* 16 (May 1960): 442–49 ("Why Have Our Children Become So Disobedient?" 442); John E. Gibson, "What Teen-Agers Are Really Like," *Catholic Digest* 25 (June 1961): 61–63;

Donald F. Miller, C.S.S.R., "Why and How Teen-Agers Need Parents," *Liguorian* 49 (August 1961): 41–45; Dr. Lois Lundrell Higgins, "Parish and Diocesan Youth Programs to Combat Juvenile Delinquency," *American Journal of Catholic Youth Work* 2 (September 1961): 16–21; Leo J. Trese, "The Special Problems of Adolescence," *Marriage* 44 (March 1962): 24–31; Theodore J. Vittoria, S.S.P., "The Priest and the Challenge of Youth," *Pastoral Life* 8 (September–October 1964): 35–38; William Grace, "Young People Today: Are They Too Smug?" *Saint Anthony Messenger* 70 (September 1962): 15–17. I should stress that this is the merest fraction of the literature on the "youth problem" in American Catholicism in the middle years of the century.

29. Sister Mary Consilia, O.P., "The Religious Practices of Children," *Journal of Religious Instruction* 8 (February 1938): 497–512; quotes appear on p. 498.

30. Rev. Gerald T. Brennan, *Angel Food: Little Talks to Little Folks* (Milwaukee: Bruce Publishing, 1939), 22.

31. Brendan Mitchell, O.F.M., "Symposium: The Teaching of Liturgy in Elementary Schools," *Report of the Annual Meeting . . . NCEA,"* 1939, 167–71; quotes appear on p. 167.

32. Mitchell, "Symposium." Mitchell's notion of "intimate participation" occurs on p. 169. "Preparing for Communion," *Junior Catholic Messenger* 31 (28 April 1944): 243c.

33. Articles by Catholic educators, lay and religious, about how best to introduce children to the Mass are simply endless—there are hundreds of them, published in many different periodicals for many different Catholic audiences (for teachers, for parents, for parish priests, and so on). What follows is the smallest example of such reflections, beginning in the 1920s, which is when the most concerted effort to make the Mass approachable to children got under way among American educators, priests, and nuns: Rev. William R. Kelly, *The Mass for Children* (New York: Benzinger Brothers, 1925); Rev. Daniel F. Cunningham, "Teaching Children the Mass," *Report of the Proceedings . . . NCEA* 27 (November 1930): 352–59; Sister Estelle, O.P., "The Liturgy and Religious Instruction in the Grades," *Orate Fratres* 5 (28 December 1930): 64–69; C. C. Martindale, S.J., " 'Teaching Mass' to Children," *Orate Fratres* 7 (9 September 1933): 443–46; Sister Jane Marie, O.P., "At Holy Mass for the Primary Child," *Journal of Religious Instruction* 7 (April 1937): 731–37; Sister M. Agnesine, S.S.N.D., "Teaching the Mass to Children," *Report of the Proceedings . . . NCEA*, 1933; 391–400; A School Sister of Notre Dame, "Teaching the Mass to Children," *Catholic School Journal* 33 (September 1933): 205–9; A Sister of the Precious Blood, "Liturgy in the Classroom," *Orate Fratres* 11 (February 1937): 150–51; Sister M. Rosalia, "Methods of Teaching the Mass to Public School Pupils of the Elementary School Grades," *Journal of Religious Instruction* 9 (January 1939): 405–15; Felix M. Kirsch, O.F.M., Cap., "A Method of Teaching the Mass," *Journal of Religious Instruction* 9 (January 1939): 365–69; Mother Margaret Bolton, "Teaching Holy Mass to Children at First Communion Level," *Journal of Religious Instruction* 9 (May 1939): 722–37; Gerald A. Meath, "Liturgy and the Child," *Blackfriars* 20 (March 1939): 195–200; Sister Agnes Helen, S.I., "A Third Grade Unit on the Mass," *Journal of Religious Instruction* 12 (October 1941): 145–50; "What Is Wrong with Our Teaching of the Mass?" *Journal of Religious Instruction* 13 (Jan-

uary 1943): 323–24; Sister Marie Imelda, "The Kindergarten Child and the Liturgy," *Journal of Religious Instruction* 13 (January 1943): 351–56; Daniel A. Lord, S.J., *A Child at Mass* (New York: Devotional Publishing, 1945); Sister M. Wilfrid, O.S.F., "The Adoring Bees of Holy Mass," *Catholic School Journal* 45 (May 1945): 142; Brother George, F.S.C., "An Experiment in Making Mass Meaningful for School Life," *Orate Fratres* 19 (9 September 1945): 467–74; Sister Mary Jane, O.S.B., "The Sixth Grade Learns the Missal," *Journal of Religious Instruction* 17 (November 1946): 295–300; Sister M. Janice Egan, O.S.B., "Bringing the Liturgy into the Classroom," *Journal of Religious Instruction* 17 (April 1947): 700–703; "The Apostolate: Suffer Little Children," *Worship* 28, no. 2 (January 1954): 94–96; Joan Schibler, "Youngsters at Mass," *Family Digest* 9 (February 1954): 57–60; Sister M. Malachy, "How Can One Teach a First Grader about 'Our Church,' " *Catholic School Journal* 58 (September 1958): 55; Sisters of Mercy, "These Children Live the Liturgy," *Catholic School Journal* 59 (January 1959): 37; Owenita Sanderlin, "Baby Goes to Mass," *Crosier Missionary* 34 (August 1959): 32–36; Thomas Schaffer, "Mass Is for Children Too!" *Marriage* 42 (April 1960): 23–26; Joy Marie Hoag, "Preparing Your Child for Mass," *Marriage* 42 (September 1960): 16–19; Sister Mary Loyola, P.V.M.I., "Young Members and Mass," *Ave Maria* 94 (8 July 1961): 28–29; Michael W. Ducey, O.S.B., "Explaining the Mass to Children," *Marriage* 43 (August 1961): 39–41; Sister Mary Rosamond Walsh, O.P., "This Is Our Life: A Fifth Grade Activity," *Catholic Educator* 33 (September 1962): 114–17 (this is accompanied by extraordinary pictures of children playing mass in school). On the children's mass, see Emil W. Dunn, O.F.M., Cap., "The Children's Mass," *Journal of Religious Instruction* 12 (May 1942): 746–50, and Msgr. John L. Belford, "The Children's Mass," *Homiletic and Pastoral Review* 23 (April 1935): 691–97. For a study of children playing Mass in Dutch Catholicism see Paul Post, " 'An Excellent Game . . .': On Playing the Mass" (trans. D. Mader), in Charles Caspers, Gerard Lukken, and Gerard Rouwhorst, eds., *Bread of Heaven: Customs and Practices Surrounding the Holy Communion. Essays in the History of Liturgy and Culture* (Kampen, the Netherlands: Kok Pharos Publishing House, 1995), 185–214.

34. The comment about getting sick from the smell of incense at mass was made by UE-F-54-Howells, Ne./Newman Grove, Ne.-5/29/01, and was seconded by her husband, EE-M-59-Norfolk, Ne./Newman Grove, Ne.-5/29/01.

35. The various instructions for receiving Communion in this paragraph are taken from "At the Communion Rail," *Junior Catholic Messenger* 9, no. 17 (6 January 1943): 99; "What We Should Do," *Junior Catholic Messenger* 8, no. 35 (20 May 1942): 281; "Manners in Church," *Junior Catholic Messenger* 10, no. 28 (31 March 1944): 223c. This article bravely concludes that the "Mass does not seem long" to children who behave properly. This was incentive. Again, the person quoted at the end of this paragraph is UE-F-54-Howells, Ne./Newman Grove, Ne.-5/29/01.

36. "This Is Tommy Twistneck," *Junior Catholic Messenger* 6, no. 9 (24 January 1940): 156; "Harry-in-a-Hurry," *Junior Catholic Messenger* 6, no. 20 (31 January 1940): 164; "Halfway Harry O'Kneel," *Junior Catholic Messenger* 6, no. 37 (29 May 1940): 300; "Whispering Willie," *Junior Catholic Messenger* 7, no. 1 (11 September 1940): 4; "Vestibule Charlie," *Junior Catholic Messenger* 7,

no. 23 (26 February 1941): 180; "Turnabout Mary," *Junior Catholic Messenger* 7, no. 28 (2 April 1941): 220; "Mummo the Clam," *Junior Catholic Messenger* 8, no. 5 (8 October 1941): 36; "Danny Divebomber," *Junior Catholic Messenger* 10, no. 3 (24 September 1943): 22; "Phillip Flip," *Junior Catholic Messenger* 9, no. 26 (10 March 1943): 156; "Don-Drop-It," *Junior Catholic Messenger* 9, no. 30 (10 April 1943): 180; "Timmy-the-Termite," *Junior Catholic Messenger* 9, no. 36 (22 May 1943): 216; "Wilfred Waster," *Junior Catholic Messenger* 10, no. 1 (10 September 1943): 6; and "Bertie Bumper," *Junior Catholic Messenger* 10, no. 20 (4 February 1944): 158-B.

37. Daniel F. O'Leary, *Pre-school Children and God* (St. Louis: Queen's Work, 1961), 19.

38. Little John's story is told in Miriam Mason, "The Boy Who Watched," *Junior Catholic Messenger* 9, no. 7 (21 October 1942): 41–42. John goes back to the church because, as he says, "I know what it is to be lonely." Pietro Camporesi reflects on the European tradition of stories about prodigies and miracles of the host in "The Consecrated Host: A Wondrous Excess," in *Fragments for a History of the Human Body*, ed. Michael Feher, part 1 (New York: Zone, 1989): 221–37.

39. CR-F-74-New Orleans, La./Harahan, La.-10/16–00; LB-F-74-Franklin, La./Harahan, La.-10/16/00; KL-F-73-New Orleans, La./Harahan, La.-10/16/00; OL-F-74-New Orleans, La./Harahan, La.-10/16/00; IV-F-74-New Orleans, La./Harahan, La.-10/16/00.

40. "In Between Times," *Junior Catholic Messenger* 9, no. 36 (22 May 1943): 215. The suggestion about making lists of prayers as gifts is from "Something to Do," *Junior Catholic Messenger* 7, no. 33 (7 May 1941): 260.

41. For example S.M.R., "Do's and Don'ts in the Teaching of Religion," *Catholic School Interests* 8 (April 1929): 20–21, 26; Sister M. Borromeo, S.S.J., "The Ideal Attitude of the Religious Teacher toward Her Pupils," *Catholic School Journal* 35 (November 1935): 288–89; Rev. Richard J. Quinlan, "Self-Examination for Religious Teachers," *Journal of Religious Instruction* 7 (September 1936): 39–45 (this includes a "teaching personality" self-examination quiz); Sister M. Viola, O.S.F., "Praise as a Factor in Religious Education," *Catholic School Journal* 38 (September 1938): 199–202; Sister Dolores Schorsch, O.S.B., "Fear in Religious Instruction: Avoiding Harmful Fear," *Journal of Religious Instruction* 11 (October 1940): 125–26.

42. A School Sister of Notre Dame, "Devotion to the Queen of the Rosary," *Catholic School Journal* 33 (October 1933): 234–38; quotes appear on p. 235.

43. Sister M. A. Merici, S.S.N.D., "I Believe in the Communion of Saints," *Catholic School Journal* 30 (November 1930): 394–99, quotes on p. 397; "The Forgotten Soul," *Junior Catholic Messenger* 2, no. 10 (3 November 1935): 76.

44. Brennan, *Angel Food*, 110.

45. This was reported to me by adults ranging in age from the late forties into the eighties in all parts of the country and in various ethnic groups. The practice was not ethnically specific or regional; it belonged to midcentury Catholic childhoods in the United States.

46. Rev. Henry P. Sullivan, "Instructing Little Children: Some Notes on 'Morning and Night Prayers' and 'Prayers before and after Meals,' " *Journal of Religious*

Instruction 7 (April 1937): 739; "Father Brown Says," *Junior Catholic Messenger* 9, no. 1 (9 September 1942): 36; "Dick the Dreamer," *Junior Catholic Messenger* 7, no. 3 (25 September 1940): 20; "Windmill Willie," *Junior Catholic Messenger* 9, no. 1 (9 September 1942): 4.

47. Sister M. A. Merici, S.S.N.D., "Devotion to the Holy Guardian Angels," *Catholic School Journal* 31 (October 1931): 349–54; quoted phrase appears on p. 350; prayer on p. 352. For examples of the place of angels in the way adults represented the faith to children, see Rev. Gerald T. Brennan, *Angel City: A Book for Children from Six to Sixty* (Milwaukee: Bruce Publishing, 1941); Daniel A. Lord, S.J., *Stories of the Angels* (New York: Devotional Publishing, 1948).

48. "She Saw Her Angel," *Junior Catholic Messenger* 4 (29 September 1937): 20. Lord holds out the same promise of seeing the angels, *Stories of the Angels*.

49. Lord, *Stories of the Angels* (the volume is unpaginated).

50. "Your Guardian Angel," *Junior Catholic Messenger* 8 (1 October 1941), and "She Saw Her Angel."

51. Brennan, *Angel Food*, 37.

52. "Things Needed for Mass," *Junior Catholic Messenger* 9 (18 November 1942): 63.

53. MM-F-73-Cinncinnati, Oh./Bloomington, In.-3/4/97.

54. SDK, Ph.D., to Robert Orsi, April 8, 2002. The writer also observed of her own childhood, "I have no doubts about the memories of having to wear blue dresses for Mary to school every day in May and the shame when my Mom couldn't come up with enough different blue dresses in our family of six to 'break Mary's heart, turn your back on the Blessed Mother' by not wearing a blue dress. . . . I remember my dad missing my brother's First Communion because he was president of the Holy Cross Alumnae Sodality and the priest moderator wouldn't excuse him from his duties there. In sixth grade I remember fainting from hunger because we had a Martyr's Club with prizes for those who practiced the most self-sacrifice—Sister suggested fasting and we even cut like stigmata and stuck thorn bushes in our school uniforms at Sister's suggestion."

CHAPTER FOUR
TWO ASPECTS OF ONE LIFE: SAINT GEMMA GALGANI AND MY GRANDMOTHER IN THE WOUND BETWEEN DEVOTION AND HISTORY, THE NATURAL AND THE SUPERNATURAL

1. The best introduction to Gemma's life in English is the recently published volume by Rudolph M. Bell and Cristina Mazzoni, *The Voices of Gemma Galgani: The Life and Afterlife of a Modern Saint* (Chicago: University of Chicago Press, 2003).

2. Walter Benjamin famously commented on the decline of storytelling as a condition of late modernity in "The Storyteller: Reflections on the Works of Nikolai Leskov," in Benjamin, *Illuminations*, 83–109.

3. LL-F-56-Superior, Az./Phoenix, Az.-2/13/01. Luisa told me, "[My grandmother] always lived in Mexico. We always traveled back and forth, back and forth, with her. My religion actually came from my grandmother. It was this one little picture that was always there—it was a Sacred Heart of Jesus that she had

that was a very important picture for me which I now have above my bed. The very same picture. When she passed away, that was all I wanted from the things that she had was that one particular portrait of the Sacred Heart of Jesus."

4. Alphonse M. Schwitalla, S.J., "Patron Saints of Catholic Hospitals," *Hospital Progress* 39 (April 1958): 81.

5. The description of Gemma bleeding at the table is from Herbert George Kramer, S.M., *Crucified with Christ* (New York: P.J. Kenedy, 1949), 103; the second quotation in the paragraph is from Rev. Leo Proserpio, S.J., *St. Gemma Galgani* (Milwaukee: Bruce Publishing, 1940), 99. Father Kramer's source for this story is not clear. Other writers on Gemma emphasize that she hid her wounds from others, wearing gloves to the dinner table, for instance, or excusing herself when she felt an imminent ecstasy. The point remains, though: the passage from everyday life to heavenly engagement was not simple for Gemma.

6. A Sister of Saint Joseph, *The White Flower of the Passion, a Drama in Three Acts* (Boston: E.J. Powers Press, 1940), 21.

7. For a helpful account of the complex processes of canonization, see Kenneth L. Woodward, *Making Saints: How the Catholic Church Determines Who Becomes a Saint, Who Doesn't, and Why* (New York: Simon and Schuster, 1990); on Gemma's canonization, see the chapter by Bell, "Canonization," in Bell and Mazzoni, *The Voices of Gemma Galgani*, 159–92. Padre Germano's boast is cited on p. 161.

8. Edna Beyer, "Gemma Galgani: Saint and Mystic," *Ave Maria* 55 (18 April 1942): 497. Schwitalla calls Gemma "this very modern Saint of our day," in "Patron Saints of Catholic Hospitals," 81.

9. Gemma's "heroic virtues" are cited in Richard Walsh, "The Power behind the Tiara," *Catholic World* 158 (March 1944): 555. Proserpio's discussion of Gemma's virtues can be found in *St. Gemma Galgani*, 116–27; the phrase "chastening of the flesh" and the sentence about Gemma's rejection of pleasure both appear on p. 122. St. Gemma of the Visitation is quoted by Bishop Proserpio on p. 127; the notion that Gemma was beyond both human and divine reproach appears in "On Being Misunderstood," *Catholic Charities Review* 27 (May 1943): 139.

10. Proserpio, *St. Gemma Galgani*, 11.

11. This paragraph and the next draw on Proserpio, *St. Gemma Galgani*, 113, 3, 7; *The White Flower of the Passion*, 11; and Beyer, "Gemma Galgani," 495.

12. Schwitalla, "Patron Saints of Catholic Hospitals," 81.

13. This paragraph is based on Hilary Sweeney, C.P., "St. Gemma and the Passion," *Sign* 39 (November 1959): 45; Therese Elizabeth Alexander, "A Saint Uncrowned," *Ave Maria* 34 (12 December 1931): 753–55, quotation on p. 755; *The White Flower of the Passion*, 60; Kramer, *Crucified with Christ*, 104; Proserpio, *St. Gemma Galgani*, 197.

14. Gemma's account of her Confirmation is quoted in Sister Saint Michael, S.S.J., *Portrait of Saint Gemma: A Stigmatic* (New York: Kenedy, 1950), 4; also cited in this paragraph are Proserpio, *St. Gemma Galgani*, 15; *The White Flower of the Passion*, 35 ("this was the beginning") and 17.

15. *The White Flower of the Passion*, 35.

16. See Kane, " 'She Offered Herself Up': The Victim Soul and Victim Spirituality in Catholicism."

17. The phrase "holy and mysterious vocation for suffering" is on p. 588 in Mary Fabyan Windeatt, "Lily of Lucca," *Sign* 19 (May 1940): 586–88. Also cited in this paragraph, in the order of quotation, are Kramer, *Crucified with Christ*, 101; Bruno M. Hagspiel, S.V.D., for the story of Gemma wishing to trade her suffering for the "lady of the house," on p. 98 in "A New Hospital Patroness: St. Gemma Galgani," *Hospital Progress* 21 (March 1940): 97–98; Gemma's "superhuman suffering" is described in Windeatt, "Lily of Lucca," 598.

18. Jesus' desire for Gemma to "suffer continually" is quoted in Sister Saint Michael, *Portrait of Saint Gemma*, 93, as is his invitation to Gemma to die on the cross, p. 197. The story of the well-rope is told by Proserpio, *St. Gemma Galgani*, 70, and the comment about Gemma suffering for the "sins of priests" is on p. 146. The quotation from *The White Flower of the Passion* is on p. 60.

19. Proserpio describes the occasion when Gemma's enraged brother, distraught at her notoriety, punches her in the eye, *Saint Gemma Galgani*, 83–84, see also pp. 123–24 for instances of Gemma's neighbors mocking her. Joseph Casper Husslein mentions the taunting in *Heroines of Christ* (Milwaukee: Bruce Publishing, 1939), 47. Beyer notes that Gemma's closest relatives did nothing to protect her for the obloquy of others, "Gemma Galgani: Saint and Mystic," 496. Beyer, p. 496, is the source for the last quotation in the paragraph. On Gemma's siblings see Bell, "The Historical Setting," in Bell and Mazzoni, *The Voices of Gemma Galgani*, 1–17.

20. Gemma's reflections on the burning fire of Jesus' love is taken from Proserpio, *Saint Gemma Galgani*, 190 and 191. Gemma's comment to Father Germano is on p. 130.

21. Jay Dolan points out that because of the high costs of secondary education, Catholic parishes did not customarily sponsor high schools. Instead, "the central high school serving a citywide population became the more common pattern." By 1959, according to Dolan, there were 2,428 Catholic high schools in the United States, with a total enrollment of 810,763. The enrollment in elementary schools that year was twice this number (*The American Catholic Experience*, 399). To set Catholic practice toward adolescents into a wider context, see Jeffrey P. Moran, *Teaching Sex: The Shaping of Adolescence in the Twentieth Century* (Cambridge: Harvard University Press, 2000); Harvey J. Graff, *Conflicting Paths: Growing Up in America* (Cambridge: Harvard University Press, 1995); and John Modell, *Into One's Own: From Youth to Adulthood in the United States, 1920–1975* (Berkeley and Los Angeles: University of California Press, 1989).

22. Windeatt, "Lily of Lucca," 587; Gabriel Francis Powers, "Two New Saints," *Sign* 19 (July 1940): 749–51 (The comment about Gemma in the teeth of the modern world is on p. 749); Walsh, "The Power behind the Tiara," 555. "By her prayers," Walsh also says, Gemma was "playing the part of the weak things of the world which confound the strong" (557). On the theme of Gemma's hiddenness, see also Proserpio, *St. Gemma Galgani*, 104–5, 144.

23. Jesus' instruction to Gemma about love is from Sister Saint Michael, S.S.J., *Portrait of Saint Gemma*, 45; the vision of Jesus offering Gemma the chalice of his Passion is on p. 60. The passage from *The White Flower of the Passion* is

taken from p. 7. The poem cited is by James Gallagher, "Saint Gemma Galgani," *Sign* 22 (May 1943): 598. Gallagher writes, "She took away His very Breath, / So beautiful her soul had grown." Jesus' desire to possess Gemma's soul entirely is quoted in Sister Saint Michael, *Portrait of Saint Gemma*, 60; Zia Elena's cry of distress is from *The White Flower of the Passion*, 38, as is Gemma's report of Jesus' claim on her.

24. Gemma's preparations for the feast of suffering are described by Sister Saint Michael, *Portrait of Saint Gemma*, 109, as is her confession to Volpi. Gemma's cry of love is from Proserpio, *St. Gemma Galgani*, 99. Gemma's prayer to be an "oblation . . . to the point of immolation" is quoted by Sister Saint Michael, *Portrait of Saint Gemma Galgani*, 179. This latter is also the source for the scene of Gemma kissing her crown of thorns, p. 154.

25. The dream is quoted in Sister Saint Michael, *Portrait of Saint Gemma Galgani*, 160.

26. There is a very substantial devotional literature on Padre Pio but no scholarly work yet. For devotional accounts, see, for example, John McCaffery, *Tales of Padre Pio, the Friar of San Giovanni* (Garden City, N.Y.: Image Books, 1981) and Dorothy M. Gaudiose, *Prophet of the People: A Biography of Padre Pio* (New York: Alba House, 1974).

27. Gemma's comments to Father Germano are quoted by Sister Saint Michael, *Portrait of Saint Gemma*, 89, as is her effort to console herself with the thought that even if Jesus does not look at her, she will always look at him.

28. Gemma's cry in the empty room is cited in Sister Saint Michael, *Portrait of Saint Gemma*, 213. Sister's reflection on Jesus' reserving the "last and the greatest" pain is on p. 211.

29. Proserpio reports Gemma's longing to be "one victim" with Jesus in *St. Gemma Galgani*, 147; the metaphor of pain as consummation appears in Sister Saint Michael, *Portrait of Saint Gemma*, 154, as does Gemma's plea to "suffer in company" with Jesus, p. 172 (which was overheard by the ever-vigilant Cecelia). The description of Gemma's last night is also from Sister Saint Michael, 218. Gallagher writes, "One day He sent His chauffer Death / And brought her brightness to His own," "Saint Gemma Galgani," 598. Gemma's death cry is cited by Kramer, *Crucified with Christ*, 114.

30. Alexander, "A Saint Uncrowned," 755.

CHAPTER FIVE
"HAVE *YOU* EVER PRAYED TO SAINT JUDE?"
REFLECTIONS ON FIELDWORK IN CATHOLIC CHICAGO

1. Critics of ethnography would have some questions about the specific tropes employed in this opening description. Why am I in the back of the church? What does this suggest about my sense of place in the community and how does it position the reader in relation to what follows? What is the point of the oppositions cold/warm, dark/light, outside/inside? Does the appearance of the young woman in the bomber jacket disclose an erotic current or a voyeuristic impulse? Why have I emphasized the "abandoned" quality of the neighborhood—so I can fill it with my own desires?—and the "diminishing" of the old ethnic neighborhoods—to

establish myself as a postethnic Catholic? To secure the neighborhoods' sense of otherness in the reader's mind? To anchor my authority as a person who has bravely gone into a marginal urban neighborhood? The locus classicus of such contemporary anxieties and suspicions about what's going on in a particular piece of ethnographic rhetoric is, of course, James Clifford and George E. Marcus, eds., *Writing Culture: The Poetics and Politics of Ethnography* (Berkeley and Los Angeles: University of California Press, 1986).

2. Devotion to Saint Jude is the subject of my book *Thank You, Saint Jude: Women's Devotion to the Patron Saint of Hopeless Causes.*

3. One can encounter the phrase "lived experience" in many different places. I draw it from Jean-Paul Sartre, *Search for a Method*, trans. Hazel E. Barns (New York: Vintage Books, 1968) and from Michael Jackson, *Paths towards a Clearing: Radical Empiricism and Ethnographic Inquiry* (Bloomington: Indiana University Press, 1989). By "empirical" in the last sentence of this paragraph I do not mean "realistic" or "objective," and this is not a call for a return to the old positivist orientation of the social sciences. My use of the word "empirical" is always inflected by the radical critiques mounted against the notion by a number of modern and postmodern philosophical traditions. Nonetheless, I want to retain the word to mean an encounter with human beings in the everyday circumstances of their lives, of which religious practices constitute one part (not discrete). The specific interpersonal nature of this encounter, the relationship between the researcher and the people among whom he or she works, is a concern of this chapter.

4. The anthropologist Jack Kugelmass, who has reflected systematically in his various writings on the implications of working in one's own cultural world (more or less), describes the fantasy that possessed him of being the "repository" of the vanishing world of the elderly South Bronx Jews he was studying. See *The Miracle of Intervale Avenue: The Story of a Jewish Congregation in the South Bronx* (New York: Schocken Books, 1986), 202. The synagogue continued on its fragile way long after Jack's work was finished there. For an account of Kugelmass's ongoing relationship with this community after his book was published, see his essay "Moses of the South Bronx: Aging and Dying in the Old Neighborhood," in Orsi, ed., *Gods of the City*, 231–56. James Clifford calls this fieldwork fantasy of the "disappearing object" "salvage ethnography," in "On Ethnographic Allegory," in Clifford and Marcus, eds., *Writing Culture*, 112–13.

5. This parenthetical comment reflects the influence in my thinking of Bonnie G. Smith, *The Gender of History: Men, Women, and Historical Practice* (Cambridge: Harvard University Press, 1998). Smith's excellent notes led me on to Marianne DeKoven, *Rich and Strange: Gender, History, Modernism* (Princeton: Princeton University Press, 1991); Rita Felski, *The Gender of Modernity* (Cambridge: Harvard University Press, 1995); Donna Haraway, *Primate Visions: Gender, Race, and Nature in the World of Modern Science* (New York: Routledge, 1989); Peter Middleton, *The Inward Gaze: Masculinity and Subjectivity in Modern Culture* (New York: Routledge, 1992); Londa Schiebinger, *The Mind Has No Sex: Women in the Origins of Modern Science* (Cambridge: Harvard University Press, 1989); and Schiebinger, *Nature's Body: Gender in the Making of Science* (Boston: Beacon Press, 1993).

6. Dipesh Chakrabarty, *Provincializing Europe: Postcolonial Thought and Historical Difference* (Princeton: Princeton University Press, 2000), 16.

7. Grant Wacker, *Heaven Below: Early Pentecostals and American Culture* (Cambridge: Harvard University Press, 2001), x.

8. Chakrabarty, *Provincializing Europe*; the definition of "historicism" is on pp. 247 and 243; Chakrabarty's discussion of Marx in this context is on p. 245 (see also the book's second chapter, "The Two Histories of Capital"); "decisionism" is introduced on p. 247.

9. The primary literature on renewal among women religious in this period is substantial. In thinking about this, I have been helped by Sister Gertrude Joseph Donnelly, S.S.J.O., *The Sister Apostle* (Notre Dame, Ind.: Fides, 1964); Sister Mary Hester Valentine, S.S.N.D., *The Post-Conciliar Nun* (New York: Hawthorn Books, 1968); Sister Charles Borromeo Muckenhirn, C.S.C., ed., *The Changing Sister* (Notre Dame, Ind.: Fides, 1965); Muckenhirn, ed., *The New Nuns* (New York: New American Library, 1967); Sisters of Charity, B.V.M., *Proceedings of the Institute on the Problems That Unite Us: July 31–August 20, 1965, Mundelein College, Chicago* (Mount Carmel, Iowa: Sisters of Charity, B.V.M., 1966). My understanding of this period in the history of American sisters was deeply informed by many conversations with Amy Koehlinger. *The New Yet Old Mass* is the title of a renewal handbook by Father Joseph M. Champlin (Notre Dame, Ind.: Ave Maria Press, 1977). On the notion of "reform" (versus revolution) in Catholic history, see Gerhart B. Ladner, *The Idea of Reform: Its Impact on Christian Thought and Action in the Age of the Fathers* (Cambridge: Harvard University Press, 1959) and John W. O'Malley, *Trent and All That: Renaming Catholicism in the Early Modern Era* (Cambridge: Harvard University Press, 2000). I first discussed the ideas that follow in the next several pages of this chapter in " 'The Infant of Prague's Nightie': The Devotional Origins of Contemporary Catholic Memory," *U.S. Catholic Historian* 21 no. 2 (Spring 2002): 1–18.

10. Daniel Berrigan, S.J., "The New Spirit of Modern Sacred Art," *Critic* 20 (July 1962): 30–33, quotes in the text from p. 30; in another article from this same period, to cite just two of countless such sources, this one about religious music, Rev. Frater Carlos Gonsalves, O.F.M., proclaims "the weight of centuries has engulfed the vitality of the Church" ("Religious Hymns and Parish Renewal," *Priestly Studies* 28 [Spring 1961]: 45–64, citation in the text from p. 45). Other instances of Catholic contempt for the past in this period and the sense of the past as inauthentic and useless include Hugh Tasch, O.S.B., "Vernacular in the Liturgy," *Altar and Home Pocket Missal* 1 (March 1961): 53–57; Don Fisher, "Contributions to Ugliness," *Catholic Property Administration* 26 (August 1962): 23; on the use of the developmental metaphor for this discredited past, see, for example, "Acting Our Age," *Today* 18 (October 1962): 2 (this was the periodical of the Chicago Inter-student Catholic Action Organization); Rev. James Killgallon and Rev. Gerard Weber, "The Mature Christian," *Ave Maria* 96 (24 November 1962): 11–14; Abbot Basil C. Butler, "The Church Speaks to Us as Adults," *Critic* 24 (February–March 1966): 18; Elmer Von Feldt, "A Call to Maturity," *Columbia* 46 (April 1966): 3; Robert T. Francoeur, "The Priest of the Future," *Jubilee* 14 (October 1966): 20–23; Andrew M. Greeley, "Adolescent American Catholicism," *Sign* 46 (November 1966): 15–18.

1. McAvoy's comment about fearing to open the door to the past is from "The *Ave Maria* after 100 Years," *Ave Maria* 101, no. 18 (1 May 1965): 6–9, 21; the quoted remark is on p. 6. The saints and objects associated with them were in many cases simply thrown away: there is a contemporary organization called the Vestment Exchange run by Episcopalian nuns dedicated to rescuing the artifacts of mid-twentieth-century American Catholic devotionalism from the junkyards, head shops, and taverns where they have been turning up for the last four decades. The founder of Vestment Exchange is Sister Elias Freeman and her website is http://www.vestmentexchange.org.

12. Michel-Rolph Trouillot, *Silencing the Past: Power and the Production of History* (Boston: Beacon Press, 1995), 15.

13. On the early apprehensions about the study of religious history among modernizing historians see Joyce Appleby, Lynn Hunt, and Margaret Jacob, *Telling the Truth about History* (New York: W.W. Norton, 1994), 38.

14. Information about *Late Nite Catechism*, which was conceived and produced by Maripat Donovan (who also originated the role of "Sister") and Vicki Quade, can be found on the website http://www.latenitecatechism.com. The description of the production on the website notes, "the authoritarian whims of Sister steer the course of the evening as she doles out glow-in-the-dark rosaries at one moment and confiscates lipsticks and candy at the next." (See http://www.latenightcatechism.com/Inc-skip.html.)

15. Examples of the photographs described here in the text may be found in the separatist newsletter, *Sangre de Cristo Newsnotes*, nos. 66–67, 15 November 1979, 6–7.

16. Crapanzano, *Tuhami*, 144.

17. On the proliferation of banners in the post-Conciliar sacred space, see Paul Hendrickson, *Seminary: A Search* (New York: Summit Books, 1983), 36–37.

18. Bronislaw Malinowski, *A Diary in the Strict Sense of the Term* (New York: Harcourt, Brace, and World, 1967), 41.

19. Sartre, *Search for a Method*, 91. Sartre, in an interview in the *New York Review of Books* (26 March 1970), identified this as his understanding of freedom.

20. Clifford Geertz, "Deep Play: Notes on the Balinese Cockfight," in *The Interpretation of Cultures*, 449.

21. Jackson, *Paths toward a Clearing*, 20.

22. Stanley A. Leavy, *The Psychoanalytic Dialogue* (New Haven: Yale University Press, 1980), 30, 29–30. Paul Rabinow, writing about anthropological research, notes that understanding is "mutually constructed" by ethnographer and informant in a process that transforms both, in *Reflections on Fieldwork in Morocco* (Berkeley and Los Angeles: University of California Press, 1977): 38.

23. John Comaroff and Jean Comaroff, *Ethnography and the Historical Imagination* (Boulder: Westview Press, 1992), 10.

24. Comaroff and Comaroff, *Ethnography and the Historical Imagination*, 11.

25. Jackson, *Paths toward a Clearing*, 4. For Jackson, this exercise reveals "the grounds of a common humanity," "the continuity of experience across cultures and through time." A powerful account of the use of one's own experience in the process of understanding another person's (in this case in a culture different from

the ethnographer's), is Renato Rosaldo, "Grief and a Headhunter's Rage: On the Cultural Force of the Emotions," in *Text, Play, and Story: The Construction and Reconstruction of Self and Society,* ed. E. M. Bruner (Proceedings of the American Ethnological Society, Washington, D.C., 1984), 178–95. See also Ruth Behar, *The Vulnerable Observer: Anthropology That Breaks Your Heart* (Boston: Beacon Press, 1996).

26. Gananath Obeyesekere, *The Work of Culture: Symbolic Transformation in Psychoanalysis and Anthropology* (Chicago: University of Chicago Press, 1990), 230.

27. Obeyesekere, *The Work of Culture,* 226.

28. Sartre, *Search for a Method,* 72.

29. Jonathan Z. Smith, "Fences and Neighbors: Some Contours of Early Judaism," in *Reimagining Religion: From Babylon to Jonestown* (Chicago: University of Chicago Press, 1982), 6.

CHAPTER SIX
SNAKES ALIVE: RELIGIOUS STUDIES BETWEEN HEAVEN AND EARTH

1. My discussion of the history of the modern Western study of religion is based on a rich literature on the subject that has begun to emerge in the past decade (with some distinguished predecessors). Among the works that have most shaped my understanding are Talal Asad, *Genealogies of Religion: Disciplines and Reasons of Power in Christianity and Islam* (Baltimore: Johns Hopkins University Press, 1993); David Chidester, *Savage Systems: Colonialism and Comparative Religion in Southern Africa* (Charlottesville: University Press of Virginia, 1996); Richard King, *Orientalism and Religion: Post-colonial Theory, India, and "the Mystic East"* (New York: Routledge, 1999); Hans G. Kippenberg, *Discovering Religious History in the Modern Age,* trans. Barbara Harshay (Princeton: Princeton University Press, 2002); Bruce Lincoln, *Theorizing Myth: Narrative, Ideology, and Scholarship* (Chicago: University of Chicago Press, 1999); Donald S. Lopez Jr., *Prisoners of Shangri-La: Tibetan Buddhism and the West* (Chicago: University of Chicago Press, 1998); Lopez, *Curators of the Buddha: The Study of Buddhism under Colonialism* (Chicago: University of Chicago Press, 1995); Russell T. McCutcheon, *Manufacturing Religion: The Discourse on Sui Generis Religion and the Politics of Nostalgia* (New York: Oxford University Press, 1997); Tomoko Masuzawa, *In Search of Dreamtime: The Quest for the Origin of Religion* (Chicago: University of Chicago Press, 1993); Nandy, *Intimate Enemy*; Nandy, *Time Warps: Silent and Evasive Pasts in Indian Politics and Religion* (New Brunswick, N.J.: Rutgers University Press, 2002); Mary Louise Pratt, *Imperial Eyes: Travel Writing and Transculturation* (New York: Routledge, 1992); J. Samuel Preus, *Explaining Religion: Criticism and Theory from Bodin to Freud* (New Haven: Yale University Press, 1987); Schmidt, Hearing Things; Jonathan Z. Smith, *Imagining Religion: From Babylon to Jonestown* (Chicago: University of Chicago Press, 1982); Smith, *Drudgery Divine: On the Comparison of Early Christianity and the Religions of Late Antiquity* (Chicago: University of Chicago Press, 1990); Michael Taussig, *Shamanism, Colonialism, and the Wild Man: A Study in Terror and Healing* (Chicago: University of Chicago Press, 1987); Ann Taves, *Fits,*

Trances, and Visions: Experiencing Religion and Explaining Experience from Wesley to James (Princeton: Princeton University Press, 1999); Taylor, *Critical Terms for Religious Studies*; Peter van der Veer, *Imperial Encounters: Religion and Modernity in India and Britain* (Princeton: Princeton University Press, 2001); Steven M. Wasserstrom, *Religion after Religion: Gershom Scholem, Mircea Eliade, and Henry Corbin at Eranos* (Princeton: Princeton University Press, 1999).

2. On the history of the gothic in American culture see Mark Edmundson, *Nightmare on Main Street: Angels, Sadomasochism, and the Culture of Gothic* (Cambridge: Harvard University Press, 1997) and Edward J. Ingebretsen, *Maps of Heaven, Maps of Hell: Religious Terror as Memory from the Puritans to Stephen King* (Armonk, N.Y.: M.E. Sharpe, 1996). For a powerful study of the eruption of this ancient memory of religious horror in the present see Lawrence Wright, *Remembering Satan* (New York: Knopf, 1994).

3. Dennis Covington, *Salvation on Sand Mountain: Snake Handling and Redemption in Southern Appalachia* (Reading, Mass.: Addison-Wesley, 1995). For other accounts of this culture that include some trenchant criticism of Covington's work see David L. Kimbrough, *Taking Up Serpents: Snake Handlers of Eastern Kentucky* (Chapel Hill: University of North Carolina Press, 1995) and Fred Brown and Jeanne McDonald, *The Serpent Handlers: Three Families and Their Faith* (Winston-Salem: John F. Blair, Publisher, 2000).

4. Covington, *Salvation on Sand Mountain*, describes the "sweet savor" of the snakes, a phrase used by the handlers themselves, on p. 162; the description of Punkin' Brown at the service is on p. 234, as is the comparison of Brown's "haaagh" with the underground vent. When he first introduces Brown, Covington tells readers that the preacher is "mired in the Old Testament, in the enumerated laws and the blood lust of the patriarchs" (209).

5. Covington, *Salvation on Sand Mountain*, 235.

6. Covington, *Salvation on Sand Mountain*, 239. The Tennessee minister is quoted by Brown and McDonald, *The Serpent Handlers*, 20.

7. On this point see also Smith, *Imagining Religion*, 6.

8. George M. Marsden, *The Soul of the American University: From Protestant Establishment to Established Nonbelief* (New York: Oxford University Press, 1994), 31, 85, and 89.

9. Marsden, *The Soul of the American University*, 85.

10. Marsden, *The Soul of the American University*, 93, 177, 329. On this early generation of Christian university professors in search of a new moral and intellectual vision see Murray G. Murphey, "On the Scientific Study of Religion in the United States, 1870–1980," in *Religion and Twentieth-Century American Intellectual Life*, ed. Michael J. Lacey (Washington, D.C.: Woodrow Wilson Center Press; Cambridge: Cambridge University Press, 1989), 136–37, and Robert M. Crunden, *Ministers of Reform: The Progressives' Achievement in American Civilization*, 1889–1920 (Urbana: University of Illinois Press, 1984).

11. Marsden, *The Soul of the American University*, 243; D.G. Hart, *The University Gets Religion: Religious Studies in American Higher Education* (Baltimore: Johns Hopkins University Press, 1999), 29.

12. Frederick Morgan Davenport's survey of the 1905 religious landscape is *Primitive Traits in Religious Revivals: A Study in Mental and Social Evolution*

(New York: Macmillan, 1905), viii. The best history of this tense engagement of the academic study of religion with broader social anxieties in American culture is Taves, *Fits, Trances, and Visions.*

13. H. L. Seneviratne, *The Work of Kings: The New Buddhism in Sri Lanka* (Chicago: University of Chicago Press, 1999), 2 and passim; on this subject see also Stephen R. Prothero, *The White Buddhist: The Asian Odyssey of Henry Steel Olcott* (Bloomington: Indiana University Press, 1996).

14. See John P. Burris, *Exhibiting Religion: Colonialism and Spectacle at International Expositions, 1851–1893* (Charlottesville: University Press of Virginia, 2001) and Richard Hughes Seager, *The World's Parliament of Religions: The East/West Encounter, Chicago, 1893* (Bloomington: Indiana University Press, 1995).

15. See Eric J. Sharpe, *Comparative Religion: A History,* 2d ed. (LaSalle, Ill.: Open Court, 1986), 266–93.

16. Sharpe, *Comparative Religion,* 310–11; Sam Gill, "The Academic Study of Religion," Journal of the American Academy of Religion 62 (Winter 1994): 969–70. Gill is here specifically criticizing the way "comparison" is understood in the discipline by some, but he clearly intends his remarks to have broader force.

17. Hart, *The University Gets Religion,* 241.

18. Stanley Hauerwas, "Christians in the Hands of Flaccid Secularists: Theology and 'Moral Inquiry' in the Modern University," paper presented at the conference on the Revival of Moral Inquiry in American Scholarship, Woodrow Wilson International Center for Scholars, Washington, D.C., 15–16 May 1995, cited with permission; Hart, *The University Gets Religion,* 251.

19. Warren A. Nord, *Religion and American Education: Rethinking a National Dilemma* (Chapel Hill: University of North Carolina Press, 1995), 8. Marsden, *The Soul of the American University,* 429–30.

20. Brown, *Mama Lola,* 241.

21. David L. Haberman, *Journey through the Twelve Forests: An Encounter with Krishna* (New York: Oxford University Press, 1994).

22. Haberman, *Journey,* 168–69.

23. Haberman, *Journey,* 169.

INDEX

altar boys, 82; the "altar boy problem,"
89–91; ambiguity of, 88–109; image of,
83; visibility of, 86. *See also* American
Catholic children
American Catholic children: and adults,
17, 77; the "age of," 79–81; and Ameri-
canization, 84–85; bodies of as media
of religious materialization, 74–78, 91;
and "children's mass," 94; clerical
abuse of, 15–16; disciplining the bodies
of, 92–99; and guardian angels, 103–6;
and the mass, 92–99, 130; and persons
with disabilities, 78–79; and Pius X, 80–
81; and prayer, 99–103; as representations of cultural interiority, 78; as saints,
81; and schooling, 82; spiritual and
moral status of, 88–109; and teenagers,
84, 91–92; visibility of, 86, 102. *See also*
altar boys; American Catholic culture;
Fontgalland, Guy de, nuns; Third Plenary Council
American Catholic culture: as alternative
to American Protestant culture, 33, 129;
changes of registered in corporal experience, 54; and conflict over media of presence, 51–54; culture of childhood in,
82–106; culture of pain and suffering in,
21–24, 30–31, 42, 129–31; liturgical
changes in, 8; modernist paradigm of, 9.
See also American Catholic children;
American Catholic memory; physical
distress; Protestants
American Catholic Hospital Association, 39
American Catholic memory, 54, 58; and
Catholic separatists, 155–56; and children's experience of mass, 94–95, 98;
and the conjunction of saints' and family
stories, 112–16, 138–45; contemporary
consequences of, 108; and contemporary
memory, 105, 107; and decisionism,
153, 157; as defined by its relationship
to the sacred, 152, 154–55; and desire,
35; devotionalism in, 153–58; and formation of children, 76–77, 106–7; and generational affiliations, 66–67; and immigration, 66–67, 107; as interpreted in

Late Night Catechism, 155–56; relationship of to forgetting, 156. *See also* American Catholic culture; modernity
American Catholic popular journalism,
205–7
American Catholic separatists, 155–56
Anthony, Saint, 37, 115
anti-Catholicism: and study of religion,
179–80; and the Virgin Mary, 65
Aquinas, Thomas, 193
Ave Maria, 26–28, 43, 86, 118, 154

Bakhtin, Mikhail, 170
Barth, Karl, 193
Benjamin, Walter, 59, 218n.14
Berger, Peter, 169–70. *See also* religious
studies
Berrigan, Daniel, S.J., 153
Blessed Margaret of Castello, 10, 13; as
"articulatory pivot," 45–46, 74; as case
for canonization, 37–38, 46; image of,
36; story of, 35–37; U.S. shrines of,
212n.59
Blessed Mother, 9–10, 13; and American
patriotism, 64–65; ancient and modern
names for, 67, 70–71; apparitions of (to
children), 79–80; apparitions of at
Lourdes, 60; and Catholic unity and dis-
unity, 65–67; in Clearwater, Florida, 10;
and devotional activities 52; and *Divine
Mirrors* exhibition, 58, 65, 70; and
human relationships, 60–63, 68; at
Knock, Ireland, 49, 62; at Oliveta Citra,
62, 64; as Our Lady of Fatima, 1; as
Our Lady of Lourdes, 1, 49; mysteries
of, 67–68; persistence of devotion to,
58–60; as portrayed in art, 69–70; as a
protean figure, 48–50, 61–65. *See also*
devotionalism; saints
Blue Army of Mary, 19–20
Brennan, Father Gerald, 92, 101; and
guardian angels, 106
Brown, Karen McCarthy, 4–5; and Haitian
Vodou, 195–96; and *Mama Lola: A
Vodou Priestess in Brooklyn*, 195. *See
also* religious studies